The Mariology of Cardinal Newman

THE MARIOLOGY OF CARDINAL NEWMAN

BY
REV. FRANCIS J. FRIEDEL, S. M., M. A., S.T.D.
(MARIANIST)

With a new Foreword by

DAVE ARMSTRONG
Author of *The Quotable Newman,* and other works.

MEDIATRIX PRESS

𝔍𝔪𝔭𝔯𝔦𝔪𝔦 𝔓𝔬𝔱𝔢𝔰𝔱
    L. A. Yeske, S. M.
    Praepos. Prov. Cincinnatensis

𝔑𝔦𝔥𝔦𝔩 𝔒𝔟𝔰𝔱𝔞𝔱
    Arthur J. Scanlan, S. T. D.
    Censor Librorum

𝔍𝔪𝔭𝔯𝔦𝔪𝔞𝔱𝔲𝔯
    ✠ Patrick Cardinal Hayes
    Archbishop of New York

NEW YORK, AUGUST 21, 1928.

ISBN: 978-0-359-58911-1

©Mediatrix Press, 2019.

The Mariology of Cardinal Newman was originally published in 1928 by Benziger Bros. The current edition has been retypeset in complete conformity with the original text. All rights reserved. No part of this work may be reproduced in electronic or physical format without the express permission of the publisher except for quotations in journals, blogs, and classroom purposes.

Cover design: ©Ryan Grant, 2019.

Mediatrix Press
607 E. 6th Ave.
Post Falls, ID 83854
www.mediatrixpress.com

Table of Contents

PREFACE xi

LIST OF ABBREVIATIONS xv

FOREWORD xix

PART I
    PSYCHOLOGICAL EVOLUTION OF NEWMAN'S MARIAN DOCTRINE AND DEVOTION

CHAPTER I
    PRINCIPLES AND OBSTACLES (1816–1839) 1

    I. Twofold Current 1
    II. Sound Belief in the Incarnation with its Consequences. 3
    III. Belief in the Communion of Saints 10
    IV. Attitude towards the Roman Church. 18
    V. Influences of Froude and Keble on his devotion ... 28
    VI. Conclusion: Character of Newman's devotion during this period 33

CHAPTER II
    TOWARDS THE LIGHT (1839–1845) 41

    I. Tract 90 41
    II. Dr. Russell and Newman 49
    III. The "Essay on Development"; difficulties vanish 58

CHAPTER III
    CATHOLIC DAYS (1845–1890) 71

    I. Devotion as shown in his life 71
    II. Devotion as portrayed in his writings. 76

CHAPTER IV
THE LETTER TO PUSEY 87

I. Pusey's *Eirenicon*; the occasion of the *Letter to Pusey*. 87
II. Brief analysis of the Letter 103

PART II
NEWMAN'S MARIAN DOCTRINE

CHAPTER I
MARY, MOTHER OF GOD 119

I. Newman's interest in the Incarnation. 119
II. Purpose of the Incarnation 120
III. Nature of the Incarnation 122
IV. The Divine Maternity 127
V. Theotokos, safeguard of the Incarnation 129
VI. History of the Title 142

CHAPTER II
MARY, SECOND EVE 151

I. Importance of this doctrine in Newman's Mariology 151
II. Scripture View of Blessed Virgin 152
III. *Prima facie* of her in Antiquity; its Scriptural basis 153
IV. Testimony of Justin, Irenaeus, Tertullian 159
V. Value of their Testimony 162
VI. Mary's merit of this position 167

CHAPTER III
MARY EVER-VIRGIN 177

I. Newman and the Virginal Birth 177
II. Nature and Importance of the Dogma 179
III. Preparation for the Virgin Birth 180
IV. The fact of the Virgin Birth: Virgo ante partum 182
V. Its Propriety 183

  VI. Virgo in partu 188
  VII. Virgo post partum 189

CHAPTER IV
  DIGNITY OF MARY 197

  I. Relation to Eve 197
  II. Elevation of Christians in general 198
  III. Mary's dignity as shown by her relations with Jesus;
    her knowledge also a result of this 200
  IV. *Quid Mihi et Tibi?* 204
  V. Scripture testifies to Mary's exaltation 209
  VI. Objection to Newman's interpretation 213
  VII. Justification of his interpretation 217
  VIII. Reason for comparative silence of Scripture about
    Blessed Virgin 219

CHAPTER V
  SANCTITY OF MARY 225

  I. Holiness proportionate to dignity of Mother of God
    225
  II. Fulness of grace in the Second Eve 228
  III. Sinlessness, a negative condition of holiness;
    patristic testimony to the contrary explained
    231
  IV. Virtues of the Blessed Virgin 238
  V. Consequences of her sanctity 241

CHAPTER VI
  THE IMMACULATE CONCEPTION 245

  I. The dogma should present no difficulties 245
  II. Protestant view of original sin, a source of difficulty
    249
  III. Nature of Immaculate Conception 250
  IV. Inference from doctrine on Second Eve 252
  V. A necessary preparation for the divine maternity;
    consequence of freedom from venial sin 256
  VI. Unreasonableness of objecting to dogma if doctrine

   is admitted..258

CHAPTER VII
 THE ASSUMPTION 261

 I. Nature of the Doctrine 261
 II. The fact of Mary's death and Assumption............263
 III. The doctrine is consistent with the rest of
   revealed teaching 268
 IV. The Assumption and the Divine Maternity 269
 V. The Assumption and the Immaculate Conception
  270
 VI. An extrinsic, historical proof............................271

CHAPTER VIII
 INTERCESSORY POWER OF THE BLESSED VIRGIN............273

 I. Based on the doctrine of prayer................................274
 II. And also on the Communion of Saints 276
 III. Mary's special intercession because of
   her sanctity and dignity..................................280
 IV. Exercise of Mary's intercession............................284

CHAPTER IX
 DEVOTION TO THE BLESSED VIRGIN 289

 I. Newman's peculiar fitness to treat this question .289
 II. Devotion is the consequence of doctrine 291
 III. Foundation of present devotion of Catholics
   laid in Antiquity..295
 IV. The Greek Church witnesses to it 297
 V. Psychological analysis of devotion to Mary 300
 VI. Misconception removed: devotion to Mary docs not
   interfere with honor due to God...................304
 VII. Superstitions doctrinally explained 309
 VIII. Attitude toward abuses 311
 IX. Character of devotion...315

CONCLUSION..321

PREFACE

INCE the death of the illustrious Cardinal Newman, his cult, if it may so be styled, has grown by leaps and bounds. Not only in his native England, but in America and other English-speaking countries as well, his name is held in veneration, his works are studied and meditated upon, and his spirit is imbibed. France and Germany also have contributed in ever-swelling numbers their quota of Newman devotees. Vigorous and original thinker as he was, Newman presents many points of view from which he may be studied. By some he is regarded, and that justly, as a prince of the English language, as a writer of the highest rank; by others as theologian, historian, apologist, and philosopher. To Catholic and non-Catholic alike, he appeals by his profound convictions, his lofty sentiments, and his candid simplicity. The nobility of his character shines through every page of his works.

Intellectual as he was, Newman takes his place among devotional writers as one of the most prominent of modern times. He has become the master and leader for many who, guided by the principles he has laid down, have given of their best to add to the treasure of devotional literature.

In all sincerity he could lay claim to a *true* devotion to our Lady while he was still Anglican. It is said that only humble minds can grasp fully this devotion and practice it in an eminent degree. Newman was too intellectual not to recognize the dangers of Intellectualism. He detested intellectual pride as the greatest of sins, and united a keen exercise of the intellect with a lively sense of its limitations. Because of this humility of mind which characterized him, he could enter into a perfect realization of true devotion to our Lady.

Combined with this humility was a deep penetration into the mystery of the Incarnation which reveals the great love of God for men. In order to save fallen humanity, God sent His only-begotten Son into the world, not with an angelic or celestial nature, but clothed with a frail human nature which he took from the Virgin Mary. Newman stood in awe at the thought that God is man, that God had a Mother. Profoundly penetrated with the spectacle of the creature's elevation in Mary, he cannot conceive of her but as the most awfully gifted of the children of men. The devotion to which these considerations gave rise was held in check for a long time by the ordinances of the Anglican Church. But, once the barriers were broken down, it burst forth like the mighty waters when the sluices are opened, not uncontrolled, not violent, not exaggerated, but powerful and energetic, yet subdued.

What Bishop O'Dwyer has said of Newman finds its particular application when there is question of his Marian doctrine: "It has always been a source of wonder and admiration to observe the extraordinary insight of Newman into Catholic theology and the almost preterhuman power and grasp and, at the same time, prevision and caution, with which he, a convert, dealt so fully with almost every phase of Catholic life." (*Newman and the Encyclical "Pascendi Gregis"* 5.)

The following study is an attempt to analyze the principles and factors which gave the orientation to his attitude concerning the Blessed Virgin Mary during his Anglican and Catholic days. This represents the First Part. The Second is occupied with a synthesis of his doctrine.

This work was undertaken under the kindly direction of Msgr. J. P. Kirsch, Professor at the University of Fribourg, Switzerland, to whom I wish to express my heartfelt gratitude for friendly advice and constant encouragement. My thanks also go out to Father Francis Bacchus, of the Birmingham

Preface

Oratory, for many valuable suggestions, and assistance in procuring certain necessary works. Finally, special thanks are addressed to Dr. E. Neubert, S.M., and to the Reverend Superiors of the Society of Mary for facilities in bringing the work to a successful conclusion.

FRANCIS J. FRIEDEL, S.M.

University of Dayton, Ohio
Feast of the Assumption, 1928

LIST OF ABBREVIATIONS

Apo.	*Apologia* (1921).
Ari.	*The Arians* (1919).
Ath.	*St. Athanasius,* 2 vols. (1911).
Call.	*Callista* (1891).
Cath. Enc.	*Catholic Encyclopedia.*
D. A.	*Discussions and Arguments* (1918).
Denz.	Denziger, *Enchiridion Symbolorum et Definitionum* Fribourg, 1914).
Dev.	*Development of Christian Doctrine* (1920).
Diff.	*Difficulties of Anglicans,* 2 vols. (Vol. I, 1901; Vol II, 1900).
I Eir.	*An Eirenicon, in a Letter to the Author of the "Christian Year,"* by E. B. Pusey, D.D. (1865).
II Eir.	*First Letter to the Very Rev. J. H. Newman, D.D., in Explanation Chiefly in Regard to the Reverential Love Due to the Ever-blessed Theotokos and the Doctrine of Her Immaculate Conception,* by E. B. Pusey, D.D. (1869).
Ess.	*Essays Critical and Historical,* Vol. II (1919).
G. A.	*Grammar of Assent* (1913).
H. S.	*Historical Sketches,* Vol. II (1917).
Jfc.	*Lectures on Justification* (1914).
Keble	*Correspondence of John Henry Newman with John Keble and Others.* Edited by the Birmingham Oratory (1917).
L. G.	*Loss and Gain* (1906).
M. D.	*Meditations and Devotions* (1914).

Mix.	*Discourses to Mixed Congregations* (1921).
Moz.	*Letters and Correspondence of J. H. Newman*, edited by Anne Mozley (1920).
P. G.	Migne, *Patrologia Graeca*.
P. L.	Migne, *Patrologia Latina*.
Pusey	*Life of Pusey*, by H. P. Liddon, 4 vols. (1893–1897).
Prepos.	*Present Position of Catholics in England* (1918).
P. S.	*Parochial and Plain Sermons*, 8 vols. (I, 1920; II, 1918; III, 1916; IV, 1919; V, 1917; VI, 1918; VII, 1920; VIII, 1920).
S. D.	*Sermons on Subjects of the Day* (1909).
S. N.	*Sermon Notes of J. H. Newman* (1914).
T. T.	*Tracts Theological and Ecclesiastical* (1913).
T. Ti.	*Tracts for the Times.*
U. S.	*Oxford University Sermons* (1909).
V. M.	*Via Media*, 2 vols. (I, 1918; II, 1914).
V. V.	*Verses on Various Occasions* (1918).
Ward	*Life of John Henry Cardinal Newman*, by Wilfrid Ward, 2 vols. (1921).

All the works of Newman used in this study are published by Longmans, Green and Co. *The Correspondence of Newman, Ward's Life of Newman, Liddon's Life of Pusey,* are published by the same firm.

Bibliography

In addition to the works cited above in the List of Abbreviations, the following were also used for consultation:

Alès, *Dictionnaire Apologetique de la Foi Catholique.*
  -*Théologie de Tertullien* (Paris, 1905).
Allo, O. P., *St. Jean, l'Apocalypse* (Paris, 1921).
Bardenhewer, *Geschichte der Altkirchlichen Literatur* (Freiburg I. Br., 1902, 1903, 1924).
Brémond, *Newman, essai de biographie psychologique* (Paris, 1906).
Cabrol, *Dictionnaire d'Archéologie Chrétienne.*
Campana, *Marie dans le dogme catholique* (Montrejeau, 1913).
Chaminade, S. M., *Petit traité de la Connaissance de Marie* (Paris, 1927).
Chapman, O. S. B., "The Age of Christ according to Papias." *Journal of Theol. Studies*, IX (1908).
Cousin, S. M., *Marie, notre vraie Mère* (Paris, 1923).
De la Broise, S. J., "Mulier amicta sole." *Études*, T. 71, pp. 289–308.
Del Prado, O. P., *Divus Thomas et Bulla Dogmatica "Ineffabilis Deus"* (Fribourg, 1919).
De Montfort, *Traité de la Vraie Dévotion à la Ste. Vierge* (Luçon, 1918).
Eberle, *Die Mariologie des hl. Cyrillus von Alexandrien* (Freiburg i. Br., 1921).
Ehrhard, *Die altchr. Literature u. ihre Erforschung von 1884–1900* (Freiburg i. Br., 1900).
Flachaire, *La Dévotion à la Vierge dans la littérature catholique au commencement du XVII siècle* (Paris, 1916).
Friedrich, *Die Mariologie des hl. Augustinus* (Cologne, 1907).
Garriguet, *La Ste. Vierge* (Paris, 1916).
Harnack, *Lehrbuch der Dogmengeschichte* (Leipzig, 1894).
  -*Geschichte der altchr. Literatur bis Eusebius* (Leipzig, 1893).
Hugon, O. P., *La Mère de Grace* (Paris, 1904).
Junglas, "Die Irrlehre des Nestorius." *Katholik*, 1913, pp. 437–447; 135–139.
Keble, *The Christian Year* (The World's Classics, 1914).
Kirsch, *Die Lehre von der Gemeinschaft der Heiligen im christl.*

Alterthum (Mainz, 1900).
Loughran, "The Theology of the Immaculate Conception," *Ecclesiastical Review,* May 1925, pp. 518–521.
Marin-Sola, O. P., *L'Evolution homogène du Dogme catholique* (Fribourg, 1924).
McCormick, "The Doctrine of the Virginal Birth and Some of Its Consequences," *Ecclesiastical Review,* May 1924.
Morgott, *Die Mariologie des hl. Thomas von Aquin* (Cologne, 1878).
Neubert, S. M., *Marie dans l'Église anté-nicéenne* (Paris, 1908).
Niessen, *Die Mariologie des hl. Hieronymus* (Münster, 1913).
Parsons, S. J., "The Virgin Birth of Christ." *America,* Jan. 5, 1924, pp. 273–274.
-"The Modernists and the Virgin Birth." *America,* January 12, 1924, pp. 297–298.
Petavius, S. J., *Dogmata Theologica* (Paris, 1866).
Prat, S. J., *La Théologie de S. Paul* (Paris, 1912).
Przywara-Karrer, *Einfürung in Newman's Wesen und Werke.*
Quentin, O. S. B., *Essais de Critique Textuelle* (Paris, 1926).
A. R., "The Immaculate Conception and the 'Contracting of Sin'," *Ecclesiastical Review,* Jan. 1925, pp. 76–82.
Reilly, O. P., "Quid Mihi et Tibi?" *Ecclesiastical Review,* Feb. 1911, pp. 169–203.
Renaudin, O. S. B., *La Doctrine de l'Assomption de la T. S. Vierge* (Paris, 1901).
Rickaby, S. J., *Index to the Works of J. H. Newman* (London, 1914).
Robinson, *St. Irenaeus, The Apostolical Preaching* (London, 1920).
Rouët de Journel, *Enchiridion Patristicum* (Freiburg i. Br., 1913).
Schultes, "Die Häresie des Nestorius." *Katholik,* 1913, pp. 126–134.
-"Die Bewährungslehre des Nestorius." *Ibid.,* pp. 233–247.
Schweitzer, "Das Alter Des Titels, Theotokos." *Katholik,* 1903, pp. 97–113.
Terrien, S. J., *La Mère de Dieu et la Mère des Hommes,* 4 vol. (Paris, 1902).
Thureau-Dangin, *La Renaissance catholique en Angleterre au XIX siècle* (Paris, 1899).
Vacant, *Dictionnaire de Théologie Catholique.*

FOREWORD

by

DAVE ARMSTRONG[1]

LESSED [soon-to-be-Saint] John Henry Cardinal Newman held to a very high Mariology even before he was received into the Catholic Church in 1845, at the age of 44, after a very distinguished career as an Anglican clergyman and Church historian. As was the case with G. K. Chesterton in his splendid book, Orthodoxy, written in 1908, fourteen years before he became a Catholic, so also Cardinal Newman was clearly Catholic in spirit in many ways before he was in a canonical sense. In a letter to Henry Wilberforce, dated 12 January 1848 he stated: "I have ever been under her shadow, if I may say it."

Like Martin Luther, he had no problem accepting, for example, Mary's Immaculate Conception (in the Catholic sense), or else something very similar to it, as early as 1832:

> Who can estimate the holiness and perfection of her, who was chosen to be the Mother of Christ? If to him that hath, more is given, and holiness and Divine favour go together (and this we are expressly told), what must have been the transcendent purity of her, whom the Creator Spirit condescended to overshadow with His miraculous presence? What must have been her gifts,

---

[1] Dave Armstrong is also the author of *The Quotable Newman*, which is available from Sophia Press.

who was chosen to be the only near earthly relative of the Son of God, the only one whom He was bound by nature to revere and look up to; the one appointed to train and educate Him, to instruct Him day by day, as He grew in wisdom and in stature? This contemplation runs to a higher subject, did we dare follow it; for what, think you, was the sanctified state of that human nature, of which God formed His sinless Son; . . .? (*Parochial and Plain Sermons*, vol. ii, Sermon 12: "The Reverence Due to the Virgin Mary," 25 March 1832; in his Apologia of 1864, he observed about this sermon: "I had a true devotion to the Blessed Virgin, in whose . . . Immaculate Purity I had in one of my earliest printed Sermons made much of.")

In the same sermon he strongly implied that Our Lady ought to be venerated:

> In her the destinies of the world were to be reversed, and the serpent's head bruised. On her was bestowed the greatest honour ever put upon any individual of our fallen race. God was taking upon Him her flesh, and humbling Himself to be called her offspring; — such is the deep mystery!

He recognized, accordingly, that the Blessed Virgin Mary intercedes for us:

> [I]f the Intercessions of the Saints have influence with Christ, surely it is not any extreme position to suppose that the greater Saints have greater influence – or that St Mary, as being our Lord's Mother, is a greater Saint. (Letter to an Unknown Correspondent, 12 Jan. 1844)

His beliefs regarding Mary as the Mother of God (Theotokos) were firmly in place at the time of his *Essay on the Development of Christian Doctrine*: completed in 1845, right before he was received (therefore, entirely written while he was an Anglican). Four years later, he elaborated upon the dogma:

> [T]he Mother of God has ever been the bulwark of our Lord's divinity. And it is that which heretics have ever opposed, for it is the great witness that the doctrine of God being man is true....

Preface

> The truth is, the doctrine of our Lady keeps us from a dreaming, unreal way. If no mother, no history, how did He come here, etc? He is from heaven. It startles us and makes us think what we say when we say Christ is God; not merely like God, inhabited by, sent by God, but really God; so really, that she is the mother of God because His mother. (Sermon Notes of John Henry Cardinal Newman: 1849-1878, "Maternity of Mary," 14 October 1849)

In the same year he wrote very eloquently about Mary's glorious Bodily Assumption:

> It was surely fitting then, it was becoming, that she should be taken up into heaven and not lie in the grave till Christ's second coming, who had passed a life of sanctity and of miracle such as hers.... Who can conceive, my brethren, that God should so repay the debt, which He condescended to owe to His Mother, for the elements of His human body, as to allow the flesh and blood from which it was taken to moulder in the grave?... Why should she share the curse of Adam, who had no share in his fall? "Dust thou art, and into dust thou shalt return," was the sentence upon sin; she then, who was not a sinner, fitly never saw corruption. She died, then, as we hold, because even our Lord and Saviour died... by the grace of Christ which in her had anticipated sin, which had filled her with light, which had purified her flesh from all defilement, she was also saved from disease and malady, and all that weakens and decays the bodily frame. Original sin had not been found in her... If the Mother of Emmanuel ought to be the first of creatures in sanctity and in beauty; if it became her to be free from all sin from the very first, and from the moment she received her first grace to begin to merit more; and if such as was her beginning, such was her end, her conception immaculate and her death an assumption... (Discourses Addressed to Mixed Congregations, Discourse 18: "On the Fitness of the Glories of Mary")

A little later he developed his existing views regarding Mary's preeminent intercession, to a fuller doctrine of Mary Mediatrix. For example:

> Our Lord died for those heathens who did not know Him; and

His Mother intercedes for those Christians who do not know her; and she intercedes according to His will, and, when He wills to save a particular soul, she at once prays for it. I say, He wills indeed according to her prayer, but then she prays according to His will. Though then it is natural and prudent for those to have recourse to her, who from the Church's teaching know her power, yet it cannot be said that devotion to her is a sine-quâ-non of salvation. (Certain Difficulties Felt by Anglicans in Catholic Teaching Considered, vol. ii, Letter to Pusey, ch. 5, 1865)

One could go on and on, immersed in these extraordinarily moving expressions of Cardinal Newman's theology and spirituality regarding the Blessed Virgin Mary. I have sought to give readers just the "tip of the iceberg," so to speak. In this spirit, I'm happy to enthusiastically recommend this new edition of a wonderful work, written by Rev. Francis J. Friedel in 1928: *The Mariology of Cardinal Newman*. I hope and pray that it is read far and wide, as we celebrate the long-awaited canonization of this extraordinarily influential Churchman: Cardinal Newman.

PART I
Psychological Evolution of Newman's Marian Doctrine and Devotion

CHAPTER I
Principles and Obstacles (1816–1839)

I. Twofold Current

T FIRST sight, there seems to be something contradictory in Newman's position relative to the Blessed Virgin during the greater part of his Anglican career. Two currents of opinion have developed, which flow on in parallel streams, apparently incapable of uniting, until the barriers keeping them apart are broken down.

The two points of orientation may be thus formulated in his own words: "At least during the Tract Movement, I thought the essence of her (the Roman Church's) offence to consist in the honors which she paid to the Blessed Virgin and the Saints, and the more I grew in devotion, both to the Saints and to our Lady, the more impatient was I at the Roman practices, as if those glorified creations of God must be gravely shocked, if pain could be theirs, at the undue veneration of which they were the objects. Such devotional manifestations in honor of our Lady had been my great *crux* as regards Catholicism."[2]

Let it be remarked that he speaks of *growing* in devotion to Mary. In another passage he characterizes his devotion, indicating the second current of which mention was made. "In spite of my ingrained fears of Rome, and the decision of my reason and conscience against her usages ... I had a secret

---

[2] Apo. 53, 195.

longing love of Rome, the Mother of English Christianity, and I had a true devotion to the Blessed Virgin, in whose College I lived, whose Altar I served, and whose Immaculate Purity I had in one of my earliest printed Sermons made much of."[3] As Anglican, then, he professed a *true* devotion to the Mother of God and advanced in it, while at the same time its external manifestations proved to be a source of great difficulty to him and even hindered him from giving his adhesion to the Church of Rome when once he was convinced that the Established Church was in schism. To the average Catholic, who scarcely gives the subject any further consideration, such an attitude is well-nigh incomprehensible. Later on, Newman will associate devotion and devotional manifestation,[4] but he had a long way to traverse before he could reconcile these two points which seemed so decidedly at variance with each other. He was making a distinction with which the Catholic scarcely concerns himself; yet for him it was vital. To go to Rome with practical doubts harassing his mind would have been acting contrary to the dictates of his conscience; only when his difficulties were solved could he think of making the decisive step.[5]

His religious instinct drew him naturally to the Blessed Mother of God, but reason and conscience, formed by his education and loyal attachment to the Anglican communion, which reprobated the cultus of saints, forbade his giving expression to these sentiments. Any one with a correct notion of the Incarnation must necessarily have some devotion to the Blessed Virgin. It will be evident in the sequel that, as he became more involved in the Oxford Movement, his categoric statements on usages discountenanced by his Church began to ring with a tone of uncertainty, until the moment came when he no longer dared to express himself on the subject.

---

[3] Ibid. 165. Newman refers to the sermon preached on March 25, 1832, on "The Reverence Due to the Virgin Mary." Cf. P. S. II, 132.

[4] Diff. II, 26: "By devotion I mean such religious honors as belong to the objects of our faith, and the payment of those honors."

[5] Diff. I, 368 sqq.

II. SOUND BELIEF IN THE INCARNATION WITH ITS CONSEQUENCES.

Prior to the age of fifteen, Newman had formed no definite religious convictions, but after his "conversion," as he calls it, he was guided by several principles that explain clearly his attitude. In examining them and comparing them with his conduct, consistency is manifest throughout. The time will come, it is true, when he is not so sure that certain of his guiding principles are correct. He will have to reconstruct parts of his religious system; on other points his principles will undergo no modification whatsoever. The study of Butler's *Analogy* in 1825 had helped considerably to place his doctrinal views on a broad philosophical basis, with which an emotional religion could have little sympathy.[6]

Dogma was the fundamental principle of his religion.[7] Such a basis was of capital importance, particularly when it is recalled that influential men such as Dr. Whately and Dr. Arnold of Rugby and hosts of lesser lights were leading the way to absolute liberalism. In fact, the quarrel of the Tractarians was with the anti-dogmatic theory that rejects anything concerned with definite religious principles, which are entirely independent of individual judgment.[8] The Liberal movement was very pronounced at Oxford, and it was Keble who turned the tide and brought the talent of the university round to the

---

[6] Moz. I, 107.

[7] "I know no other religion, I cannot enter into the idea of any other sort of a religion; religion, as a mere sentiment, is to me a dream and a mockery. As well can there be filial love without a father, as devotion without a Supreme Being. Even when I was under Dr. Whately's influence I had no temptation to be less zealous for the great dogmas of the faith, and at various times I used to resist such trains of thought on his part as seemed to me (rightly or wrongly) to obscure them." *Apo.* 49.

[8] "Liberalism is the mistake of subjecting to human judgment those revealed doctrines which are in their nature beyond and independent of it, and of claiming to determine on intrinsic grounds the truth and value of propositions which rest for their reception simply on the external authority of the Divine Word." *Ibid.* 288.

old theology.⁹

When Newman accepted the principle of dogma as the basis of his religion, there were four doctrines which he held as certain truths—namely, those of the Holy Trinity, of the Incarnation, of Predestination, and of the Lutheran apprehension of Christ.[10] The first three remained indelible through all his changes of opinion, whereas the fourth departed from his mind after a time. Due to the fact that he had a precise notion of what was meant by the Incarnation, he could lay the foundation of a solid and true devotion to the Mother of God. Without this dogma there would be no more reason for honoring the Blessed Virgin than for venerating any other saint. Newman justly considered it so vital as to make the existence or ruin of a Church depend on it.[11]

He held unfalteringly to the doctrine that God the Son, existing from all eternity, chose to be born in time, becoming the son of Mary and taking upon Himself our human nature.[12] "He submitted to be the offspring of Mary, to be taken up in the hands of a mortal, to have a mother's eye fixed upon Him, and to be cherished at a mother's bosom. A daughter of man became the Mother of God—to her, indeed, an unspeakable gift of grace, but in Him what condescension."[13]

Such firm convictions on the Incarnation were by no means general in Newman's time, for mere Protestants have seldom any real perception of the doctrine of God and man in one person. They are rarely if ever willing to commit themselves to the full import of the Catholic dogma; they will evade a clear expression of their belief by assuming that the subject is too deep to be inquired into without being subtle or technical.[14] Christ for them is a being made up of God and man, partly one and partly the other, or a being between both, or a man in

---

[9] Ibid. 289.

[10] Moz. I, 110.

[11] U. S. 35.

[12] P. S. VI, 55.

[13] P. S. VIII, 252.

[14] Cf. Mix. 345, 6.

whom the Divine Presence specially dwells. In the early Church men understood that the "Word was made flesh", that Jesus Son of Mary was Son of God, and so the mystery was treated with reverent brevity; but when faith grew cold, discussions and doubts arose, and the Church was compelled to formulate its doctrines in exacts terms so as to give no leeway to heresy.[15] Later on, Newman can explain how all these heresies, centering about the Incarnate Word, receive their death-blow by the simple statement that Mary is the Mother of God.

In 1834 Newman seems almost to hesitate about calling the Blessed Virgin Mother of God. He says: "Thus He came into this world, not in the clouds but born of a woman; He, the Son of Mary, and she (if it may be said) the Mother of God."[16] This parenthetical expression may have served simply for emphasis. One is at a loss to explain this apparent hesitation. Perhaps he felt that Mother of God went beyond *Theotokos*. He may have hesitated to proclaim her unqualifiedly as Mother of God, though of course the title was confirmed by the Council of Ephesus, which was accepted by Anglicans; there may have been danger of arousing some liberal spirits round about Oxford by too direct a statement. If Newman seems to hesitate about the title he has no difficulty whatever about the *fact* of the divine maternity; a little later he simply claims that all but heretics have ever called her the Mother of God.[17]

In face of the great anti-dogmatic tendencies manifest in the Anglican Church in the early nineteenth century, it is refreshing to witness Newman's attachment to the Virginal Birth—a doctrine that is attacked and speedily thrown overboard as soon as men begin to go astray in their own rationalistic delusions. Mary was the mother of Jesus, but she was not like other mothers, as was fitting, for her Son was not as other sons; He was in truth the Son of God. The Prophet had

---

[15] P. S. II, 36, 37.

[16] Still, in his sermon of 1832 he says that Gabriel "was sent to tell her that she was to be the Mother of our Lord," or again: "God was taking upon Him her flesh, and humbling Himself to be called her offspring."

[17] D. A. 223, written in 1838.

announced that a Virgin should conceive and bear a Son whose name was Emmanuel.[18] Newman never seems to tire of insisting on the fact that Christ was born of a Virgin[19] "pure and spotless";[20] He had no earthly father and abhorred to have one.[21] To Newman's mind it was inconceivable that the all-holy Son of God should have been born according to the ordinary laws of nature—"The thought may not be suffered that He should have been the son of shame and guilt; He came by a new and living way; He selected and purified a tabernacle for Himself, becoming the immaculate seed of the woman, forming His body miraculously from the substance of the Virgin Mary."[22]

Virginity was the first condition for Mary's becoming the mother of God. For such a lofty position mere physical integrity is not sufficient; she had to be endowed with gifts of nature and grace in proportion to her sublime dignity. Holiness and divine favor go together—such is Newman's principle. God does not choose any human instrument for accomplishing His designs upon humanity without endowing him with a measure of grace suitable to the function to be fulfilled. But is there any creature that had a role to perform comparable to that of her who is the most highly favored of women? Is it possible to gaze upon her holiness in all its fulness, if even St. John, who saw the Word in the flesh, was tempted to fall down before an Angel, and if Daniel at sight of one of these heavenly spirits fell flat to the ground?[23] Newman considers it a mercy of God to our feebleness that so little is revealed about the Blessed Virgin, though of her there are "many things to say, yet they are hard to be uttered, seeing ye are dull of hearing."[24]

Scripture tells us that "that which is born of the flesh is

---

[18] Is. 7:14.

[19] P. S. VI, 187.

[20] Ibid. 285.

[21] Ibid. 62; II,31.

[22] Ibid. II, 31; VI, 61, 64, 79; II, 142; VII, 187, 75.

[23] Dan. 8:18; Apoc. 19:10; 22:8.

[24] Heb. 5:11; cf. P. S. II, 135; D. A. 223.

flesh" and that none can bring a clean thing out of an unclean.[25] Starting out from Mary's closeness to the Word of God, Newman is led to so lofty a conception of her sanctity that he asks himself: "What must have been the transcendent purity of her whom the Creator Spirit condescended to overshadow with His miraculous presence? ... This contemplation runs to a higher subject, did we dare follow it; for what, think you, was the sanctified state of that human nature of which God formed His sinless Son?"[26] Notwithstanding his apparent reserve in suggesting the conclusion most natural to his mind, he was understood fully by his hearers to speak of the Immaculate Conception and was accused of holding it.[27] No dogma of faith had been the object of so much bitter discussion for centuries, and still the Anglican Newman found no difficulty in admitting it twenty years before it was imposed upon Catholics as an article of faith. Basing himself upon the doctrine that Mary is God's Mother, no condition was more proper for her than that same sinlessness in which Eve came from the hands of the Creator. The Immaculate Conception imposed itself upon him as a necessary condition for Christ's coming into the world free from sin, though, of course, the mere fact of the hypostatic union would have precluded such a possibility. When Newman in the same sermon speaks of Mary as "by nature a sinner,"[28] he wishes to imply only that she too would have fallen under the curse of sin had not grace been beforehand with sin and prevented its taking possession of her, for she had been raised above the condition of sinful beings.

Newman was so impressed with our Lady's *dignity* that he seemed dazzled by its splendor. If all the saints are the, special work of the Holy Ghost,[29] how much more must she not be the special fruit of His divine operations in order to make her a fitting tabernacle wherein could repose the Son of God? On her

---

[25] John 3:6; Job 14:4. Cf. P. S. II, 132.
[26] P. S. II, 132.
[27] M. D., 78, 79.
[28] PS. II, 135.
[29] Ibid. I, 72.

was bestowed the greatest honor ever put upon any individual of our fallen race.[30] It seems almost impossible to regard her without a "certain perversion of feeling,"[31] because of the peculiar place she holds—in intimate relationship with God and yet but a creature. She seems to lack a place in our feeble intelligences, which cannot identify her with the Creator and still cannot put her on the same level with fallen humanity. "We cannot combine in our thoughts of her all we should ascribe with all we should withhold."[32]

Notwithstanding the enthusiastic admiration of Newman for this creature "above all creatures blessed", so that he seems hardly able to find words in order to give vent to his sentiments, still there is a certain restraint, as if he were unable to find the line of demarcation between what he ought to ascribe to her and what he ought to withhold. He remarks that were we able to contemplate Mary in all the fullness of her grandeur, we should certainly be tempted to fall before her in worship, since she is above all the angels and saints. But he refers it to a merciful Providence that so little is told about her, lest we lose sight of the Creator in the wonderful gifts bestowed upon the creature. Why this restraint, it may be asked. The sequel of our study of this period will bring this out in a clear light.

It may cause no little surprise to see the hardihood with which Newman extols the incomparable dignity of the Virgin Mary. Even granting that the hearers to whom the sermon on Annunciation day, 1832, was addressed, were just as solidly grounded in their belief in the Incarnation as he was, it is not so certain that they were prepared to hear the Blessed Virgin exalted to such an extent. It is true, he at once puts them on their guard, cautioning them to remember that she is but a creature and that whatever she is or has, redounds to the glory

---

[30] Ibid. II,128.
[31] Ibid.135.
[32] Ibid.

of her divine Son.³³ He holds up to them the example of their Church, which commemorates no feast of the Blessed Virgin unless it is also associated with some event in our Lord's life.³⁴

Even the germ of Newman's later teaching on the Second Eve may be found in his Anglican days, though not in so pronounced a manner as for the other doctrines already exposed. Through her instrumentality the Seed of the woman, announced to guilty Eve, was at length appearing on the earth and was to be born of her. "In her the destinies of the world were to be reversed, and the serpent's head bruised."³⁵ Unwittingly Newman indicates what will eventually be the center of his Mariology. He merely touches on the comparison which is so important in his Catholic apologetics in defense of devotion to our Lady. Though he had already begun to read the Fathers,³⁶ nevertheless he had not yet been struck by the fact that what may be called Irenaeus' Recapitulation Theory represents the primitive view of the Blessed Virgin, who was chosen by God to be an active voluntary agent in the restoration of mankind as Eve was instrumental in bringing about its ruin. Newman is already aware that through Mary the curse pronounced on Eve was turned into a blessing, for through childbirth original sin is communicated to all succeeding generations; through the Childbirth *par excellence,* man is saved. The very punishment of the fall, the very taint of the birth-sin, admits of a cure by the coming of Christ through Mary. Likewise through her, the subjection of woman to man as foretold in the Garden had been freed from the odious character which it possessed in large part before the coming of Jesus.³⁷ The fulness of development of Mary's role in the

---

[33] One of his first Marian sermons preached as a Catholic is "The Glories of Mary for the Sake of Her Son." Mix., Discourse XVIII.

[34] The same preoccupation may be noticed in one of Keble's sermons preached on the same feast. It was published as Tract 54.

[35] P. S. II, 128.

[36] Newman began a systematic reading of the Fathers in 1828. Cf. Apo. 25; Moz. I, 112.

[37] P. S. II, 129–131.

restoration of fallen humanity must await the period when Newman's practical difficulties are removed; in this period the Blessed Virgin remains for him largely the channel by which the Son of God came into the world, though not merely a physical instrument.

Newman's Marian doctrine during this period may be summed up as follows: A clear perception of the nature of the Incarnation led him to a firm belief in the divine maternity, a dignity surpassing all the conceptions of our feeble understanding. The most fitting way for the all-holy God to come to earth through a woman was by a new and living way; He was to be born through the operation of the Holy Spirit. In consequence of the high dignity conferred upon Mary, she had to be endowed with special graces, in particular, a transcendent holiness which included not merely the possession of virtues in a superior degree, but a sinlessness that extended to the first moment of her existence.

III. BELIEF IN THE COMMUNION OF SAINTS

The second principle which lies at the basis of Newman's Mariology, though not carried at once to its logical conclusion, is the "teaching that there is a visible Church with sacraments and rites which are the channels of invisible grace."[38] What Newman calls the sacramental system, he derived from a study of Butler, and broadened its scope under the influence of Keble. This doctrine as thus enlarged, embraces not only what Anglicans (of the orthodox variety) as well as Catholics believe about sacraments properly so called, but also the article of the Communion of Saints, and likewise the mysteries of faith. The doctrine of the Communion of Saints is of primary importance in this study, for it led to the belief in the intercessory power of our Lady and to the admission of invocation. This consequence is, however, not immediate. Newman laid the premises of his syllogism in this period of his Anglican career; the second

---

[38] Apo. 49.

period will supply the conclusion.[39] Hence, it is necessary to analyze the principle held in 1828 which leads to its consequences only towards 1844.

Besides the Church visible, consisting of members living upon earth, there is also an invisible Church, composed of the body of the elect, as it already exists in paradise and as it will be hereafter. Besides the Church militant upon earth, there is the invisible Church.[40] In the visible Church, the Church invisible is gradually moulded and matured.[41] The spirits of the just made perfect and already sealed for heaven encourage the individual Christian to combat, to go forward in the paths of self-denial; they sympathize with him, they spur him on by their example. In the Communion of Saints, an article of the Creed, is opened to the Christian a world of sympathy and comfort.

There is a union between the creature and the Creator by the mere fact of existence, for "in Him we live and move and are."[42] But far higher, more intimate and more sacred is the indwelling of God in the hearts of His elect people—so intimate that, compared with it, God may almost be said not to inhabit other men at all, since His presence is specified as the characteristic privilege of His own redeemed servants.[43] Christ formed his Apostles into a visible society, but the Holy Spirit made them one, organs of one unseen power; their persons were grafted upon and assimilated to the spiritual body of Christ.

Salvation is only possible in "that great invisible company [of those] who are one and all incorporate in the one mystical body of Christ and quickened by one Spirit; by adhering to the visible ministry which the Apostles left behind them, we approach unto what we see not, to Mount Zion, to the heavenly Jerusalem, to the spirits of the just, to the first-born elected to

---

[39] Ath. II, 195.
[40] P. S. III, 223.
[41] Ibid. 240, 244, 245.
[42] Acts 17:28.
[43] P.S. IV, 169.

salvation, to Angels innumerable, to Jesus the one Mediator, and to God. This heavenly Jerusalem is the true spouse of Christ and the virgin Mother of Saints."[44]

Thus, there is a bond of union between the faithful upon earth and the blessed in heaven. Of these latter undefiled followers of the Lamb, the Blessed Mary is the chief.[45] She must necessarily be above them all, for on her was bestowed the greatest honor ever put upon any creature. Happiness in heaven is measured by the merit acquired upon earth; merit in its turn is determined by holiness and charity, but "who can estimate the holiness and perfection of her who was chosen to be the Mother of Christ?"[46] Ordinary creatures by means of the Incarnation are elevated so high, gifted with a measure of all those perfections which Christ has in fulness, "partaking each in his own degree of His Divine Nature so fully, that the only reason (so to speak) why His saints are not really like Him, is that it is impossible; yet still so, that they are all but divine, all that can be made without violating the incommunicable majesty of the Most High. They are made all but gods, higher than Angels or Archangels, in heaven and in Christ, and on earth tending to the same high blessedness."[47] What, then, must be the glory, blessedness, and honor conferred upon her in heaven who was so closely related to the Blessed Trinity during her mortal life? Spotless, immaculate, as she was to become a fit tabernacle of the Most High, what must have been the abundance of her merit and sanctity? Raised above every creature, above Angels and Saints on earth, her fitting place in heaven must be after her Divine Son, the Incarnate Word, the Sovereign Mediator. Such were the deductions to which Newman was led in his contemplation of the mystery of the divine indwelling in the soul of the Christian who while on

---

[44] P. S. IV, 174. It is unnecessary to investigate here what Newman understood by the Church as it is constituted on earth. His opinions on this score underwent several notable transformations.

[45] Ibid. II, 137.

[46] Ibid. 132.

[47] Ibid. VIII, 253.

earth remains in communion with the body of elect, already in possession of the Beatific Vision.

The question naturally presents itself to us as well as to Newman: What is the occupation of the elect and what is the nature of the intermediate state, i.e., the state of the elect who have departed this life and consequently are destined to enjoy the Beatific Vision?[48] Is the Communion of Saints a mere vague term, implying, it is true, a certain grouping of those who are saved and those who are still on their trial, all of them, knit with Christ—the former irrevocably, the latter with a possibility of missing their final destiny; or is it something living, calling for a real intercommunion of the blessed in heaven and the faithful upon earth and an exchange of good offices, the former interceding and the latter invoking their aid? The answer to this will determine as exactly as it is possible, how Newman stood on the important question of intercession, though it would not determine his attitude on invocation. These two points are distinct and must be kept apart, and thus they were ever distinguished by Newman.[49] It may be affirmed that Newman would have been prepared to accept the intercession of our Lady and of the Saints as early as 1834,[50] yet it was only towards 1841 that he was willing to admit a limited amount of invocation that would at the same time be in keeping with the prescriptions of the Anglican Church.

Consequently, the second question of invocation must be relegated for separate consideration. We must take up directly Newman's speculations on the position of the Blessed Virgin and Saints in their glorified state—speculations they are, since the Anglican communion did not insist upon this point in her teachings and left the individual free to resolve the question according to his interpretation of Scripture.

---

[48] In this period of his career Newman held that the elect did not enter into the possession of the Beatific Vision until after the General Judgment.

[49] Cf. L. G. 246; Keble 230.

[50] Cf. P. S. II, 214. "It may be that Saints departed intercede for the victory of the Truth upon earth, and their prayers above may be as really indispensable conditions of that victory, as the labors of those who remain among us." This sermon was preached towards the end of 1834.

Those who have gone before us are not entirely separated from us, and though worldlings may think the departed losers of the questionable pleasures of this life, the true Christian cannot think slightingly of the vessels of future glory. "Shall we doubt for a moment, though St. Paul was martyred centuries upon centuries since, that he who even while in the body was present in spirit at Corinth when he was at Ephesus, is present in the Church still, more truly alive than those who are called living, more truly and awfully an Apostle now upon a throne than when he had fightings without and fears within, a thorn in his flesh and a martyrdom in prospect? ... Shall we not dimly recognize amid the aisles of our churches ... by the eye of faith, the spirits of our fathers and brethren, past and present, whose works have long been known to God?"[51]

Does such a belief in the abiding presence among us of the Church invisible interfere with the Scriptural assurance that it is at rest? Human nature, Newman supposes, is unequal to incessant watchfulness and when it dies, is said to fall asleep. The condition of the faithful departed is then a "state of repose, rest, security; but a state more like paradise than heaven—that is, a state which comes short of the glory which shall be revealed in us after the Resurrection, a state of waiting, meditation, hope, in which what has been sown on earth may be matured and completed."[52]

Newman seems to infer that the Saints have this time to grow in holiness and perfect the inward development of the good seed sown in their hearts, to mature that fruit of grace but partly formed in this life. "As we are expressly told that the spirits of the just are perfected on their death, it follows that the greater advance each has made here, the higher will be the line of his subsequent growth between death and the Resurrection." Such a position must be taken by one who

---

[51] P. S. IV, 179, 180.
[52] P. S. III, 377.

rejects Purgatory[53] and at the same time admits that "nothing defiled can enter heaven." Still, Newman does not precisely say how the elect will purify themselves, who have "much in them unsubdued—much pride, much ignorance, much unrepented sin, much inconsistency, much irregularity in prayer, much lightness and frivolity of thought."[54]

Admitting the text of the Apocalypse which states that the Saints will rest from their labors,[55] he reconciles their repose with their presence in the Church. The latter does not involve any labor or toil, any active interference. "Though they live unto God and have power with Him, this does not imply that they act, or are conscious of their power. Yet they may be active promoters of the Church's welfare as by prayer, though we know not how they are active, or how they are at rest or how they can be both at once."[56] The same earnest gropings are evident from another passage of a sermon; Newman seems desirous of penetrating the mystery insofar as it is possible from the data furnished by Scripture: "Christ went to intercede with the Father; we do not know, we may not boldly speculate,—yet it may be that Saints departed intercede, unknown to us, for the victory of the Truth upon earth; and their prayers above may be as really indispensable conditions of that victory as the labors of those who remain among us. They are taken away for some purpose surely; their gifts are not lost to us; their soaring minds, the fire of their contemplations, the sanctity of their desires, the vigor of their faith, the sweetness and gentleness of their affections, were not given without an object. Yea, doubtless they are keeping up the perpetual chant in the shrine above, praying and praising God day and night in His Temple like Moses upon the Mount, while Joshua and his host fight with Amalek. Can they be allotted

---

[53] He calls this doctrine a "frightful notion," though he adds that he would accept it on faith were it what the Anglican formularies imply it is not, a doctrine sanctioned by the Catholic Church. Cf. P. S. III, 372; also IV, 88.

[54] P. S. III, 377.

[55] 6:11.

[56] P. S. IV, 182.

greater blessedness than to have a station after the pattern of that Savior who has departed hence? Has *He* no power in the world's movements because He is away? And though He is the living and exalted Lord of all, and the government is on His shoulder, and they are but His servants without strength of themselves, laid up, moreover apart from the conflict of good and evil in the paradise of God, yet so much light as this is given us by the inspired pages of the Apocalypse, that they are interested in the fortunes of the Church."[57]

At least up to 1837, then, Newman's ideas are not very clear on the intercession of the Saints. Nevertheless, he takes some of his co-religionists to task for ridiculing the Roman Catholics who claim that the Saints cannot hear our prayers unless Almighty God reveals our requests to them so that they might ask them back for us. "We are using," says he, "an unreal, because an unscriptural argument, Moses on the Mount having the sin of his people first revealed to him by God, that he in turn might intercede with God for them. Indeed it is through Him ... that we are able even in this life to hear the requests of each other, and to present them to Him in prayer."[58]

If he hesitates about the intercession of the Saints, he has no doubt whatever about the intercessory power of the just upon earth. There is too much evidence in Scripture on that point.[59] He declares formally that it is the privilege of mortals in the friendship of God to intercede for others.[60] Intercession is the characteristic of Christian worship, the privilege of the heavenly adoption, the exercise of the perfect and spiritual mind.[61] One cannot doubt the power of faith and prayer to effect all things with God. Nothing is so powerful with Christ as continual intercession, which distinguishes a Christian from such as are not Christians. Indeed, intercession is the function

---

[57] Ibid. II,214.

[58] V. M. II, 102.

[59] Cf. P. S. II, 198; III, 351, 352.

[60] P.S. III, 362.

[61] Ibid. 350.

of the justified.⁶² In view of this frequent and explicit testimony by which Newman affirms that the just on earth are intercessors, mediators between God and man, it is difficult to understand why he should have hesitated about admitting that the Saints who have already merited their rewards have a still greater power of intercession before the throne of God. The only explanations that present themselves are the fact that the doctrine of intercession of the blessed is not clearly brought forth in Scripture, as Newman thought, and especially there is the fact that the Anglican Church did not pronounce upon the subject.⁶³

As for any direct reference to the intercession of our Lady, Newman expresses himself only to condemn in a forceful manner the teachings of some Roman Catholics who seem, to him at least, to ascribe to the Blessed Virgin a power of intercession so great as to dispense from Christian living. As a matter of fact, the citations he makes, do not at all give such an impression.⁶⁴ He quotes from a tract by the Jesuit Crasset, who in catechetical form expounds the doctrine on Mary's intercessory power. In the answers quoted, the Jesuit states that the devout client of Mary has a morally infallible guarantee of salvation and that the Blessed Virgin has fetched souls out of hell. On the face of it, it may seem that a Protestant would have reason to be shocked, but on closer investigation it is seen that the Jesuit has given a satisfactory explanation.⁶⁵

---

⁶² Ibid. 348, 353, 354, 358.

⁶³ In 1840 Newman declares that he considers the intercession of Saints a question left open by the Prayer Book. Moz. II, 276.

⁶⁴ Cf. V. M. II, 122.

⁶⁵ The work referred to by Newman is *"La véritable dévotion envers la Sainte Vierge, établie et défendue,"* which appeared in 1675 at Paris. This book was one of a great number of refutations directed against the *Monita Salutaria B. V. M. ad cultores suos indiscretos* attributed to a certain Adam Widenfeldt, a Cologne lawyer but imperfectly converted from Protestantism. He composed the work under the inspiration of the Jansenists with whom he had been acquainted at Ghent and later on at Paris. Catholics were scandalized, while Protestants acclaimed it in all countries and at once translated it into various languages. The work was condemned as was the Apology which succeeded it. For more detailed

Newman finds fault particularly with the ascription to the Blessed Virgin of power to command her divine Son. Crasset gives an answer to the question whether God ever refuses anything to the Blessed Virgin: "The prayers of a Mother so humble and respectful are esteemed a command by a Son so sweet and so obedient. Being truly our Savior's Mother as well in heaven as she was on earth, she still retains a kind of natural authority over His person, over His goods, and over His omnipotence; so that, as Albertus Magnus says, she can not only entreat Him for the salvation of her servants, but by her motherly authority can command Him; and, as another expresses it, the power of the Mother and of the Son is all one, she being by her omnipotent Son made herself omnipotent." Newman's only answer to these supposedly exaggerated statements is the words of the Master Himself: "Woe to the world because of offences! for it must needs be that offences come, but woe to that man by whom the offence cometh!"[66]

When Newman expressed himself on this question, he felt his position secure in the Anglican Church and was trying to find a theological basis for Anglicanism, the Via Media between Romanism and Protestantism. Here he finds that he has a case where Rome condemns herself out of her own mouth, where the ground on which English Catholics stood was not in accord with the exaggerations of others of the Faith. Thus, he cites the curse upon him "who believes the Virgin to be more than a creature ... who honors her above her Son or believes that she can in any way command Him."[67]

IV. ATTITUDE TOWARDS THE ROMAN CHURCH.

Another principle must be taken into consideration to understand what may be called Newman's negative attitude on devotion to the Blessed Virgin. This investigation will explain

---

information cf. Terrien, *La Mère de Dieu et la Mère des Hommes*, IV, 378 sqq. Note.

[66] V. M. II, 122.

[67] Ibid. 128–130.

Principles and Obstacles (1816-1839)

the second current of which mention was made, and at the same time show to some extent the influence exerted upon him by the Fathers, who represent Tradition or Antiquity. Thereby the key will be furnished to the difficulties which he experienced in reference to devotion to the Mother of God. The point in question is his view of the Church of Rome, particularly during the first period of the Oxford Movement from 1833 to 1839.

His *crux*, as for others,[68] lay precisely in the inability to reconcile the worship of the Blessed Virgin and Saints with the teachings of Antiquity as he understood them.[69] Unlike the Protestants, he did not hold the Bible as the sole rule of faith; with the Catholic, he held Tradition besides the Scriptures, but the divergence lay in the interpretation of the authority of Antiquity. His *a priori* principle (if it may be so called) was this: the foundation of Anglican faith is Antiquity,[70] which is the true exponent of the doctrines of Christianity.[71] He supposed that Anglicanism stood midway between the doctrinal excesses of Protestants and the practical corruptions of Roman Catholics. Hence his attempt to elaborate a Via Media theory, which was calculated to steer a middle course between these two extremes. Because of the position of Anglicanism, Newman thought that "Romanist," heretic, and infidel were uniting with one another in opposing it as they did the orthodoxy of the first centuries.[72] He was sincerely convinced for a time that the Anglican church was the most perfect reproduction of the primitive Church among the different communions.

---

[68] Pusey in his *Eirenicon* also speaks of "that vast system as to the Blessed Virgin, which to all of us has been the special *crux* of the Roman system." p. 101.

[69] Another ground for objection is the claim that the worship of Mary interferes with that due to God alone. However, Newman conceded that this might not have been true in individual cases.

[70] V. M. I, 70.

[71] Apo. 26.

[72] V. M. I, 60.

He and other Tractarians had striven to put an effective check to the spread of Protestant doctrines in England by a strong and clear-cut affirmation of Catholic dogma proved from Scripture. The Roman Catholic, however, was not to be met on the same ground, but must be encountered on that of Antiquity. Newman felt certain that the latter could not prove his special doctrines to be found in Primitive Christianity. The tradition of Catholics, declared Newman, "is not really such, it is a tradition of men, not continuous, it stops short of the Apostles, the history of its introduction is known." Antiquity, then, was his stronghold, and his doctrine, the primitive.

Still, he acknowledged that the primitive truth seemed to be virtually lost in the nineteenth century and, by proceeding along a Via Media, he hoped to attain, the "nearest approximation to that primitive truth which Polycarp and Ignatius enjoyed."[73] At once a certain inconsistency is manifest, which, however, was not apparent to the logical Newman. He first claims to have Antiquity on his side and to be in possession of the primitive truth, and then is willing merely to *approximate* primitive doctrine if he could not possess it absolutely. He would be content then if the Fathers did not contradict him,[74] thus trying to hold on to the Fathers as well as the Anglican divines.

In his estimation there were two elements in operation in the Roman system. As far as it is Catholic and Scriptural, it adheres to the Fathers; as far as it is a corruption, it finds it necessary to supersede them.[75] Modern Catholicism, he thought, presents a contrast with the Primitive Church in teaching, conduct, worship, and polity;[76] further, there is even a difference between its formal teachings and its popular and political manifestations. He argues the case somewhat in this fashion:

---

[73] V. M. I, pp. xxv, 7.

[74] V. M. I, pp. xxv, 7.

[75] Ibid. I, pp. xliv, 83.

[76] Ibid. p. xxxvii.

Principles and Obstacles (1816-1839)

The Roman Catholic has a tradition[77] unlike other traditions; its beginnings go back to the very Apostles of Christ. The Fathers are witnesses to this tradition; the beliefs of the Church today must be those of the Primitive Church. But the Roman Catholic, while recognizing the Fathers[78] and ascribing a certain authority to them, admits that they are of use only as they prove the Roman doctrines; they are allowed in no way to interfere with the conclusion adopted by his Church; they are of authority if they agree with Rome; of none if they differ. They held what the Church of Rome holds today; if not, then they were out of joint with the Church of their own day, for the Church of Rome today is the logical continuation of the early Church. Her own writers claim that she has deprived herself of the means of introducing innovations, that she not only submits to Scripture but binds herself to interpret it in what concerns faith and morals according to the sense of the Holy Fathers, from which she professes never to depart.[79]

For Newman there was no question here of abstract arguments, original views, or moral interpretations, but of simple historical fact, and the Anglican had only to hold tenaciously to his position, considered absolutely impregnable.[80] He accused Rome of ruthlessly thrusting aside the Fathers because she lays claim to a higher authority,—an infallible one,—which stands above that of any individual. An Anglican could not admit this, for such an acknowledgment would be branding his own Church with the stigma of schism, if not of heresy. The Fathers, according to the Roman view, have great weight when a dogma is to be defined, since they are the spokesmen of Tradition, which must go back to ancient times, nay, to the Apostles themselves. Their authority is, however, not so much individual as collective; to them was not given or

---

[77] Cf. Renaudin, *La Doctrine de l'Assomption de la T. S. Vierge*, 84. The author exposes a defense of tradition and of the Fathers according to St. Augustine.

[78] Ess. II, 17.

[79] V. M. I, 68, 78.

[80] Ibid. 79.

promised infallibility, but to the successor of Peter. With just reason, then, can a Catholic prefer the teaching of a Pope to that of a thousand Augustines and Jeromes.

Both Roman and Anglican claim the same foundations for doctrines that are contrary. The former admits the *Cultus Sanctorum,* a special worship of the Blessed Virgin, Purgatory, etc., because these teachings are found in germ in Scripture and Antiquity; the latter denies them because he affirms that Antiquity did not hold these beliefs; for the latter the Vincentian canon implied a certain rigidity in religious doctrine and practice.[81]

At least during the Tract Movement, Newman considered the essence of Rome's offence to consist in what he called the extreme honors which she paid to the Blessed Virgin and to the Saints;[82] in his estimation the cult to the Virgin could not be proved from Antiquity. He admits, it is true, that St. Ephrem may have invoked the Mother of God, Gregory may have besought the intercession of a Basil, but he asks, what is the testimony of one or two Fathers when so many others are silent?[83] These invocations might be merely rhetorical; and, as isolated facts, need not represent the general belief of Antiquity.

Newman recognized the claim Rome had on his admiration, but conscience demanded that he protest with all his might against these usages. His line of action was clear before him, since Rome was going, as he thought, far beyond the scope of Scripture and Tradition.[84] The dominant errors he condemned were the actual popular beliefs and usages sanctioned by Rome over and above the dogmas which it maintains.[85] Rome, he thought, had departed from Primitive Christianity by a practical idolatry, namely, virtual worship of the Virgin and the Saints and by the degradation of moral truth and duty which

---

[81] V. M. I, 31–35; Apo. 203; Diff. I, 371–372.

[82] Apo. 53.

[83] V. M. I, 52.

[84] Apo. 54, 106–107 (1839–1841).

[85] Ibid., 78

flow from these.⁸⁶ This accusation occurs again and again: "If the note of schism, on the one hand, lies against England, an antagonist disgrace lies upon Rome, the note of idolatry. ... The Roman Church practices what is so like idolatry ... that we do seriously think that members of the English Church have a providential direction given them, how to comport themselves towards the Church of Rome, while she is what she is."⁸⁷ "We cannot join a Church, did we wish it ever so much, which does not acknowledge our orders, refuses us the Cup, demands our acquiescence in image-worship, and excommunicates us if we do not receive it and all other decisions of the Tridentine Council."⁸⁸ Elsewhere he indicates the path to follow: "Our Lord said of false prophets, 'By their fruits you shall know them,' and however the mind may be entangled theoretically, yet surely it will fall upon certain marks in Rome which seem to convey to the simple and honest inquirer a solemn warning to keep clear of her while she carries them about her. Such are her idolatrous worship of the Virgin, her image-worship, etc. Surely we have more reason for thinking that her doctrines concerning images and the Saints are false, than that her decision that they are Apostolical is true."⁸⁹ Under such conditions, then, union with Rome is impossible.⁹⁰

Idolatry he holds is the specific difference between Rome and Anglicanism.⁹¹ Catholics, Newman assumes, may attempt to repudiate this assertion, but their arguments are useless, he claims, since facts are against them: "Whatever may be said in defense of the *authoritative documents* of the faith of Rome, this imputation against her authorities, that they have countenanced and established doctrines and practices from which a Christian mind, not educated in them, shrinks; and that

---

⁸⁶ Ibid., 111.

⁸⁷ Ibid. 113 (1841).

⁸⁸ Ibid. 111 (1836).

⁸⁹ V. M. I, 265; II, 415 (1837, 1841).

⁹⁰ ⁸⁹ Moz. II, 59 (1834).

⁹¹ L. G. 176; Ess. II, 367, Prepos. 13.

in the number of these, a worship of the creature which to most men will seem to be a quasi-idolatry, is not the least prominent."[92]

"Romanism," Newman affirms, has the truth of Primitive Christianity, but in many instances the truth is overlaid with corruptions which are dangerous to the multitude but which the better instructed might be able to counteract.[93] Nay, he goes further; it is not merely a corruption, but a perversion, a distortion of true Catholicity; a misdirection and abuse of right principle, so much so that it stunts or distorts the growth of the soul in spiritual excellence.[94] "In place of the Blessed Trinity and the future life, it sets the Blessed Virgin and purgatory before the people as centers of their spiritual lives, to the exclusion of fundamental dogmas."[95] The principal corruptions or additions centering in the Blessed Virgin and Saints are, as Newman avers, image-worship, veneration and invocation. The first so-called addition, he claims to have been made in 787 at the Seventh General Council, held at Nice, which sanctioned the worship of images; it was the first that presumed to rest the proof of its decree on ground short of Scripture, the first that violated the doctrine of adhesion to the practice or received opinion of Antiquity.[96] Newman claimed with the Homilist that no images were exposed publicly during the first seven hundred years, when Christianity was still pure,[97] and that English Catholics refrained from this practice during times of persecution as a matter of expedience, though it is expressly

---

[92] 91 Ess. II, 368.

[93] V. M. I, 40.

[94] Ibid 106.

[95] V. M. II, 368–370. Cf. these lines of *The Christian Year*, p. 246:
> She mourns that tender hearts should bend
>> Before a meaner shrine,
> And upon Saint or Angel spend
>> That love that should be Thine.

[96] Ess. II, 7.

[97] V. M. II, 333.

Principles and Obstacles (1816-1839)   25

recommended by the Council of Trent as an edifying usage.[98]

Newman admitted a certain form of veneration of the Blessed Virgin which consisted in reverence for her dignity and a silent contemplation of her grandeurs with the imitation of her virtues. But any external demonstration was discountenanced, as though our Lady would he shocked at the veneration of which she is the object.

The invocation of our Lady was the practice particularly condemned by Newman. In a sermon preached in 1837 he indicates the reasons why Anglicans abstain from such a usage:[99]

1. The practice, he holds, is not primitive, but an addition made when the world had poured into the Church. "Can the Romanist imagine," he asks elsewhere, "St. Paul offering up his addresses to St. Mary and vowing some memorial to her, if she would be pleased *deprecare pro illo filium Dei* or, using the language of Bellarmine or others, *Laus Deo Virginique Matri*."[100] Such a doctrine, Newman claims, cannot be traced to the age of the Apostles or at least to the period immediately following the Apostolic Age. If the Apostles did teach the worship of Saints, why did they not transmit their doctrines to the generations following?

2. The second reason is based upon Scripture, in which we are told to pray to God alone. Invocations may easily be corrupted into prayer and then become idolatrous—such is the assumption. "Scripture speaks clearly and solemnly about Christ as the sole mediator. When prayer to the Saints is recommended at all times and places as ever-present guardians, and their good works pleaded in God's sight, is not this such an infringement upon the plain word of God, such a violation of our allegiance to our only Savior, as must needs be an insult to Him? His honor He will not give to another. Can we with a safe conscience do it? Should we act thus in a parallel case even

---

[98] Cf. V. M. II, 112, 113, 118. The homily "On the Peril of Idolatry" ridicules the veneration of images. Cf. ibid. 295, 302.

[99] P. S. IV, 183.

[100] Ess. II, 13, 14.

with an earthly friend? Does not St. John's example warn us against falling down before angels? Does not St. Paul warn us against a voluntary humility and worshipping of angels?

And are not these texts indications of God's will, which ought to guide our conduct? Is it not safest not to pay them this extraordinary honor?"[101]

3. As is evident, Newman's difficulty was a real one, which touched his conscience very closely. The two reasons given above have their confirmation in another which in the final analysis had the greatest weight with him, namely, that invocation of our Lady and of the Saints was not sanctioned by his Church, which forbade it as contrary to Scripture and Tradition. Even when Newman was convinced to a certain extent that his other reasons had no sufficient basis, he still refrained from invocation and dissuaded others from it. Obedience to his Church counted for very much with him; even when he knew that his Church was in the wrong, he was convinced that his adherence to it was an indication from on high how he ought to act in the matter.

He felt that the Tridentine Decrees which declare that "it is good and useful suppliantly to invoke the Saints, and that the images of Christ, the Blessed Virgin and the other Saints should receive due honor and veneration," might possibly have a good interpretation but that danger lurked in following the prescription exactly. As a matter of fact, it seemed to him that in certain countries and in certain instances the worship rendered by the people was positively idolatrous, or at least not far from it. He could not comprehend the attitude of the Roman Church, which did not seem to take heed of the situation and failed to repress the abuses that may have crept in, thereby giving a free hand to superstitions practices. The ecclesiastical authorities appeared to have closed their eyes instead of using the power that was at their disposition.[102]

To prove his point most effectively, Newman cites Bossuet, the eminent Bishop of Meaux, as an example of the teaching of

---

[101] V. M. II, 111, 112.

[102] V. M. II, 119. In answer to this cf. ibid. I, p. lxviii–lxxvii.

Roman Catholics on the question of invocation and veneration of Saints. He admits that Bossuet "seems to have been nearly the first who put on the Tridentine Decrees a meaning more consonant with Primitive Christianity, distinguishing between the doctrines of the Church, and of the Schools. This new interpretation has been widely adopted by the Romanists."[103] The eminent prelate played a doubly important role in Marian devotion, first by combating with all his might the tendency of an exaggerated and almost puerile devotion fostered by certain religious organizations,[104] and on the other hand by presenting in a clear, concise manner, that could give no offence to Protestants, the exact doctrine of the Church on the privileges of the Blessed Virgin, the power of her intercession, and the bond linking her with her faithful clients. Nevertheless, Newman, recognizing the unquestioned authority of Bossuet, finds in the latter an argument to sustain his opposition to Roman devotional manifestations in honor of the Mother of God. It is unnecessary to detail here the nature of the supposed difference or resemblance between the doctrine of Bossuet and that of the Jesuit Crasset, spoken of above.[105] Newman places Bossuet on the horns of a dilemma; either he agrees with Crasset or not. If he agrees, then his teaching is to be condemned, for one need only consult the citations given. If he does not, then his conduct is inexplicable in letting the statements of Crasset pass without questioning them. Further, Newman cites the words of Bossuet, comparing the texts of two editions of his "Exposition of the Faith." In a subsequent edition of the Tract in which these excerpts occur, Newman, by that time a Catholic, accuses himself of making unfair insinuations

---

[103] Ibid. 123.

[104] Cf. Flachaire, *La Dévotion à la Vierge dans la littérature catholique au commencement du XVII siècle*, p. 9. The author signalizes the efforts of some writers to develop a devotion in which "l'effusion sentimentale s'accompagne toujours de multiples et minutieuses pratiques." Others like Olier and St. John Eudes seemed to run into theological adventures. Men like Bossuet, St. Francis de Sales and the Oratorians counteracted the tendencies towards a merely sentimental devotion. Cf. also 141.

[105] V. M. II, 121.

with reference to the private impression of Bossuet's "Exposition."[106]

V. INFLUENCES OF FROUDE AND KEBLE ON HIS DEVOTION

The preceding section presents quite a contrast between Newman's attitude on invocation and veneration of the Blessed Virgin, and that solid doctrinal foundation which presents her as the highest of creatures and thus deserving of our reverent esteem and faithful imitation. He acknowledges possessing a *great* devotion to our Lady during this period. Whence did he derive it? The answer to this question leads us to examine the sources, or rather the source, which can be traced to two persons, who exerted a most profound influence on him. Newman had the happy faculty of throwing himself into the mind of others and, while influencing others, he himself imbibed something of the character of the other individual. Subsequent to the beginnings of the Oxford Movement, it was his personality that drew others after him; he furnished the principles of individual conduct to many, but in his younger days he was rather in a receptive position, being influenced strongly by the dominating personalities of certain men, whose memory he evoked with deepest gratitude and fondest affection in the *Apologia*. With his usual precision and insight he traced the sources of his principles. He developed a strong, tender, loyal devotion to the Mother of our Lord under the genial influence of Richard Hurrell Froude.[107]

---

[106] Ibid.125.

[107] Froude was born in 1803, and was brought up in the High Church traditions. He was a pupil of Keble in 1821, and in 1823 followed the latter to his country parish to complete his preparations for the university examinations. As a young man he had a remarkable prestige for his distinguished manners, and, unknown to those about him, continually exercised himself in asceticism, something practically unknown at that time to Anglicans. He was elected Fellow of Oriel in 1826 and sought to spread the ideas of his master. Ill health compelled him to voyage in Southern Europe accompanied by Newman. With his usual enthusiasm he threw himself heart and soul into the Oxford Movement; his criticisms were particularly sought for by the writers of the Tracts, especially by

"He fixed deep in me the idea of devotion to the Blessed Virgin," says Newman of his friend.[108] Froude was a man brimful of ideas and views, with an intellect as critical and logical as it was speculative and bold. It is curious to find these two men attracted towards each other already in 1826. Newman was still under the influences of Evangelicalism, with a leaning towards the liberalism of his master Whately. Froude, on the contrary, considered Newman a bit suspect doctrinally, even heretical, being himself firmly attached to High Church principles. He had been formed by Keble, and it seems fairly certain that the devotion to the Blessed Virgin was taught him by Keble. Unlike most other High Churchmen, Froude had no particular attachment to the Primitive Church, but was drawn towards the Medieval Church; he criticised the English Church for having departed from Antiquity on several points and for having severed with the Universal Church. He did not hesitate to express his admiration for the Church of Rome and as strong an aversion for the so-called Reformers.

Froude held Tradition as a main instrument of religious teaching and further had "a high, severe ideal of the intrinsic excellence of virginity; and he considered the Blessed Virgin its great pattern. He delighted in thinking of the Saints; he had a vivid appreciation of the idea of sanctity, its possibility and its heights."[109] With his intense ardor, he had the courage to draw the ultimate conclusions of all the principles he accepted. He helped gradually to turn Newman from his Evangelicalism and Liberalism, though not convincing him on certain points, for example, that Rome was not anti-Christian. Froude was the one who strove to counteract Newman's idea concerning the honors paid to the Blessed Virgin and the Saints. Thus he writes: "I think people are injudicious who talk against the Roman Catholics for worshipping Saints and honoring the Virgin and images, etc. These things may be idolatrous, I

Keble and Newman. He died on Feb. 28, 1836, just at a time when his services to the Oxford Movement could have been most appreciated.

[108] Apo. 25.

[109] Ibid. 24.

cannot make up my mind about it; but to my mind it is the Carnival that is real practical idolatry."[110]

This continual check upon Newman's almost violent denunciations of Rome, did not hinder Froude from expressing his own dissatisfaction at the Roman system and just on the very question of so-called idolatry. He was struck on his tour abroad by what he considered a degeneracy among Italian Catholics.[111] His ardor for Roman Catholicism was slightly dampened by his contact with exuberances that shocked his English nature. "Since I have been out here," he writes, "I have got a worse notion of the Roman Catholics than I had. I really do think them idolators. ... What I mean by calling the people idolaters, is that I believe they look upon the Saints and the Virgin as good-natured people, that will try to them let off easier than the Bible declares, and that as they don't intend to comply with the conditions on which God promises to answer prayers, they pray to them as a come-off."[112]

Froude, though directly influencing Newman in devotion to the Blessed Virgin, was merely the channel carrying it from the real source, which was John Keble,[113] from whom he had imbibed the ideas of a visible Church, apostolic succession, the sacramental principle, the Communion of Saints; at the same time he reacted upon his master in completing his principles in a more Catholic direction, and drawing all the possible

---

[110] Apo. 53.

[111] Ibid.25.

[112] V. M. II, 214.

[113] John Keble was born in 1792 and brought up in the traditions of the Non-jurors. He was elected Fellow of Oriel and, as if fearing the dangers of intellectual vanity, took up a post as vicar of a small country parish. His piety was of such a nature as to seem to keep him in the continual thought of God's presence. His volume of verses which appeared in 1827 under the title of *The Christian Year* did much to inculcate forgotten Catholic principles. Pusey even ascribes the beginning of the Oxford Movement to this little work. Newman places it in Keble's sermon on the "National Apostasy." Keble helped to keep many in the Established Church who would otherwise have drifted into infidelity. He was unable to follow Newman in the decisive step which brought the latter to Rome. He died March 29, 1866.

consequences of the principles placed.[114] Froude was likewise instrumental in bringing Keble and Newman together.

In his Catholic days Newman has described in a most delicate manner the beautiful Marian devotion which one would naturally expect to encounter in the master of Hurrell Froude. "If there be one writer," wrote Newman shortly after his conversion, "in the Anglican Church, who has discovered a deep, tender, loyal devotion to the Blessed Mary, it is the author of the 'Christian Year'. ... His mind and heart seemed to have been formed upon the Vision of the Virgin and Child, for as a young man already, he loved to adorn the walls of his room with pictures of the Madonna."[115]

Who could forget the touching lines penned for the feast of the Annunciation:

> Ave Maria! thou whose name
> All but adoring love may claim![116]

Are these but the raptures of a poet or are they not rather the fruits of convictions born of continual meditation on the Divine Economy? To Keble, Mary is the "Mother blest, favor'd beyond Archangels' dream," the "Lily of Eden's fragrant shade," the "sole earthly care" of Jesus, her divine Son. Three times in the same poem he salutes her with the words that spring so naturally to a Roman Catholic's lips, but which were held almost in abomination by Anglican and still more by the out-and-out Protestant. Newman explains that the "Ave Maria" might pass as mere poetry in 1827 but a little later it would be rejected as savoring of "Romish superstition."[117]

Keble's devotional feeling towards the Blessed Virgin simply became more decided, more firmly based in reason, as he advanced in life.[118] This is abundantly proved by his *Lyra Innocentium* written at a time when he had grown weary of

---

[114] Thureau-Dangin, op. cit. I, 16.
[115] Ess. II, 452, 453.
[116] *Christian Year,* p. 197.
[117] Ess. II, 440.
[118] Ibid.439.

looking at the imperfections of the English Church and turned to neutral ground where he could contemplate tranquillity and peace—the blissful period of childhood. From the consideration of infancy he is instinctively drawn to the Divine Child and His Maiden Mother. He introduces her again and again, and sometimes expressly, when it would scarcely be expected; he expatiates on the worship offered by infants and asks:

> "How in Christ's anthem fails the children's part
> While Mary bears Him throned in her maternal heart?"[119]

He is prodigal in the use of titles that give expression to his tender devotion; this is but the result of his clear understanding of her part as instrument in Christ's miracles of mercy.[120] Still, in order not to give offence to his fellow-Anglicans, he abstains from certain terms and even introduces the idea of Mary's condition of creature when there seems hardly any call for it. May we not assume that Keble held the Immaculate Conception and that it was from him Newman learned to speak of the "transcendent purity of her, whom the Creator Spirit condescended to overshadow with His miraculous presence ... the contemplation of which leads to a higher subject did we dare to follow it." Keble too speaks of this spotless Mother, first of creatures, "whom the awful blessing lifted above all Adam's race."[121]

> "Who can express the love
> That nurtur'd thee so pure and sweet,
> Making thy heart a shelter meet
> For Jesus' holy Dove?"[122]

A firm believer in the Communion of Saints, he placed Mary and the Saints near the soul in prayer:

---

[119] Ibid. 437.
[120] Ibid. 447.
[121] Ess. II, 438.
[122] *Christian Year*, 197.

> "The Mother of Our Lord is there
> And Saints are breathing hallowed air,
> Living and dead to waft on high our feeble prayer,"[123]

and if our eyes were purged we could trace "God's unseen armies hovering near."[124]

Nevertheless, as Newman, he too held that Rome had allowed corruptions to taint the founts of her doctrine, that she "upon Saint or Angel spend that love that should be Thine."[125] He taught his fellow-countrymen their duty with regard to Rome, a duty of kindness and loving sympathy which would bring her back, as he thought, to the purity of her ancient teachings:

> "Speak gently of our sister's fall:
> Who knows but gentle love
> May win her at our patient call
> The surer way to prove."[126]

The prayer of Newman that Mary would obtain for her loving client the grace of conversion was never realized.

VI. CONCLUSION: CHARACTER OF NEWMAN'S DEVOTION DURING THIS PERIOD

Having examined the principles that guided Newman's doctrine and personal devotion, together with the influences directing his devotion, it remains to characterize the devotion of Newman during this period of his Anglican life. What did he understand precisely by devotion, for he speaks of a *great* devotion, of *growing* in devotion, and of finding devotional manifestations to our Lady his great *crux?*

The word devotion in general may mean addiction, eager inclination, strong attachment, ardent love, affection, or zeal. It may specially represent feelings towards God, appropriately expressed by acts of worship, or it may be prayer, an act

---

[123] Ess. II, 438.

[124] *Christian Year,* 225.

[125] Ibid. 247.

[126] Ibid. 248.

evincing devotedness, a form of prayer or worship, a consecration or dedication. As a Catholic, Newman distinguishes between faith and devotion. He defines devotion, then, as "religious honors that belong to the objects of our faith and the payment of those honors." There is a real distinction between faith, which is the Creed and assent to it, and devotion. The former may exist without the latter, but not vice-versa.

In Newman's Anglican life, he distinguished neatly between the honors belonging to the objects of faith and the payment of these honors. Devotion for him may be tersely summed up in the first part of his definition, namely, reverent esteem paid to the objects of faith; the payment of this honor he usually styled devotional manifestation[127] or, at other times, when there is question of Saints or Angels, he speaks of "undue reverence" or "veneration,"[128] "excessive honor."[129]

That Newman had a truly intense devotion to our Lady as an Anglican is undeniable. One has but to read casually his elegant sermon on "The Reverence Due to the Virgin Mary"[130] to be convinced of this fact. He who had at an early date been brought under the shadow of our Lady,[131] and whose altar he served at St. Mary's was necessarily attracted by the contemplation of her dignity and her ineffable gifts and could not restrain the profound admiration that was seeking an outlet, but which was held in check by loyalty to his Church. He had to limit his devotion to a silent contemplation of this most wondrous of creatures.

He finds in the silence of Scripture a powerful lesson and at the same time an approbation of the Anglican's position in regard to our Blessed Lady. How little, in truth, is to be found in Holy Writ about God's Mother. The circumstances attending Christ's birth and infancy, one or two events in His public life

---

[127] Apo. 195.

[128] Ibid. 53.

[129] P. S. II, 358.

[130] Ibid. Sermon XII.

[131] Oriel College is dedicated to St. Mary.

and Passion, and once after the Ascension—these are the only data furnished concerning her. This silence, in Newman's view, seemed to show that God wished to bring to our notice and for our edification only those creatures that have some connection with the special course of His providence and are instruments of His purposes. The intimate relation existing between Jesus and His holy Mother was too sacred a thing to be exposed to the public gaze of a curious world. Her feelings, sentiments, and virtues were not to be exploited. Newman brings out this thought beautifully in speaking of the silence of the Gospels about the Blessed Virgin after the Resurrection of Jesus: "She, who was too pure and holy a flower to be more than seen here on earth, even during the season of her Son's humiliation, was altogether drawn by the Angels within the veil on His Resurrection and had her joy in Paradise."[132]

There is another consideration that gave a special color to all his devotion to the Blessed Virgin, namely, he thought that it was dangerous to expose the sanctity and beauty of Mary in all its splendor. This is the continual objection made by Protestants, and Newman was sincerely convinced of its force. He supposed that there was a continual risk that the honor received by the Blessed Virgin from God should eclipse in our minds the honor due to the Divine Giver Himself.[133] She would be honored, her gifts would be seen, and God would be lost sight of; because then she would seem to exist for her own sake and not as an instrument appointed for realizing the divine plan. The Blessed Virgin could not be revealed except insofar as she ministered to the mystery of the Redemption, so that we in our feebleness might not stop at her, but rather go on from her to the purpose for which she was chosen, and thus we should be led on to God Himself. Otherwise we should rest perchance in the thought of her and think of the creature more than of the Creator. Particularly is this the case with reference to the Blessed Virgin, because of her high gifts. The higher the gifts, the less fitted they are to be seen; what greater favor can

---

[132] P. S. IV, 341.
[133] Ibid. II, 133.

be conceived than to be associated not merely mystically with Christ, but physically, for Christ derived His humanity from the very substance of Mary?[134]

What, then, is the best way to honor the Blessed Virgin? Newman answers this by using two authorities as a basis—Scripture and the practice of the Anglican Church. As Scripture shows us the Blessed Virgin ever associated with her divine Son and never for any reason that concerns herself alone, he suggests that we "had better only think of her with and for her Son, never separating her from Him, but using her name as a memorial of His great condescension in stooping from heaven and not abhorring the Virgin's womb."[135] In like manner the Anglican Church never separates the two, commemorating only those feasts in honor of the Blessed Mary as may also be festivals in honor of our Lord; thus, it has retained only two of the ancient feasts of the Blessed Virgin, the Purification, which is also the Presentation of Jesus in the Temple, and the Annunciation, which recalls at the same time the mystery of the Incarnation.

The duties of reverence to the Blessed Virgin, as for other Saints, consist in reading of her in Scripture, making mention *of* her in prayer, thanking God for her, praising God with her, and praying God to visit us in His mercy as he visited her, insofar as it is possible.[136] She must be contemplated silently for our edification, so that her example may serve to encourage our faith, enliven our patience, shelter us from thoughts of ourselves, keep us from resting on ourselves.[137] She must be a pattern of faith and sanctity, for she is set before us to excite and guide us in our religious course.[138] She, more than the other Saints, leads us on to our Lord, for she was more modelled after His pattern than any other.

Devotion must limit itself to this silent contemplation,

---

[134] P. S. II, 133.
[135] Ibid. 135.
[136] P. S. III, 250.
[137] P. S. III, 387.
[138] Ibid. II, 399.

reverence, and imitation, and must be watched over lest it lead to "superstitiously" honoring her. Newman was a docile son of his Church and so refrained from anything that might savor of disloyalty or disobedience. Article 22 says: "The Romish doctrine concerning worshipping and adoration, as well of images as of relics and also invocation of saints, is a fond thing vainly invented, and grounded upon no warranty of Scripture, but rather repugnant to the Word of God." Had he not been convinced of the further ground that these devotional manifestations were not primitive and that they might easily become "idolatrous"[139] he would, nevertheless, have abstained because of the formal prohibition of the Church. This was evidenced in the second period of his career. "Such," he says, "is the almost incredible perverseness of men, that instead of glorifying God in His Saints, Christians came to pay them an honor approaching to divine worship."[140]

He cautions Anglicans not to honor the Saints "superstitiously, or wilfully to rely on them, lest they be a snare."[141] But he can find a psychological reason why men had recourse to the Blessed Virgin and the Saints. "The humble and contrite believer coming to Christ for pardon and help, perceives the great strait he is in, in having to address the God of heaven. This perplexity of mind it was which led convinced sinners in former times to seek refuge in beings short of God; not as denying God's supremacy, or shunning Him, but discerning the vast distance between themselves and Him and seeking some resting places by the way ... because of the height of God's mountain, up which the way of escape lay. And then gradually becoming devoted to those whom they trusted, Saints, Angels, or good men living, and copying them, their faith had a fall, and their virtue trailed upon the ground, for want of props to rear it heavenward. We Christians, sinners though we be like other men, are not allowed thus to debase our nature, or to defraud ourselves of God's mercy, and though

---

[139] Ibid. IV, 183.
[140] Ibid. II, 395.
[141] P. S. III, 387.

it be very terrible to speak to the living God, yet speak we must, or die; tell our sorrows we must, or there is no hope; for created mediators and patrons are forbidden us, and to trust in an arm of flesh is made a sin."[142]

Newman sees why men should find it easier to appeal for aid to a Saint, but forgets that the Saints are invoked as intercessors. They are not an end in themselves but merely a means. It is inexplicable, however, why he should see in invocation and confidence in the Saints a debasing of one's nature and, as consequence, the loss of faith and lack of virtue. He probably entertained the notion to which Froude gave expression when he claimed that Catholics called upon the Saints in order to spare themselves the effort of practicing good Christian lives.

Profound psychologist as he was, Newman did not lose sight of the value of exteriorizing one's sentiments. He objected to the worship and veneration of images, it is true, but admitted in word and conduct that pictures, emblems, ceremonies, etc., are powerful incentives to virtue and piety. For example, he insisted on placing a picture of the Madonna in the room of his younger brother Frank, when the latter came to Oxford. To the latter's protests, the future Catholic Cardinal simply replied by vigorously denouncing the Protestants who forget the sacred words "Blessed art thou among women."[143]

Newman ever insisted on the necessity of devotional manifestation when there is question of God. Devotion in this instance always embraced the religious honor owed to God and the payment of this honor. He affirmed that "practical devotion to the ever-blessed Son has precluded difficulties in faith"; declarations, Creeds and such like "rouse in us mingled feelings of fear and confidence, affection and devotion towards Him."[144] And again: "forms of devotion are parts of devotion—like body and soul. No one can really respect religion and insult its

---

[142] P. S. I, 146.

[143] This incident is related by Francis Newman himself. **Cf.** Brémond, *Newman, Essai de biographie psychologique*, p. 296.

[144] P. S. II, 27, 29.

forms."[145] Man is so constituted that he must give expression to his inmost sentiments and convictions, but the so-called Reformers wished to reduce religion to a dry, impersonal, insipid worship; this is what they called worshipping in spirit and in truth. The same Protestanizing influences were at work in the Anglican Church, so that Newman could later complain that many no longer merely stopped at discountenancing honor to the Saints, but went a step further and railed at all religious usages as superstitious. Newman had learned by experience that when the visible body goes, religion itself goes.[146] Externals of faith, stimulants of devotion, were abolished by Protestants, and in due time the essential dogmas of Christianity follow in their wake.

Newman saw the dangers resulting from a lack of psychology in supplying the wants of human nature, which craves excitements to devotion. In the eyes of Tractarians "Methodism and Popery" are the refuge of those whom the Anglican Church stints of the gifts of grace; "they are the foster-mothers of abandoned children. The neglect of the daily service, the desecration of festivals, the Eucharist scantily administered, insubordination permitted in all ranks of the Church, orders and offices imperfectly developed, the want of societies for particular religious objects, and the like deficiencies, lead the feverish mind, desirous of a vent to its feelings and a stricter rule of life, to the smaller religious communities, to prayer and Bible meetings, and ill-advised institutions and societies, on the one hand—on the other, to the solemn and captivating services by which Popery gains its proselytes."[147] Newman himself could not repress his admiration for Rome, which like a true mother supplies the wants of its children from the devotional viewpoint, but he had to cry out at the same time: "Oh, that Rome were not Rome! but I seem to see as clear as day that union with her is

---

[145] Ibid. 75.

[146] P. S. II, 77.

[147] Advertisement to Vol. I of the Tracts for the Times.

impossible."[148] "The Christian system there is deplorably corrupt; it upholds a religion that is polytheistic, degrading, idolatrous."[149] Yet to Rome he owed a debt of gratitude for the faithful custody of the Faith through so many centuries.[150] She is as "a sister or mother towards whom we feel so tenderly and reverently, and whom nothing but some urgent reason in conscience could make us withstand so resolutely."[151] It was precisely the forms of devotion which he considered as not sanctioned by Antiquity that forced him to hold aloof from Rome. There was a contrariety of claims between the Anglican and the Roman Church, and the history of his conversion was simply the process of working it out to a solution.[152]

He understood only later that if Rome had guarded the faith so zealously during the centuries, it was just because it was so devoted to the Blessed Mother of God. His objections vanished when he learned that merely the title "Mother of God" would put an end to all heresies connected with Jesus Christ, and devotion to the Blessed Virgin was the surest safeguard of devotion to her Son.[153]

---

[148] Moz. I, 338.
[149] Ibid. 341, 342.
[150] P. S. II, 390.
[151] L. G. 278, 279; Ess. II, 369.
[152] Apo. 112.
[153] Dev. 426.

CHAPTER II
TOWARDS THE LIGHT (1839–1845)

I. TRACT 90.

A NEW phase in Newman's Marian development presents itself when he first begins to entertain serious doubts about the Catholicity of Anglicanism. The history of the Monophysites, which he began to study during the Long Vacation of 1839, came as a thunder-bolt from a clear sky. Never before had he felt so secure in his position, maintaining the Via Media between Romanism and Protestantism. On the grounds of Antiquity, he opposed what he styled Rome's "corruptions," and not the least of these was her sanction of honors to the Blessed Virgin and the Saints and the veneration of their images. He had looked to Antiquity for his defense and had found the sixteenth and nineteenth centuries faithful reflections of the fifth, and himself—a Monophysite. Could anything have been more terrifying to one whose whole life was contained in the single word of loyalty to his conscience? He felt himself "turning devil's advocate against the much-enduring Athanasius and the majestic Leo."[1]

Shortly after came a second blow in the form of an article by Wiseman "On the Anglican Claims." The words of St. Augustine "Securus judicat orbis terrarum" cited in the article, struck him with a force unknown to him previously. Was Rome, after all, so full of corruption as he deemed it; had it

---

[1] Apo. 115–116.

really added to the primitive deposit confided to it from apostolic times? The step which would lead him to Rome was still far off. His difficulties against Rome had not yet been solved to his satisfaction, and reason was to be his guide, not imagination.[2] The only thing left for him was to bide his time and fall back upon the three principles spoken of in the preceding chapter; still, he found the dogmatic and sacramental principles better preserved in the Roman Church than in the Anglican communion. He was compelled almost against his will to resort to the positive charges against Rome, which determined his attitude so strongly on devotion to Mary.[3] Nevertheless, he feared to speak against the doctrines of Rome, lest in the event they should prove to be true. Hurrell Froude had warned him years before "how mistaken we may ourselves be on many points that are only gradually opening on us."[4]

In the state of doubt in which he found himself, and unable as he was to do aught for others who were in a similar condition, Newman felt that he had to take a positive stand in the defense of Anglicanism. Antiquity was the stronghold. He had to prove that Anglicans still held the old Catholic truth, which he thought was to be found in the Thirty-nine Articles. He and his followers had been accused of Popery and were asked what they could make of these Articles;[5] he thought he could interpret them in a Catholic sense, though the interpretation given them by Anglican ecclesiastical authority was Protestant.[6]

The arguments by which he sustained his opposition to the Roman Church, had as much force as ever to his mind and conscience.[7] Tract 90 was the fruit of his investigations on applying the acid-test to the Articles. Would they bear a Catholic interpretation? The thesis of his essay is stated in

---

[2] Apo. 119.
[3] Ibid. 120.
[4] Ibid. 123.
[5] Ibid. 78.
[6] Ibid. 130.
[7] Ibid. 134.

these words: "the Articles do not oppose Catholic teaching; they but partially oppose Roman dogma; they for the most part oppose the dominant errors of Rome."[8] He thus made a distinction as to what was meant by "Roman doctrine." This could be: 1. the Catholic teaching of the early centuries; 2. the formal dogmas of Rome as contained in the later Councils; 3. the actual popular beliefs and usages sanctioned by Rome, over and above the dogmas; these he called "dominant errors". He set himself to the task of placing a line of demarcation between what the Articles sanctioned and what they condemned. They did not reject the Catholic teaching, they *did* condemn "dominant errors"; they approved some and condemned others of the *formal* dogmas. Since the Articles were drawn up prior to the decrees of Trent, Newman maintained that they were not directed against the latter. When Anglicans spoke of Tridentine, they meant the "cut and dried propositions" enunciated in the decrees of Trent. The Articles, however, use the term "Romish," by which is meant something vague and indeterminate, comprising all that was taught in theological schools and from the pulpit and embodied in numberless devotional usages and practices.[9]

It is well known what a storm was raised by the publication of Tract 90. Four college tutors were the first to stir up the agitation that culminated in charges from many bishops in England. These four, who seem scarcely to have given the essay much serious study, asserted that the Tract "has a highly dangerous tendency from its suggesting that certain very important errors of the Church of Rome are not condemned by the Articles of the Church of England ... but only certain absurd practices and opinions which intelligent Romanists repudiate as much as we do."[10] Among the five points signalized by them as instances of what the Articles do not condemn, they cite the invocation of Saints and worship of images.[11] These very points

---

[8] Ibid. 79.

[9] Keble, 73.

[10] V.M.II, 359.

[11] The other three points were: Purgatory, Indulgences, Masses.

contained in Newman's eyes nearly all the differences between the two Churches which to him seemed irreconcilable.[12]

By 1840 he had made a certain degree of progress on the question of invocation insofar as it was not wrong in itself, abstractly considered, though experience proved it to be dangerous.[13] He claimed that the English Church had removed all invocations from her services because of the abuses to which the practice had led.[14] Previously he had also insisted on the dangerous character of invocation, but nowhere admitted that the practice was not evil in itself. His own conduct in the use of invocation was consistent as long as he remained in the Anglican Church. He would never use them because they were not sanctioned by ecclesiastical authority. In a letter to an enquirer he made a statement which summarizes his viewpoint in Tract 90, published a year after the letter was written: "in our daily service we say, 'O ye spirits and souls of the righteous ... bless ye the Lord,' which would seem to show that there are invocations which are not Romish."[15]

This is precisely the distinction he makes in interpreting Art. 22. It is the "Romish doctrine" which is a "fond thing." He presupposes that the "Romish doctrine" and the primitive are not the same, though there is a primitive doctrine on all these points, which was widely received and supported, though it may not have been universal. The Article, he avers, does not condemn the Tridentine Decree but rather "the received doctrine" of the day, or that of the Roman schools.[16]

Invocation, which in Newman's view was permissible, was addressing beings out of sight, such as the Angels, who are called upon in the Psalms to bless us; the *Benedicite* likewise furnishes an instance in which the Saints and the souls of the

---

[12] "The concessions which, as an Anglican, he would have demanded from Rome upon these several points were little else than capitulation with the honors of war." Keble, 76.

[13] Keble, 65.

[14] Ibid. 66; found in first edition of *Historical Sketches*.

[15] Keble, 65.

[16] V.M.II,295.

righteous are invoked. Such invocation is evidently sanctioned by Scripture and therefore could not be considered as "fond." When Newman accepts addresses to unseen beings, he relies upon the acknowledged authority of Bishop Kent, but one is tempted to ask whether the mere fact that this Bishop uses invocation justifies Newman's admission of it. However, the invocations that he seems to allow, provided nothing definite is meant by them and they are used as mere interjections, are vague, indeterminate addresses to beings "which we know cannot hear." Does not this seem a recession from the ideas he previously held on the Communion of Saints and their possible power of intercession? Had he not explained the argument that the Saints can hear our prayers if these be revealed to them by God so that they might in turn intercede for those who invoke their aid? Scripture approves of it.[17]

From a motive of discretion Newman does not explain precisely what is acceptable and what is objectionable in invocation, but leaves the reader to draw his own inferences after having gone over citations from the Homilies on "The Peril of Idolatry" and "The Place and Time of Prayer." Bishop Andrewes and Bellarmine are called upon also as authorities. According to the Homilies, the invocations that are to be rejected are those that encroach upon the incommunicable glory and honor due to God alone, for asking the aid of the Saints, is, as it were, confessing the inability or powerlessness of God to help us, so that some creature must always be associated with Him in order to give answer to our prayers. The Roman Catholic is accused of imitating the idolater as though he constitutes the Saints as so many tutelary divinities to prosper him in his enterprises, in his duties, and sufferings. Why should he use invocation when it is certain that the Saints cannot hear our prayers, that they do not read the secrets of the heart, and it may be doubted whether they know anything of what is going on upon earth? But Newman had already answered this argument as being unscriptural.

Sacrificing and falling down in worship before the Saints

---

[17] V. M. II, 351, 102.

are likewise repudiated. Catholics as well as the most orthodox Anglicans know full well that God knows what we have need of; He alone can hear our prayers and will help us. They know, too, that Christ is the all-sufficient Mediator. As Newman remarks, the Council of Trent expressly teaches that "sacrifice is not offered to the Saints, but to God alone."[18] Bellarmine[19] very concisely shows also that Catholics do not pray to the Saints as authors of divine benefits or graces, for these are beyond the power of any creature, but they may be asked to intercede for us since they have great power with God. When invocations are used, the words employed should not be examined as much as the meaning, for favors are asked of them that they might obtain them from God through their prayers.[20] Newman acknowledged the justice of Bellarmine's explanations on the question of invocation, but was not willing to commit himself to any definite conclusion on this point as on some other subjects exposed in the Tract. There was, in fact, "a vagueness and deficiency as to the conclusions he would draw from the premisses stated," for he was "more bent on laying down his principles than defining the results."[21]

If he hesitated at coming to a conclusion which his premisses required, friends and opponents did not, namely, that the *Ora pro nobis* was not necessarily included in the invocation of Saints which the Article condemns. Unwilling to state his conclusion categorically,[22] Newman simply maintained that the question whether invocation was or was not Catholic was an open one, and was left as such by the Article.[23]

His own stand in the matter was, however, definitely taken; he let it be clearly understood that, though not flatly

---

[18] Session 22.

[19] Editor's note: The work of Bellarmine that Newman examined is *On the Canonization and Invocation of the Saints*, which is also available in English from Mediatrix Press.

[20] V. M. II, 308–309.

[21] V. M. II, 390.

[22] V. M. II, 410.

[23] Ibid. 391.

condemning invocation, he felt a strong apprehension regarding the use of even modified invocation. Bishop Lloyd, whom Newman cites in his own defense, acquits the Roman Church of the charge of idolatry as far as the public formularies go, though he considers the practice unscriptural and unwarranted. "But," he adds, "we do consider the principles relating to the worship of the Virgin calculated to lead in the end to positive idolatry; and we are well convinced ... that a large portion of the lower classes are in this point guilty of it."[24]

The same reasons that Newman advances for the rejection of invocation several years before, still retain their force, though, as has just been seen, he does not now condemn all forms. Since, according to his estimation, these may lead to abuse, the best is to omit them entirely. "Every feeling which interferes with God's sovereignty in our hearts is of an idolatrous nature; and as men are tempted to idolize their rank and substance, or their talent, or their children, or themselves, so they may easily be led to substitute the thought of Saints and Angels for the supreme idea of their Creator and Redeemer, which should fill them."[25]

Newman makes a further concession in this regard, that invocations may be of use to certain persons advanced in sanctity and for whom there may be no danger, but for the rank and file there is a real peril. It is so much easier, so much less awful if ordinary persons can have recourse to creatures and so be saved the necessity of calling upon the Sovereign Majesty directly. The consequence, as Newman sees it, is that the image of the Saint will replace that of Almighty God in the mind of these individuals, who are hardly capable of many ideas at a time. A further obstacle to this practice for Newman is the supposition that the Catholics who make use of invocation do a sort of violence to themselves and their conscience in order to satisfy a certain curiosity which seeks for the strange and extraordinary in religious rites.[26]

---

[24] Ibid. 374.

[25] Ibid. 411.

[26] V. M. II, 411.

The same attitude towards veneration of images as for invocation is now to be seen in Newman. He does not reject all, for certain authoritative writers admitted accounts as veracious, of miracles wrought through the application of relics, or of a reverence paid to images. Newman precises what he would discountenance in the worship of saints: "kneeling before images, lighting candles to them, offering them incense, going on pilgrimage to them, hanging up crutches, etc., before them, lying legends about them, belief in miracles as if wrought by them through illusion of the devil, decking them up immodestly, and providing incentives by them to bad passions; and, in like manner, merry music and minstrelsy and licentious practices in honor of relics, counterfeit relics, multiplication of them, absurd pretences about them."[27] This he supposes is what the Article condemns as a "fond thing," and not any Tridentine statement, for the Council of Trent set itself sternly against any abuses and superstitious practices that may have been introduced among the simple, ignorant faithful, almost naturally inclined to excess and to superstition.[28]

Filled with a more kindly feeling towards Rome, he still felt there was no possibility of a compromise. While objecting to the political attitude of Catholics in England, there were other greater difficulties to be overcome. Thus, he wrote in a letter to a Catholic layman: "And now I fear I am going to pain you by telling you that you consider the approaches in doctrine on our part towards you, closer than they really are. I cannot help repeating what I have many times said in print, that your services and devotions to St. Mary in matter of fact do most deeply pain me. I am only stating it as a matter of fact."[29] Were a union between Rome and England possible, he argued that his own communion would as a matter of necessity be obliged to "protest against the extreme honors paid to St. Mary."[30]

---

[27] V. M. II, 304.

[28] Ibid. 305. Trid. Sess. 25.

[29] Apo. 192.

[30] Ibid.

II. Dr. Russell and Newman

Although Tract 90 had stirred up considerable and widespread opposition among members of the Anglican Church, it served as a providential means of bringing Newman into contact with the one who had, humanly speaking, perhaps more to do with his conversion than any one else. This was Dr. Russell, later on President of Maynooth. For a long time this humble Irish priest was watching the signs of the times and awaiting indications of a revival of Catholic doctrine in the Reformed Churches.[31] Associated with Dr. Wiseman, he specially followed the Oxford Movement with the greatest interest. A man of such a keen mind could realize that a movement like the one then in progress must almost infallibly bring some of its followers into the true Church, since many of them were dissatisfied with their own communion.[32] Russell had read Tract 90 and was following the discussions consequent upon its publication. He rejoiced at the general tone of the Tract, but felt deeply pained at the insinuations of Newman about the Catholic dogma of Transubstantiation. Though timid and unassuming, he at length succeeded in summing up sufficient courage to write to the great Oxford leader in order to clear up as far as was possible at least this one false impression of Newman. "It grieves me," he wrote, "to observe that ... there is to be met much misapprehension of many doctrines and practices which I have been taught since childhood to venerate, and which, were they indeed as you represent them, I should abhor as fervently as you yourself can do."[33] He proceeded then to explain how Catholics understand the presence of Christ in the Holy Eucharist.

Newman in his reply assured his correspondent that he did not wish to impute the holding of gross views on the Real Presence to all the members of the Roman communion but rather wished to explain the sense in which the term is used in

---

[31] Keble, 117–118 sqq.

[32] *Life and Times of Card. Wiseman*, I, 387, 388.

[33] Keble, 119.

the Article.[34] In admitting the doctrine as understood by himself and as held by Catholics, he concluded with the wish: "O, that you would reform your worship, that you would disown the extreme honors paid to St. Mary and the Saints, your traditionary view of Indulgences,[35] and the veneration paid in foreign countries to images."[36] Dr. Russell in return assured Newman that the latter's conceptions are ungrounded. His fears about the "traditionary system" of Rome would rapidly disappear if he had a correct idea of the Catholic doctrine on the Blessed Virgin and the Saints, the value of indulgences and the use of sacred images; he would be convinced that the honor paid to the Saints is not "extreme." "Where can the true spirit of our devotions be traced so surely as in the devotions themselves! ... Every Hymn has its doxology—every Litany begins with a prayer for mercy to the *Blessed Trinity,* and after asking the *prayers* of the *Saint* or *Saints,* closes with a supplication again for *mercy* to the *Lamb of God;* every prayer terminates by assigning the merits of our Lord as the ground of its petitions, and the Rosary, which is considered the most offensive of all, is but a series of meditations on the Incarnation, Passion, and Glory of our Redeemer."[37]

A perfectly valid argument for the legitimacy of these devotions lay in the very fact that those whom Newman would recognize as great servants of God, were "in the same proportion the most devoted clients of the Mother of God, and the humblest suitors for her intercession." Newman recognized that Rome admitted Scripture and Tradition, held fast to the great dogmas of faith, but that it had departed from antiquity on points which Catholics claimed were logical developments, and which Anglicans called corruptions, abuses, dominant

---

[34] He assumes that there were persons or a party that did still hold unsound views on the doctrine. Keble, 123.

[35] Indulgences were reprobated for the same reason as the cultus of Saints: 1. Christ is the only mediator; His merits are all-sufficient for the pardon of sin. 2. Indulgences were thought to be an encouragement to sin.

[36] Keble, 125.

[37] Keble, 125.

errors. England, he said, differed from Rome in questions of fact, degree, and practice.[38] Dr. Russell pressed the point which Newman evolved at greater length later on. If the question is one of fact, examine the facts and see whether in reality Catholics do lose sight of their Creator in consequence of their attention to creatures. Do they not hold all the essentials of faith received by Anglicans, and others also which Anglicans had given up long ago? Indeed, Newman had found out by bitter experience that his Church was unable to endure an injection of a more orthodox Christianity;[39] it seemed doomed to sink deeper and deeper into Protestantism. Russell pointed this out in no uncertain terms: "Even though your views were correct in point of fact as to the dangerous tendency of what you conceive to be our 'traditionary system,' how much greater the peril of salvation for an ordinary Christian in your own communion, where the blessed doctrines to which your dearest hopes, as well as mine, must cling, are barely (and, indeed, not even so) tolerated, where all your learning and all your moderation *can scarcely even* do this for them, when the very attempt has raised a storm such as our days have never seen before, and when, on the other hand, the uncatholic (and may I add, almost unchristian) views were those of the mighty majority, and most probably remain so even still, when, according to yourself, there is no positive creed (but only articles of peace) upon many points which I cannot conceive how any one, once admitting, can regard as unessential. ..."[40]

The correspondence between Dr. Russell and Newman continued at a period when, as Newman confessed, he was on his deathbed with regard to Anglicanism.[41] His notes to his correspondent continually manifested the same fear entertained of Rome's traditionary system. Even though the Roman Church might reform, he could not as yet see any reason for abandoning his own communion, in which he had

---

[38] Ess. II, 168.

[39] Advocated by Tract 90. Cf. Apo. 130–131.

[40] Keble, 125, 126.

[41] Apo.147.

been placed by divine Providence. Under the nine headings in which he sums up his "position in the view of duty" there is one which gives his principal reason for remaining in the English Church: "I could not go to Rome while she suffered honors to be paid to the Blessed Virgin and Saints which I thought in my conscience to be incompatible with the Supreme, Incommunicable Glory of the One Infinite and Eternal."[42] Elsewhere he expressed the same thought in this manner: "As to the present authoritative teaching of the Church of Rome, to judge by what we see in public, I think it goes very far indeed to substitute another Gospel for the true one. Instead of setting before the soul the Holy Trinity, and hell and heaven, it does seem to me as a popular system, to preach the Blessed Virgin and the Saints and the Purgatory."[43] In the former citation Newman omits mention of Purgatory, because probably his feelings on this point were not so keen as on the cultus of Saints.[44]

It was Dr. Russell's task, then, to convince Newman that devotional manifestations to the Blessed Virgin and the Saints did not in the least interfere with the worship of God. He accomplished this with a tact to which Newman renders homage when he says: "He was always gentle, mild, unobtrusive and uncontroversial. He let me alone."[45] Russell sent him a few books, among others a volume of sermons by St. Alphonsus. Newman was acquainted with this work from extracts which had tended only to accentuate his prejudices against Rome because of the so-called "Mariolatry" evidenced in them. Surprised not to find the objectionable passages in the book he had received, he made inquiries and found out from his friend that some parts were certainly omitted as being

---

[42] Ibid. 148. On p. 184 he makes a similar remark: "I could not go to Rome while I thought what I did of the devotions she sanctioned to the Blessed Virgin and the Saints."

[43] V. M. II, 368, 369.

[44] Keble, 167. As early as 1826 Pusey asked Newman whether it was allowable to pray for the departed. Cf. Pusey, I, 112.

[45] Apo. 194.

unsuitable for English Catholics. Newman went so far as to promise that if he were ever convinced that he had been wrong in speaking on this subject of devotions to the Blessed Virgin and the Saints, he would not hesitate to make a public avowal of the fact.

He went through the Exercises of St. Ignatius, which bring the soul in direct contact with its Maker. Some other small books of devotion were sent him from Rome by Dr. Russell. All of them surprised Newman by the conspicuous absence of what he sought for in them to justify his assertions. Still, he remained unconvinced for some time. Even when in February, 1843, he retracted his anti-Catholic statements, there is not the slightest allusion to the public avowal of which he had spoken to Dr. Russell.[46]

His whole prejudice had its root in a sincere "zeal for God." From his boyhood on, he had been led to consider that God and he were the beings, "luminously such, *in rerum natura*. The soul is face to face, *solus cum solo*, in all matters between man and his God."[47] Thus, his whole life was centralized in God, in the face of Christ. How, then, could he mistake the members of Christ for Christ Himself? The incommunicable glory of the Eternal was his sole preoccupation,[48] and his conscience told him that devotions to Mary and the Saints interfered with this glory. He had obtained a key to his difficulty, but he had not yet reached the stage where he could acknowledge in all tranquillity and sincerity, "that the Catholic Church allows no image of any sort, material or immaterial, no dogmatic symbol, no rite, no sacrament, no Saint, not even the Blessed Virgin herself, to come between the soul and its Creator."[49]

At the same time his thoughts began to be directed towards the problem of development and he came to realize that the idea of the Blessed Virgin had been *magnified* in the Church as so many other doctrines, the Blessed Eucharist, for example.

---

[46] Keble, 168.

[47] Apo. 195, 196.

[48] Cf. Przywara-Karrer, *Einführung in Newmans Wesen und Werk*, p. 89.

[49] Apo. 195.

"The whole scene of pale, faint, distant Apostolic Christianity is seen in Rome as through a telescope or magnifier."[50] The early Church possessed the sum-total of divine revelation but as it were, only in embryo or germ, which would require centuries upon centuries to grow and bring forth bud, blossom, and fruit, all contained potentially in the seed. That which seemed at first sight wholly unlike the primitive deposit, is that same deposit evolved to its logical conclusion. This is particularly the case with the doctrine on the Blessed Virgin. Scripture speaks little of her, beyond stating her position in regard to the Son of God and leaving her as it were in the background so as to emphasize the grandeur of her Divine Son. The task of discovering all the consequences to be derived from the scanty data furnished by Scripture is reserved to the religious instincts of the faithful in succeeding ages. This doctrine concerning the Mother of God forms part of a harmonious whole and cannot be removed out of its context without disrupting the unity of the ensemble of Christian teaching.

Newman gave himself to the study of development in 1842. He was now reaching a conclusion contrary to the one he had maintained in the heyday of his Anglican career. He formulates it as follows: "1) I am far more certain that we *are* in a state of culpable separation than that developments do *not* exist under the Gospel and that Roman developments are not true ones. 2) I am far more certain that *our* (modern) doctrines are wrong. 3) Granting that the Roman (special) doctrines are not found drawn out in the early Church, yet I think there is sufficient trace of them in it, to recommend and prove them, *on the hypothesis* of the Church having a divine guidance, though not sufficient to prove them by itself. ... 4) The proof of the Roman (modern) doctrine is as strong (or stronger) in Antiquity, as that of certain doctrines which both we and the Romans hold, e.g., there is more evidence in Antiquity ... for the practice of Invocation than for certain books in the present Canon of Scriptures, etc. 5) The analogy of the Old Testament, and also

---

[50] Ibid. 196.

of the New, leads to the acknowledgment of doctrinal developments. ..."[51]

Meanwhile, Newman remained obedient to the ordinances of his Church, refraining from any exterior practices that are peculiar to the Roman Church, in particular the use of invocation. He assures an inquiring correspondent that there is nothing in Scripture against invocation. "It is right or wrong according as the Church allows it or not—but where it is a Church ordinance still, it may be abused." During the last years of his Anglican life, Newman was striving might and main to retain his followers in the Anglican Church, feeling that he had special responsibility in this regard before his Bishop. It is interesting to find two of his most intimate friends, not yet fully decided upon going to Rome, still seeking to give an outlet to their devotional feelings towards the Blessed Virgin and the Saints.

Ambrose St. John, Newman's inseparable companion of Catholic days, was further advanced towards Catholicism than his master in 1843; he went to Littlemore, where he was held back for some time from making the final step. He was of the opinion that the Articles, at least according to their content, condemned certain usages and modes of expressing doctrines which he believed permitted and sanctioned by God. On this belief he held that it is the will of God that we should ask the Saints for their prayers, and especially those of the Blessed Virgin. He did not hesitate to style a direct, unqualified condemnation of invocation as dangerous, since it tended to keep men back from taking hold of the true doctrine of the Catholic Church.[52] Newman would hardly have dared to use such forceful language; in fact, in these last years it was his policy to say as little as possible on the subject of invocation.[53]

---

[51] Apo. 197. In 1843 he wrote: "I am very far more sure that England is in schism, than that the Roman additions to the Primitive Creed may not be developments, arising out of a keen and vivid realizing of the Divine Depositum of Faith." Addressed to Keble. Cf. Apo. 208, Keble, 219.

[52] Keble, 241.

[53] The same may be said about Transubstantiation.

Others of the party became more aggressive and began unreservedly to recommend the whole of the Roman devotional system, especially as regards the Blessed Virgin. This was assuming such alarming proportions that Keble as well as Pusey felt deeply grieved about it, but nothing could stem the tide. Feelings pent up for a long time were demanding expression and the leaders were powerless to do anything. Furthermore, Newman could not have been induced to act because of the difficult state of mind in which he found himself; he refrained from these practices himself only because of the Church ordinance and, as he said, he did not like "decanting Rome into England."[54]

In the course of 1844, Faber held correspondence with Newman on the same subject of devotion to our Lady and to the Saints. On several occasions he had asked Newman, his spiritual guide, to remove the prohibition of invoking the Blessed Virgin and Saints. His letter of November 28 is more insistent, though he is content to obey: "I want you to revoke your prohibition laid on me last October year, of invoking our blessed Lady, the Saints and Angels. Really I do not know whether I ask this in a lower and less spiritual mood than usual or whether the mere pain I feel in not speaking to the Blessed Mother of God drives me to it; but I do feel somehow weakened for the want of it, and fancy I should get strength if I did it. ... However, obedience will do me more good than invocation, so if you still think I had better refrain, then of course I will do so still."[55]

Newman was no less perplexed in the matter than Faber, because of diffidence in his own judgment; nevertheless he could not allow his penitent the use of direct and habitual invocations. He could not reject them, neither could he admit them into Anglican worship, because it seemed like mixing religions. "Observances," he wrote, "which may be very right in Saints, or in a Church which creates Saints, in a communion in which the aids of grace are such and such, may be dangerous

---

[54] Keble, 356.

[55] Bowden, *Life and Letters of F. W. Faber*, Vol. I, p. 219.

in a communion which has them not. ... What is natural in Saints and in a saintly system, becomes a mere form in others."[56] Even though this would not be a mere form in Faber, other evils might result, especially the manifestation of a spirit of insubordination to the Church's commands and a presumptuous use of private judgment. Such disobedience would be entirely out of place in one who still held office in the Anglican Church, as did Faber. However, Newman did not intend his answer to be a definite decision, but a mere suggestion for guidance in conduct, for as he said: "I am far too much perplexed myself in various ways, to feel it pleasant to give advice at all—much more to suffer what I say to be taken as a decision on the point."[57]

Like Newman, Faber thought that it was treachery and heresy too easily to question the spiritual authority under which he had been placed by divine Providence. So he had for the time being, to stifle the outbursts of filial devotion to her who for long years seemed to be haunting his spirit. Invocation was an irresistible need of his soul, but it could not be indulged in. He seemed to be entirely out of his element, for who can number the beautiful allusions to the divine Mother in his poems such as the "Styrian Lake," "Sir Lancelot," "Jesus, the Way," etc. These poetic effusions were not merely the outpourings of an overwrought imagination, but the manifestation of sentiments grounded on strong convictions. As with Newman, his devotion was hampered and held in check only to be given free scope once the barriers of prejudice and doubt had been overthrown, so that, once converted, he could in all truth proclaim that he had no other desire but to increase the fruits of the Savior's Passion and to swell the number of zealous servants of Mary.[58] It may be said that after his conversion Faber went further than Newman in the manifestation of an external devotion to our Lady. His temperament lent itself more readily to an effusiveness in his

---

[56] Keble, 357.

[57] Keble, 357.

[58] *Vie et Lettres*, I, 427.

sentiments that was quite foreign to his former spiritual director.[59]

III. The "Essay on Development"—Difficulties Vanish

Conscience from the interior and circumstances from the exterior[60] were all uniting to urge Newman's submission to Rome. But, rather than push himself forward, he was waiting for indications from on high as to the course he was to follow. He considered his conversion as a special vocation, a special light, and a direct call. He did not anticipate a general move among his followers, but began to treat the question only from a personal point of view. "Can *I* be saved in the English Church? am *I* in safety were I to die tonight? Is it a mortal sin in *me* not joining another communion?"[61] In a postscript to the letter in which he puts these questions to himself he adds: "I hardly see my way to concur in attendance, though occasional, in the Roman Catholic chapel, unless a man has made up his mind pretty well to join it eventually. Invocations are not *required* in the Church of Rome; somehow I do not like using them except under the sanction of the Church, and this makes me unwilling to admit them in members of our Church."[62]

To give a definitive answer to his questions and to leave the state of immobility, he entered resolutely upon a path which he thought would put an end to his doubts. He knew that his joining the Roman communion could not be far off. He began to put into form the solution of a vital problem in which he had become interested since several years, although it had occupied

---

[59] In his *Letter to Pusey*, Newman is obliged to animadvert on some of his friend's statements; at the same time, he renders a delicate tribute to him. Cf. Diff. II, 96.

[60] The Bishops' Charges on Tract 90, the condemnation of Ward's *Ideal*, as well as the Jerusalem Bishopric.

[61] Apo. 231.

[62] Apo.231.

his mind to a lesser extent as early as 1832.⁶³ At the beginning of 1845 he set to work to examine in detail whether the "new dogmas" with which he had reproached the Roman Church were in reality corruptions of the primitive truth or genuine developments. Corruptions, as he conceived them, were nothing but untrue developments. His first studies on the subject had already been crystallized in a lengthy sermon preached in 1843, which by a strange coincidence was delivered on the feast of the Purification of our Lady and the exordium of which was devoted to a consideration of the faith of Mary, who "pondered all these things" which she saw and heard concerning Jesus.

Anglicans used the dictum of Vincent of Lerins, "quod ubique, quod semper, quod ab omnibus" as an absolute criterion to distinguish what belongs to the Christian Church in its pristine purity and what is merely a corruption belonging to later ages. They wished to set a certain fixity and immobility in doctrine which would preclude the possibility of any development, theoretically speaking, though in practice they had to admit that their own beliefs and usages, ostensibly based on Antiquity, greatly differed from it.⁶⁴

Newman's purpose was to apply the same principle of Vincent of Lerins and give an explanation of the so-called corruptions, doctrinal and practical, of Rome.⁶⁵ He explains in brief the development of an idea which takes hold of the mind by its force and grows in it. A simple proposition results and in turn evolves into other propositions which were implicitly contained in the first. This deduction is not only a logical process, forming conclusions from certain clear premises, it is also what Newman calls "metaphysical," pertaining to man both to reason out and to feel as well.⁶⁶ In like manner Revelation gives certain facts to the mind which reflects upon them and in time gives expression to a judgment. The

---

⁶³ Cf. Apo. 197.

⁶⁴ Dev. 10. Yet Anglicans admitted the principle of development.

⁶⁵ Dev. 32.

⁶⁶ Cf. Ibid. 52, sqq.

proposition thus formulated is a theological dogma. "Reality and permanence of inward knowledge are distinct from explicit confession. The absence or partial absence, or incompleteness of dogmatic statements is no proof of the absence of impressions or implicit judgments, in the mind of the Church. Even centuries might pass without the formal expression of a truth which had been all along the secret life of millions of souls."[67] The nature of the conflict between Rome and the Anglican Church is not so much on the *principle* of development, but rather on the fact whether the developments in Rome are faithful, or simply additions and corruptions.[68]

Because of its intellectual character, Christianity had to grow and develop into a vast theological system; if there is such a development, then the Author of Revelation had to secure the

---

[67] U. S. 323.

[68] Cf. Grandmaison in *Revue pratique d'Apologetique* (avril, 1908), p. 33, for an appreciation of the *Essay*. The recent work of the Dominican, Francis Marin-Sola, on *L'Évolution homogène du Dogme Catholique* (Fribourg, 1924) is heralded as one of the most able treatments of the subject which has occupied the minds of many distinguished theologians. Father Marin-Sola, while examining the various methods used to explain the problem, proves himself an ardent champion of Newman on the question, against accusations of Modernists and others. He shows clearly that Newman is not only orthodox but traditional as well, and that it is primarily necessary to understand his terminology. Though Newman speaks of assimilation, preservation, and addition, he means nothing else but what the Scholastics call *explicatio impliciti*. "New dogmas" are not such objectively but explicitly. He says clearly: "no simply new truth has been given to us since St. John's death. The office of the Church is to guard, that noble deposit ... in its fulness and integrity." (Diff. II, 327). "Revelation is all in all in doctrine: the Apostles its sole depository, the inferential method its sole instrument, and ecclesiastical authority its sole sanction." (Idea, 233). Earlier in his Anglican life, Newman explains a theory which admits of developments which are real innovations, material, formal changes—a certain metamorphosis and recasting of doctrines into new shapes—the old and new shapes being foreign to each other, connected only as symbolizing or realizing certain immutable but nebulous principles. This theory, however, was not strictly his own, but that of a friend. Cf. Ess. I, 288; Marin-Sola, op. cit. I, 347–353. Furthermore, Newman *could* speak of transformation, assimilation, addition, in such things as Liturgy, devotions, etc., which are also considered in the *Essay*.

Depositum from perversion and corruption. Now there are what may be called additions in the Latin and Greek Churches. Newman explains his point in this manner:

"If the idea of Christianity, as originally given to us from heaven, cannot but contain much which will be partially recognized by us as included in it and only held by us unconsciously, and if again, Christianity being from heaven, all that is necessarily involved in it and is evolved from it, is from heaven, and if, on the other hand, large accretions actually do exist, professing to be its true and legitimate results, our first impression naturally is that these must be the very developments which they profess to be. Moreover, the very scale on which they have been made, their high antiquity yet present promise, their gradual formation yet precision, their harmonious order dispose the imagination most forcibly to the belief that a teaching so consistent with itself, so well balanced, so young and so old, not obsolete after many centuries, but vigorous and progressive still, is the very development contemplated in the Divine Scheme. These doctrines are members of one family, and suggestive, or correlative, or confirmatory, or illustrative of each other. One furnishes evidence to another, and all to each of them; if this is proved, that becomes probable; if this and that are both probable, but for different reasons, each adds to the other its own probability."[69]

Thus Newman lays down his principle of development: the Author of Revelation watches over the deposit of faith. What especially shows the divinity of the Catholic religion is the wonderful harmony manifest in all the doctrines; each doctrine is vitally connected with others of a series and these in turn bear a relation with others of a different group, so that the whole body of Catholic teaching forms a single harmonious whole. Devotion to our blessed Lady and the Saints finds its place in this wonderful scheme, which Newman describes succinctly but thoroughly. "The Incarnation," he says, "is the antecedent of the doctrine of Mediation, and the archetype both

---

[69] Dev. 93.

of the Sacramental principle and of the merits of Saints. From the doctrine of Mediation follow the Atonement, the Mass, the merits of Martyrs and Saints, their invocation and cultus. From the Sacramental principle come the Sacraments properly so called; the unity of the Church, and the Holy See as its type and centre; the authority of Councils; the sanctity of rites; the veneration of holy places, shrines, images, vessels, furniture and vestments. Of the Sacraments, Baptism is developed into Confirmation on the one hand; into Penance, Purgatory, and Indulgences on the other; and the Eucharist into the Real Presence, adoration of the Host, Resurrection of the body, and the virtue of relics. Again, the doctrine of the Sacraments leads to the doctrine of Justification; Justification to that of Original Sin; Original Sin to the merit of Celibacy. Nor do these separate developments stand independent of each other, but by cross relations they are connected and grow together while they grow from one. The Mass and Real Presence are parts of one, the veneration of Saints and their relics are parts of one, their intercessory power and the Purgatorial State, and again the Mass and that State are correlative. ... You must accept the whole or reject the whole; attenuation does but enfeeble, and amputation mutilate. It is trifling to receive all but something which is as integral as any other portion; and, on the other hand, it is a solemn thing to accept any part, for, before you know where you are, you may be carried on by a stern logical necessity to accept the whole."[70]

Devotion to the Blessed Virgin finds its complete justification in the *Essay on Development;* Newman's method there is patristic throughout: his reasoning is clear and unmistakable. Gradual comprehension of the nature of the Incarnation, of Christ's personality and twofold nature, in turn leads to a clearer recognition of Mary's dignity and office.

Prior to the Council of Nice, the Fathers were not too exact in the use of their terms to describe the Divinity of our Lord, to such an extent that their explanations seemed to savor of Arianism. So according to some, the Son is subservient to the

---

[70] Dev. 93, 94. The last statement was realized fully in Newman's own case.

Father in creation; He is the Instrument of God. In stressing the *Principatus* of the Father, they did not sufficiently protect the co-equality.[71] They frequently took the apparitions of heavenly spirits in the Old Testament as manifestations of the Son of God; the manifestation was called an Angel, or the Lord, or God; St. Augustine, however, introduced the doctrine that these were merely *media*, and not the Son of God whom they took as the medium; it was through these Angels that the Omnipotent Son manifested Himself. Consequently, the mediatorial acts of our Lord came to be regarded as the works of one, who, though having become man, remained God. He was looked upon more in his absolute perfections than in His relations to the First Person of the Blessed Trinity. This was the effect of Catholic polemics against the Arians, who rejected Christ's divinity.

On the other hand, the Apollinarian and Monosphysite heresies tended to the denial of Christ's humanity, the former declaring that He had no human soul, which was replaced by the Word, the latter maintaining the absorption of the humanity by the divinity. Hence the tendency to emphasize the human nature in Christ and apply to His huinanity what had previously been referred to His divinity. The natural result of these combats against heresy was the *Cultus Sanctorum,* for "in proportion as texts descriptive of created mediation ceased to belong to our Lord, so was a room opened for created mediation."[72] The Angels spoken of in Scripture received a worship insofar as they were tokens of the divine Presence or manifestations of it.[73]

Another result of these controversies, which prepared the way for worship of the Saints, was the high esteem in which man is to be held once he is regenerated through baptism and incorporated with Christ. The Son of God added nothing to His essential glory by assuming our human nature; the gain was all on our side. Our nature is elevated, glorified, divinized by its

---

[71] Cf. T. T. 208 sqq.

[72] Dev. 138.

[73] Cf. V. M. II, 112; Apoc. 19:10; 22:8; Judges 2:1; 6:11; 13:3; Dan. 10; Exod. 3:2; Acts 7:30; Josue 5:13.

union with the Word, who is in the Saints, makes them instinct with His life, divine sons, gods. The Son of God shares His titles with us; He possesses them absolutely and we by participation; He is within us in so intimate a manner that He may be worshipped in us as in His temple. What is this but the sublime doctrine of St. Paul: "Know you not that you are the temple of God."[74]

The glorified Saints will share in a certain manner the worship paid by the Angels to Christ Himself. Newman finds in this fact an explanation of the inhibition placed by the Angel on St. John the Evangelist, when the latter wished to prostrate himself in worship before the heavenly messenger.[75] It is in this text with some others that Protestants claim to find the scriptural sanction of their opposition to a cultus of the Saints. Hence to the Saints might be applied what at first sight seemed to be reserved to the Son of God.[76] We who are still in the flesh are by grace so elevated above our natural states that our souls and bodies become sacred, and to profane them is a sacrilege; in other words, we become objects of worship because of the divine indwelling and share in the incommunicable glory of God. Is it not perfectly legitimate that the Saints in heaven should likewise share in worship? Have they not a valid claim to a religious cultus?

The Arians had fallen short of the correct notion of Christ's nature when they spoke of Him as far above any creature, though not allowing Him to be God in the full sense of the term. Newman uses this as an argument to disprove the silly contention continually urged by Protestants that Catholics adore the Blessed Virgin. "Arius and Asterius did all but confess that Christ was the Almighty; they said much more than St. Bernard or St. Alphonsus have since said of the Blessed Mary, yet they left Him a creature and were found wanting."[77] Still they acknowledged that He was Creator of the universe and

---

[74] I Cor. 3:16, 17; 6:15–20; II Cor. 6:16.

[75] Apoc. 19:10; 22:8.

[76] Dev. 140, 141.

[77] Dev. 143.

was created in order to create. Accordingly, they were rightly charged by the Fathers with idolatry. They either had to hold two Gods or worship a creature, unless they denied both divinity and worship to Christ.[78] Any created substance is a creature; whatever is creature is not God. Christ was created, according to Arians, and yet they held Him worthy of worship.

The Arian controversy, besides giving a new interpretation to texts which speak of our Lord's subordination, gradually led to a further development with regard to texts which could not be applied fully to Him, and seemed to pertain more directly to a creature.[79] Accordingly, theologians looked about for another that would be the immediate object of such descriptions. Newman's language becomes exalted, poetical, in answering who this could be: "There was a wonder in heaven, a throne was seen far above all other created powers, mediatorial, intercessory; a title archetypal; a crown bright as the morning star; a glory issuing from the Eternal Throne; robes pure as the heavens; and a sceptre over all; and who was the predestined heir of that Majesty? Since it was not high enough for the Highest, who was that wisdom and what was her name, 'the Mother of fair love, and fear, and holy hope,' 'exalted like a palm-tree in Engaddi, and a rose-plant in Jericho', created from the beginning before the world, 'in God's everlasting counsels,' and 'in Jerusalem her power?' The vision is found in the Apocalypse, a woman clothed with the sun and the moon under her feet, and upon her head a crown of twelve stars. The votaries of Mary do not exceed the true faith, unless the blasphemers of her Son came up to it."[80] Newman sums up his conclusion in a few words that mark the dispelling of all his doubts and hesitations and serve as a vindication of the Church of Rome against the charges laid at its door formerly by him as well as others: "The Church of Rome is not idolatrous unless Arianism is orthodoxy."[81]

---

[78] Ath. II, 159, 160.

[79] Such, for example, the texts on Wisdom.

[80] Dev. 143.

[81] Dev. 144.

The condemnation of Arians and Semi-Arians amply prove that to exalt a creature is no recognition of its divinity. The controversy laid down certain premises which required only time for the complete expression of their conclusions. Can it be said at any time that Catholics expatiating on the prerogatives of Mary ever used language equivalent to that employed by Arians about our Lord, yet Christ remained for the latter a mere creature. Newman is led from this consideration to a profound reflection on the heretics of modern times who find fault with Catholic devotion to our Lady. "It is not wonderful considering how Socinians, Sabellians, Nestorians, and the like abound in these days, without their even knowing it themselves, if those who never rise higher in their notions of our Lord's Divinity, than to consider Him a man singularly inhabited by a Divine Presence, that is, a Catholic Saint—if such men should mistake the honor paid by the Church to the human Mother, for that very honor which, and which alone, is worthy of her Eternal Son?"[82]

From the earliest times Christians had recognized the dignity of the Mother of God, her grandeur, her privileges, but their official recognition came only as the outgrowth of the struggles against heresy which attacked directly the person and nature of our Lord. Newman has here manifested a striking originality in his study of the primitive cult of the Blessed Virgin. His own deep researches into the history of the various heresies centering about our Lord fitted him for the task of examining Mary's position in the minds of the early Christians. He had come to realize that in truth, contrary to all that he had previously supposed, Mary did hold a prominent position, and that the heresies of the fourth and fifth centuries, though opposed to one another, yet tended to her exaltation. This he sums up concisely when he asserts that Nestorianism "supplied the subject of that august proposition of which Arianism had provided the predicate."[83] The attention of the Church in the first period of her liberation had to be concentrated on the

---

[82] Ibid. 144, 145.

[83] Dev. 145.

figure of her divine Master, so as to clear it of all sorts of misconceptions. The Councils of Nice and of Constantinople occupied themselves with the divinity of Christ, but in the following century Nestorianism attacked the human nature. To secure a right faith in the manhood of the eternal Son, the Council of Ephesus declared Mary to be the Mother of God.

Heresy did not tend alone towards the exaltation of the Blessed Virgin; the early Fathers also served as the spokesmen to express the beliefs of the faithful. She is not only the *Theotokos,* but also the "new Eve," "the sacred shrine of sinlessness," "the wise woman who hath clad believers with the clothing of incorruption"; she is "full of grace" as the Angel had proclaimed her. A new vista in reality had presented itself to Newman's mind: lofty views of the Blessed Virgin as well as a cultus necessarily arising from the beliefs concerning her are to be found in Antiquity. What he had deemed corruptions are nothing but true developments, which are very pronounced as early as the fourth and fifth centuries and which have their explicit foundations in the sub-Apostolic Age, and can thereby be referred to Apostolic times.

Newman's entire treatment of Mariology in his *Essay on Development* may be summed up in three points: 1) the view of the faithful concerning her, as has just been seen, is an instance of the historical argument in favor of existing developments;[84] 2) the doctrine and devotion concerning her in the early Church are an anticipation of what is held and practiced at the present day; 3) that in matter of fact, devotion to Mary has not interfered with the worship due to God, but has really served as the bulwark of the fundamental dogmas of Christianity. A mere cursory survey of the second and third points will suffice in this place.

By becoming man, Christ incorporated us into His divinity, and by His resurrection gives us also a pledge of a future glorious resurrection. He sanctified not only the spiritual element of man, but also that which is material, corporal. Thus, the Christians were led from the very beginning to hold in

---

[84] Dev. 99.

profound veneration the relics of the martyrs; their enemies, like Protestants, taunted them with supplanting the idols of the heathen by their martyrs. From veneration of the relics to that of the persons was but a step. Images recall the persons, hence a certain cultus was also paid to these representations, though this comes later on. Protestants sometimes cite the decree of a Council of Illiberis in Spain held before that of Nice, in which images are forbidden. Newman turns the argument against Protestants by proving decisively that such a decree would not have been issued had there not been a cultus of Angels and Saints already in existence.[85] Justin, in a celebrated text, plainly confesses a worship paid to the Angels.[86]

If Angels and Saints possess the right to be worshipped, how much more she, who is far above every other created being. Mary's prerogatives received early recognition. In accord with the Fathers, Newman lays down the principle that the Blessed Virgin was not merely a physical instrument in the Incarnation but a voluntary agent in the actual work of the Redemption, just as Eve had been instrumental and responsible in Adam's fall; if Mary had been disobedient or had not believed in the message of the Angel, the Divine Economy would have been frustrated.[87] This parallel between Eve and the Blessed Virgin, so much insisted upon by the Fathers, becomes as it were, the key-stone of the argument in Newman's Letter to Pusey. Mary's position as Second Eve is sanctioned not only by Antiquity which Newman traces back to Apostolic times, but also by Scripture, which presents the Woman and her Seed as engaged in a warfare with the Serpent. She is also respresented as Patroness or Paraclete, i.e. an advocate, a loving Mother whose intercession is all-powerful with God. This view of her is manifestly spoken of already in the fifth century, exhibited by the Medieval Church and particularly accentuated in these latter times.[88]

---

[85] Dev. 410.

[86] Ibid. 415.

[87] Dev. 411 sqq.

[88] Ibid. 417, 418.

Almost the last question touched upon by Newman in his Essay is whether the honors paid to the Blessed Virgin, which have grown out of devotion to her Son, do not tend to weaken the latter devotion, and whether it is possible to exalt a creature without withdrawing one's heart from the Creator. The whole question resolves itself to one of fact. Newman had previously conceded that this devotion to our Lady, speaking in the abstract, might be tolerated or that it might not be dangerous in certain holy persons who would not be led astray by it. But now he removes the obstacle which was shutting out from his view the "blessed vision of peace."

Devotion to Mary *has been* the real safeguard of the faith of Catholics; the *Theotokos has* protected the doctrine of the Incarnation. Newman thus characterizes the result of his investigations: "If we take a survey at least of Europe, we shall find that it is not those religious communions which are characterized by devotion towards the Blessed Virgin that have ceased to adore Her Eternal Son, but those very bodies (when allowed by the law) which have renounced devotion to her. The regard for His glory, which was professed in that keen jealousy of her exaltation, has not been supported by the event. They who were accused of worshipping a creature in His stead, still worship Him; their accusers who hoped to worship Him so purely, they, wherever obstacles to the development of their principles have been removed, have ceased to worship Him altogether."[89] A truer picture of the actual condition of most Protestant communions could hardly have been drawn. These men cannot be consistent and stop at the repudiation of God's Mother; her Son must go with her. There is no metaphysical principle involved here. Absolutely speaking, Jesus is separable from His Mother, and ever remains at an infinite distance from her, for He is God as well as man; psychologically considered, however, where Jesus is, there must also be Mary. Such is a fact proved by experience. The protagonists of a pure worship forget the dual element in man, the spiritual and the material. The soul derives its knowledge through the senses. So in the

---

[89] Dev. 426.

supernatural order, the spirit of man cannot feed on mere abstractions; through the senses devotion is fostered, and where there is devotion there is worship, which in turn is the safeguard of doctrine. Newman's statements in this matter are confirmed by actual experience, for individuals among the Protestants are receding more and more from the elemental ideas of Christianity and, on the contrary, those who are striving to keep the fundamental tenets are also distinguished by efforts to revive devotion to our Blessed Lady.

Furthermore, as Newman explains, the "tone" of the devotion paid to the Blessed Virgin is of an altogether different kind from that paid to her Divine Son or to the Holy Trinity. "The supreme and true worship paid to the Almighty is severe, profound, awful as well as tender, confiding and dutiful. Christ is addressed as true God, while He is true Man; as our Creator and Judge, while He is most loving, gentle and gracious. On the other hand, towards St. Mary the language employed is affectionate and ardent, as towards a mere child of Adam, though subdued as coming from her sinful kindred."[90] To be convinced of this, it is but necessary to cast a casual glance at the liturgy, the official expression of the Church's devotion. Devotion to Mary has not at all supplanted the adoration of God. With reason Newman asks "whether the character of much of the Protestant devotion to our Lord has been that of adoration at all; and not rather such as we pay to an excellent human being, that is, no higher devotion than that which Catholics pay to St. Mary, differing from it, however, in often being familiar, rude and earthly?"[91]

---

[90] Dev. 429.

[91] Ibid. 428.

CHAPTER III
Catholic Days (1845–1890)

I. Devotion as Shown in His Life

HEN Newman was about to make his act of submission to the Church of Rome, he realized finally that devotion to our Lady had its source in devotion to our Lord. Throughout his Anglican career he was characterized by an intense personal devotion to our Blessed Savior, but not so for his devotion to the Blessed Virgin. From what has been explained, it has become evident that a precise point where this latter devotion takes its rise may be assigned. As time advances, his Catholic piety, if it may be so called, becomes more and more clear cut. He seems at first to be shielding himself against an instinctive attraction that draws him to the Mother of God. As Brémond expresses it, Newman "was in a sort of affectionate expectation, as though he foresaw that some day the ice which separated him from the Mother of the Savior would melt before him."[1] Hurrell Froude helped to rid him of his vain scruples and fixed in his mind the idea of a true devotion to Mary. The reading of the Fathers and of the Lives of the Saints did the rest. After his conversion he seemed to be desirous of paying up for time lost because of his docility to the prescriptions of the Anglican Church. Once a Catholic, he took a delight in recalling that the Blessed Virgin had practically always occupied his mind; thus, he remarks as an

---

[1] Brémond, op. cit. 296.

item of some importance, the strange inspiration that drew him to sketch a pair of beads on his verse-book at the age of ten.[2] The consolation which the thoughts had afforded him that invocations were not *required* in the Roman Church had not the slightest interest for him after his conversion. Then he loved to recall the fact that really he had been all his life under the shadow of our Lady: "My College was St. Mary's," he writes to a friend, "and my Church; and when I went to Littlemore, there, by my own previous disposition, Our Blessed Lady was waiting for me. Nor did she do nothing for me in that low habitation, of which I always think with pleasure."[3] When he entered the Church, he and his convert-friends received the residence at Old Oscott, which had been dedicated to the Blessed Virgin by Dr. Milner; with their advent it received the name of Maryvale.[4]

While in a state of uncertainty as to what line of work he was to follow in his newly found Faith, Newman gave a thought to joining the Dominicans or Jesuits, for whom he entertained a great admiration. On further consideration, he felt that his life's work lay elsewhere. For a long time the idea of establishing a theological school attracted him. He even contemplated establishing a religious Order, as he explained to Dalgairns in a letter:[5] "I sketched out the first outlines of a community under the patronage of St. Mary, 'quae sola interemisti etc.' with the object of first recognizing, second defending the *Mysteries* of Faith." Such a project does not cause the least surprise to any one who knows Newman's antecedents; his own formation had been along the historico-dogmatic line, and he felt the want of just such schools in the Roman Church. That he should have thought of choosing hte Blessed Virgin as patroness of such an undertaking is most natural, for he had discovered that she was the greatest bulwark for the truths of Christianity; to her the Church could address the unique praise of having "alone destroyed all

---

[2] Apo. 3.

[3] Ward I, 193. At his confirmation he took the name of Mary.

[4] Ibid. 120.

[5] Ward I, 125.

CATHOLIC DAYS (1845-1890)

heresies in the whole world."

Even in such an apparently insignificant question as taste regarding architecture, the Blessed Virgin enters. At Milan he was most affected by all that reminded him of the Fathers, St. Ambrose, St. Augustine, and the "great" St. Athanasius, his favorite patron Saint; the church near which he resided was of the Grecian style. This fact occasions the remark in a letter to Henry Wilberforce: "I cannot deny that however my reason may go with Gothic, my heart has ever gone with Grecian. ... There is in the Italian style such a simplicity, purity, elegance, beauty, brightness, which I suppose the word 'classical' implies, that it seems to befit the notion of an Angel or Saint. The Gothic style does not seem to me to typify hte sanctity or innocence of the Blessed Virgin, or St. Gabriel, or the lightness, grace and sweet cheerfulness of the elect as the Grecian does."[6]

Again in his visit to the Catacombs—those memorials of primitive Christianity to which he was so sincerely attached—a painting of the Virgin produced a forceful impression upon him. "At the back (of the chapel) ... is a large figure of the Blessed Virgin with her hands out in prayer (as the Priest stretches them now in the Mass)—our Lord is in her lap, *not* in prayer."[7] He finds it necessary to emphasize the point in order to show the idea Christians had of her in the early Church. These pictures serve to furnish him with a strong argument in favor of Mary's exaltation.[8]

Returning from Italy to England, he went to Loretto to receive the Blessed Virgin's blessing on his future work of the Oratory, which he intended to establish in England.[9] The Oratory at Birmingham was formally inaugurated on the Feast of the Purification, which is also the foundation day of Oriel. He chose this day expressly that the new enterprise might be under the shadow of "Maria Purificans." Of this feast Newman

---

[6] Ward I, 139.

[7] Ibid. 152. This is in the Coemeterium Majus on the Via Nomentana. Cf. Wilpert, *Die Malereien der Katakomben Roms*, II, Taf. 207.

[8] Cf. Diff. II, 55–56.

[9] Ward I, 193.

says: "To me it is *especially interesting*, for it has been my great feast-day for thirty years. Thirty years this year since I was brought under the shadow of our Lady, whom I ever wished to love and honor more. ... God has blessed us through her intercession for three years in this place."[10]

One of the earliest essays published by Newman after his conversion was a review of Keble's *Lyra Innocentium*. The work might be styled in great part a study of Keble's Marian devotion, to which reference has already been made when examining the latter's influence on Newman. In this, however, Newman did not wholly escape the tendency manifest among a certain number of the converts, of using rather strong language against the communion to which he had formerly belonged.[11] In the same way, when there is question of Keble's devotion to the Blessed Virgin, he points out certain *desiderata* in his second volume of verses. "We do not discover one *Ave Maria* throughout it, though he has used that invocation in ... the *Christian Year*. We cannot doubt it has been upon his lips; why, then, is it excluded from his book? Perhaps he feared to give scandal, or to cause distress or excitement, in the use of a form of words not sanctioned by his Church." Again, referring to the author's representing "Mary as bending to adore her Babe," he says: "No Catholic can quarrel with such an image ... but as introduced into these passages it is surely out of place, as if intended to give satisfaction to Protestants."[12] One may be tempted to demand whether Newman had already forgotten his own difficulties in this regard; he could easily have condoned any seeming neglect in his friend.

After his conversion, perhaps influenced by the almost indiscreet enthusiasm of Faber and his followers, Newman inclined somewhat to the Continental devotions which he had denounced as an Anglican. Such a proceeding, of course, may have been a natural reaction, but he gradually came to agree with Dr. Newsham and Dr. Ullathorne, who advocated fidelity

---

[10] S. N. 102–103.

[11] Cf. for example, Ess. II, 443.

[12] Ibid. 440.

to the forms of piety which were held in honor among English Catholics. Still, as his biographer remarks, "his own personal taste in devotion was always far more in sympathy with the Continental forms than was that of the old Catholics. What he deprecated was untheological exaggerations[13] which were found in some French and Italian books of devotion and which Faber and his friends affected, to the dissatisfaction of the old English Catholics."[14]

The converts, with Newman's sanction, started a series of Saints' lives. Newman's principal object in publishing them was to manifest his gratitude to the *Regina Sanctorum,* who used the Saints' lives for his own conversion. Besides trying to stir up the English Catholics themselves and reach those outside the fold, Newman thought that thereby he might promote an increase of devotion to the Madonna, to images, relics, etc. Due to the violent opposition aroused by these works, the series was discontinued at the request of Bishop Ullathorne. Though hurt by the attack of a certain Father Price on the project, Newman was certain that "somehow our Lady and St. Philip will take our part, if we do not take our own."[15]

Later on when the Achilli trial was in progress, the Dominican Sisters of Stone suggested that they would pray before the Image of our Lady for the success of Newman's cause. The latter replied with a certain amount of caution that seemed to bespeak scepticism. The correspondence that ensued throws a light on the simplicity of his devotion to our Lady, combined with a great diffidence in himself. "I smiled at the cleverness with which you are attempting to get up a miraculous image in England. Now, as to your proposal, I have this difficulty, that it is taxing our Blessed Lady unfairly—not her power, but her willingness. For observe, you are asking no *public* benefit of her. The *Church* will be quite enough

---

[13] Ward, I, 204, Cf. Diff. II, 21, 22.

[14] Ward, I, 205. Still, Newman ever preferred devotions that were most conformable to the English character. Cf. Ward II, 109, 110. Cf. Terrien, op cit. iii, 67, note.

[15] Ward, I, 209.

vindicated if I gain a moral victory, not a legal. ... Now what right have I, for the sake of my private ends, to put your image on trial? It has done everything for you,—because you have asked what you ought to ask. Now you wish me to ask a *very hard* thing, and that (in a way) *selfishly* and you make me say to our Lady, 'Do it, under pain of your image losing its repute.'

"Now I do want light thrown upon this. I assuredly have a simple faith in the omnipotence of her intercession—and I know well (not to say my Lord expressly tells me) that we can not ask too much, so that we are but importunate and unwearied in asking ... somehow, at first sight I do not like to be *unkind,* if I may use such a word to your image."[16] On being taken to task for not accepting the offer, he gives way and promises to preach a sermon in honor of the Blessed Virgin and carry her image in procession if she gains his acquittal. To the Reverend Mother Superior, who must have administered a reproof to him in this connection, he writes on the same occasion: "Recollect, that our House in Birmingham is erected under the Invocation of the Immaculate Mother of God, as beseems an Oratory of St. Philip—and is dedicated to her for ever, and that you will not please *her* by abusing *him*."[17]

The Catholic University of Ireland was undertaken under the auspices of the Blessed Virgin;[18] to the Blessed Mother of God he ascribed his ability in keeping at the work of the preparation of his lectures for the University.[19] Again, it is to our Lady and St. Philip, who seem henceforth to be inseparable, he dedicates his *Discourses on the Present Position of Catholics in England.*

Newman's devotion to our Blessed Lady was of that sane variety which was ever averse to what seemed exaggerated or affected, but it was none the less profound and tender. To her he applied the words of the hymn for Corpus Christi, "quia major omni laude, nec laudare sufficis." Yet this praise must

---

[16] In 1852. Ward, I, 288.
[17] Ward I, 289.
[18] 398.
[19] 316.

ever remain within the bounds of discretion and not lose itself in puerile sentimentalism. These words pertaining to the Eucharist were used in reply to congratulations received on the publication of his *Letter to Pusey.* There he adds: "It is still more difficult at once to praise her, and to dispraise some of her imprudent votaries."[20]

Particularly touching is the favorite devotion of Newman's declining years. When no longer able to recite the Divine Office, which he had loved so well ever since he had become acquainted with it in 1836, he found a solace and sufficient compensation in the recitation of the Rosary. Towards the end, even this consolation was denied him because of a lack of sensitiveness in his fingers. The Rosary had been his favorite devotion as a Catholic and he was generally seen with it. In this connection Father Neville mentions in his *Notes:* "From far back in the long distance of time, memory brings him forward, when not engaged in writing or reading, as most frequently having the Rosary in his hand."[21] The Rosary was to him the most beautiful of all devotions, as containing all in itself, for it so intimately associates the thought of Mary with that of her Divine Son, as she had been associated with Jesus in all the mysteries of His life. Truly, "Mary is music in our need, and Jesus light in store."[22] At this sight of the venerable old Cardinal prayerfully passing his fingers over the sacred beads, we are led to recall the youngster at the age of ten designing a pair of beads in his verse-book. The Rosary, symbol of Catholic devotion, against which he had inveighed in his Anglican career, had caught his childish fancy, and in Catholic days became his favorite companion.

II. DEVOTION AS PORTRAYED IN HIS WRITINGS.

Nowhere is one so apt to be deceived, at least in part, in trying to form the estimate of a person's character as by his

---

[20] Ward, II, 113.

[21] Ward II, 533.

[22] V. V. 280.

writings. This is more so the case in trying to adjudge the sanctity or devotion of a writer renowned for his literary abilities. One almost instinctively feels that the sentiments expressed in the works or sermons of a Lacordaire or Bossuet savor of literary attempt; though devout Catholics, they do not give a clear picture of their interior life. They seem rather to indicate what they would like to be than what they really are. It may seem that the same risk is incurred in trying to estimate Newman's devotion to our Lady from his writings, yet such is not the case, for his main preoccupation was rather to conceal his own interior dispositions as much as possible, although frequently and inadvertently he betrays himself into some revelations of his interior life. He is rather inclined to be reserved and objective in devotional matters; already as Anglican he combated any unreality in word and action. Thus, in speaking of religious journals, he says: "Useful as they often are, at the same time I believe persons find great difficulty, while recording their feelings, in banishing the thought that one day these good feelings will be known to the world, and are thus insensibly led to modify and prepare their language as if for a representation. Seldom, indeed, is any one in the practice of contemplating his better thoughts or doings without proceeding to display them to others, and hence it is that it is so easy to discover a conceited man. When this is encouraged in the sacred province of religion, it produces a certain unnatural solemnity of manner, arising from a wish to be, nay, to appear spiritual. ..."[23]

In the *Letter to Pusey* he gives evidence of the same reserve when he checks himself in his description of our Lady's dignity. "I am aware that, in thus speaking, I am following a line of thought which is rather a meditation than an argument in controversy, and I shall not carry it further. ..."[24] Even in the *Apologia,* which purports to be the history of his religious opinions and thus touches on what is most intimate in his soul, there is a characteristic modesty which is in great part

---

[23] P. S. II, 172.

[24] Diff. II, 52.

CATHOLIC DAYS (1845-1890)

responsible for the profound effect it produced on the Catholic and the non- Catholic world.

The earliest works of Newman as a Catholic are replete with references to his own particular difficulties concerning the Blessed Virgin in Anglican days. *Loss and Gain*, published in 1848 is an answer to the numerous rumors that circulated about Oxford in reference to the converts. Newman there adroitly puts into the mouth of Anglicans the objections commonly made by himself before his conversion, against Catholic devotion to the Blessed Virgin. Thus, one says: "At Rome and Naples they worship the Virgin as a goddess."[25] Reding, the hero of the tale, is summarily dealt with by the authorities of Oxford when he attempts to make a distinction between intercession and invocation—a distinction which was quite clear to Newman as an Anglican, though he was not absolutely certain how far either one was to be received.[26] Willis, another character in the story, is converted to Catholicism. He does not take the trouble to answer Bateman's statement that the worship of the Blessed Virgin is unscriptural, but admits that this devotion is likely to perplex him, since he cannot understand how it does not interfere with the supreme adoration due to the Creator alone. The enthusiastic convert refers this perplexity to a mere *a priori* judgment, for the Protestant does not judge from experience. He says that because he thinks a thing to be so, then it must be so. Willis then turns back the argument upon the Anglicans, who are accused by other sects in a similar manner. What is to prevent a Catholic from believing that he can honor our Blessed Lady as the first of creatures without interfering with the honor due to God?[27] He may be illogical, but he can make the distinction even though he is an uneducated Catholic.

The same thought of the supposed opposition between the worship of Mary and that of God is beautifully brought out in the verses entitled "The Pilgrim Queen," in which the Blessed

---

[25] L. G. 176.

[26] Ibid. 239.

[27] L. G. 312–316.

Virgin is represented as desolately wandering through merry England, which was once her own, seeking for her heir, that is, her divine Son, who was lost to this people because it had abandoned the Mother.

> "They said they could keep Him far better than I,
>   In a palace all His, planted deep and raised high.
> 'Twas a palace of ice, hard and cold were they,
>   And when summer came, it all melted away."[28]

This same theme recurs, as has been seen, in the *Essay on Development;* it is to be found likewise in the *Discourses to Mixed Congregations* and in the *Letter to Pusey,* that Mary is the surest safeguard of the doctrine concerning Jesus.

Newman's sermon on "The Glories of Mary for the Sake of Her Son" gives the doctrinal basis for the fact that devotion to Mary really guarantees devotion to and belief in her Son. If he has just reason to voice the plaints of the Mother of God against those who would separate her from Jesus, he can also prove to his audience that Mary's role in the Church is a positive one. Because of the interdependence and connection of Christian teachings, her divine Maternity protects the doctrine of the Incarnation. "The confession that Mary is *Deipara*, or the Mother of God, is that safeguard wherewith we seal up and secure the doctrine of the Apostle (that the Word was made flesh) from all evasion and that test whereby we detect all the pretences of those bad spirits of 'Antichrist which have gone out into the world'."[29] Mary does not exist for herself; her grace and her glory are not for her own sake but for her Maker; to her is committed the custody of the Incarnation.

One can readily understand that Newman should emphasize the point that Mary's glory is for the sake of her Son, since he is addressing an audience composed of Catholics and non-Catholics. His reasoning would be the most effective means of dispelling any illusions that might be entertained concerning the Catholic's veneration of the Blessed Virgin. All in Mary must be referred back to Jesus; whatever she had was from her

---

[28] V. V. 281, 282.
[29] Mix. 347.

Son and for His glory. Precisely because of her sublime office God had endowed her person with a superabundance of heavenly gifts. In fact, she was more glorious in her person than in her office; her purity was a higher gift than her relationship with God.[30] If, then, Mary is so great, so holy, is it strange, Newman asks, "that the Mother should have power with the Son, distinct in kind from that of the purest Angel and the most triumphant Saint?"[31] The prayer that Newman breathes at the close of this beautiful discourse seems to be an echo of his own experiences when he faltered at sight of this heavenly Mother, whose ravishing beauty, he learned, was not dangerous to look upon, nor could it draw him away from Jesus. "O hope of the pilgrim! lead us still as thou hast led; in the dark night, across the bleak wilderness, guide us on to our Lord Jesus, guide us home."[32] Thus, it would seem that Mary had become for him the "Kindly Light" which had led him on and brought him to the truth, and his desire was that others might be led on in the same manner.

The mysteries of our Blessed Lady's life that seem to have had an appeal to Newman's devotion were, besides the Divine Maternity, the Immaculate Conception, the Dolors, and the Assumption. In addition, he devoted a certain interest likewise to the intercessory power of Mary. Most of the sermons concerning the Blessed Virgin, as well as the Meditations and Devotions written about 1874 center about these mysteries.

We know how Newman's religious instinct, developed under the influences of Keble and Froude, led him to a firm belief in the Immaculate Conception while he was still an Anglican; it was but natural that his sentiments in this regard should become all the more precise in time. He was convinced that no holy persons ever really denied this mystery; if they seemed to deny it, it was because of a misunderstanding as to the object of the belief.[33] The Blessed Virgin serves as a bright

---

[30] Ibid. 350.
[31] Mix. 355.
[32] Ibid. 359.
[33] S. N. 106.

contrast to the world of sin.[34] Since she was to be the new Eve, she had to have at least the gifts which Eve had possessed, and among these was principally her sinlessness at creation.[35] The proclamation of the dogma of the Immaculate Conception caused great joy to the heart of the celebrated Oratorian; on the Christmas following the definition, he remarked that the feast of this year was different from others, for a crown had been given to Mary. The Oratory, above all, had every reason to be particularly interested in this event, as the Church at Birmingham was raised under the invocation of Mary Immaculate, who had showered her favors upon the Community. The feast itself was held in great honor in the Congregation, for the lives of the Oratorians ought to begin in personal holiness, just as Mary began her mortal existence in the state of perfect sanctity.[36]

Newman also loved to dwell on the sorrows of the heavenly Mother. She, the ideal of painters and poets, the flower of human nature, so holy that she inspired holiness, she too, had to suffer as did her Son; she was to be the Queen of Martyrs; she was privileged to share the acutest part of Jesus' sufferings, as she stood courageously by the cross.[37] Her sorrows were all the more intense because she foresaw them a long time in advance of their actual infliction; hers was the anguish caused by the sight of her Son's bodily suffering, which she herself was not permitted to bear in her own person.[38]

The Assumption was also a favorite topic in Newman's sermons. He draws this mystery as an immediate inference of the Immaculate Conception, in the same way that the latter dogma is derived from the belief that Mary is the second Eve. It became our Lord to raise His Mother to heaven after her death. She was not a mere physical instrument through whom the Word passed in order to come into the world; Jesus took

---

[34] S. N. 93–95; 27–29.

[35] Ibid. 107.

[36] Ibid.109.

[37] Ibid.73–75.

[38] S.N.135,136.

His body from her substance. Sanctity and a spiritual office go together, therefore she had to be full of grace, conceived without sin. If she saw no original sin, she ought not to witness corruption. Jesus could not treat this holiest of mothers worse than human sons do their mothers, who are far beneath the Mother of Jesus.[39]

Her Assumption introduces Mary to another important function, seated as she is at the right hand of her Divine Son in glory. She becomes the most powerful intercessor with Jesus. Newman centers the doctrine of our Lady's intercession on the Catholic doctrine of prayer, and any one who holds this, can find no difficulty in admitting the teaching concerning the Blessed Virgin. Mary's power is but an exemplification of the power of prayer. If any one has once convinced himself that prayer has a great influence in the supernatural order, there is nothing left but to admit that Mary can accomplish more than any other creature by the power attached to her supplications. What strong things Protestants can say about prayer and faith, we can apply to our Lady, who becomes omnipotent through prayer. Since she is the most holy and persevering of creatures, there should be nothing to astonish us in this, that she can have so much influence with Almighty God.[40] Newman is always careful to remind his audience that, though Mary is the advocate of the Church, she did not effect the Atonement—she like all others was saved by her Son, through whom she had been exalted to the office of advocate of mankind. This position conferred on her is the result of God's merciful providence, which permits us creatures to supplicate Him for the dispensation of His favors and graces.[41]

Of the Second Eve, little is to be found in his sermons, though this belief becomes the basic argument in the *Letter to Pusey*. He draws the Immaculate Conception as an immediate consequence of this office. In one place Newman carries out the parallel. The sermon was preached at the opening of May, 1851:

---

[39] Cf. S. N. 13-15; Mix. 360-376.

[40] S. N. 42-44.

[41] Ibid.118.

"She is a better Eve. Eve, too, in the beginning may be called the May of the year. She was the first-fruits of God's beautiful creation. She was the type of all beauty; but, alas! she represented the world also in its fragility. She stayed not in her original creation. Mary comes as a second and holier Eve, having the grace of indefectibility and the gift of perseverance from the first, and teaching us how to use God's gifts without abusing them."[42]

A series of meditations for each day of the month of May written and used about 1874 appeared after the Cardinal's death under the heading of *Meditations and Devotions,* which included other meditations on Christian Doctrine, an exercise of the Way of the Cross and numerous prayers. The meditations on our Lady reveal most strikingly the devotional side of the Cardinal; other works present him rather as apologist, but here he puts aside the controversial tone. Many a one, perhaps, in reading over these brief meditations on the invocations of our Lady's Litany may find them rather cold or, at most, too reasoned. Newman seems hardly ever able to give vent to his inmost feelings; sober reason seems to dominate all and holds any outburst of sentiment in check. But therein lies precisely the beauty of Newman's devotion. It reveals itself as something profound, almost too profound for expression, too serious a thing to be exhibited to the vulgar gaze of curious passersby. He had a tight grasp on the solid foundations of true devotion; what mattered it to him if others could not enter into the type of devotion that suited his own character? His was not the superficial sentimentalism that is profuse in rhetorical expression with little or no profundity of thought and still less concern to live according to belief. His was rather of the stern virile type, which is true and solid because grounded in true humility.

In sketching these almost bare outlines of meditations, Newman purposed rather to suggest certain reflections that could be developed by the pious user or the hearer. The invocations are grouped about the four phases of Mary's life

---

[42] S.N.79.

which, as was remarked, interested Newman in a special manner: the Immaculate Conception, the Annunciation, the Dolors, and the Assumption. Under these headings the pious author skilfully develops the salient points of his Mariology. The apparent reserve combined with the clarity and simplicity of these reflections simply testify the more to a devotion that is not ordinary. Had he not said that there were certain devotional manifestations into which he could not enter even twenty years after his conversion, though he was certain that he did not love our Lady the less for that?[43] A virile mind, established in humility, could not be content with a puerile devotion.

The *Notes on Athanasius* complete the sources from which may be examined Newman's Marian doctrine and devotion. These *Notes* were published just before his conversion, in connection with the Library of the Fathers. As for the doctrine concerning our Lady, he touches on the Divine Maternity and the Virginity of the Blessed Virgin. His ideas on these topics were complete in his Anglican days. Perhaps the only point in this connection that underwent modification when he revised the work in later years, was the question of a cultus to the Saints, who are "in the sight as in the fruition of the exuberant infinitude of God."[44] He then exposes this doctrine as a necessary deduction from the Divine Indwelling in the soul of the Christian, who has already merited his reward. In a few compact pages, Newman gives a concise history of the title *Theotokos*, with the teachings of the Fathers concerning the Divine Maternity as well as the virginity of Mary. Of particular interest is the defense of the latter dogma by an explanation of the text of St. Matthew, which is used by non-Catliolics to disprove the virginity of Mary *post partum*.

---

[43] Apo. 195.
[44] Ath. II, 195.

CHAPTER IV
THE LETTER TO PUSEY

HE *Letter to Pusey* (written in 1865) is the work by which Newman is best known as a writer on the Blessed Virgin. That it was a work adapted to the needs of the moment, is testified by the translations made within a short time after its appearance. It had a broad appeal to those within the fold, who understood and appreciated better the position that Mary should hold in their beliefs and devotions, as well as to those outside the Church, who were made to understand that Catholic devotion to our Lady has a strong dogmatic basis and is attested to by the earliest witnesses of Christian antiquity. If Newman was able to produce so finished a composition within the space of a few weeks, it was because he had the material ready for service a long time since. In fact, this masterpiece of Marian literature is but the systematization, the crystallization of what Newman had taught and preached since the day when he set himself to write the *Essay on Development*. In order to get complete understanding of the *Letter* it is necessary to examine the circumstances under which it was called forth; thus, many preliminary remarks made by Newman can be understood. A brief analysis of Newman's method of exposition will complete the study.

I. PUSEY'S *EIRENICON*; THE OCCASION OF THE *LETTER TO PUSEY*.

The *Letter to Pusey* purports to be an answer to this renowned Anglican's *Eirenicon*,—a letter addressed to John Keble. This in its turn had been an answer to a letter of

Manning, provoked by the following statement of Pusey in his preface to a legal decision: "While I know that a very earnest body of Roman Catholics rejoice in all the workings of God the Holy Ghost in the Church of England (whatever they think of her) and are saddened in what weakens her, who is in God's hands the great bulwark against infidelity in this land, others seemed to be in an ecstasy of triumph at this victory of Satan."[1] Manning made a public reply, followed by a rejoinder from Pusey in book form. In his volume Pusey at first merely defended the English Church against the imputations of Manning, following somewhat on the lines of Newman's Tract 90,[2] by showing that the divergences between the Articles and the Tridentine Decrees were merely differences of words. But as he reached the great point of contest, namely, Article 22, which treats of the "Romish practices such as invocation, pardons, etc.", he changed his tactics and made his answer a plea for reunion. Pusey explained his reason for this to Newman:

"I meant by this to point out or suggest what we could accept, if it could be made quite clear that, in accepting this, we did not accept what lay beyond it. I hoped that the Roman Church might agree to lay down thus much as matter of faith and not more. Such an authoritative explanation would be something wholly different from unauthoritative explanations, such as those of Milner.[3] But in order to explain what we want, we ought to explain why we want it. It would be an unmeaning thing to ask that it should be defined, that nothing more was of faith touching the Invocation of Saints than what is given in the Council of Trent, as explained by Milner, without saying why we desire this. We should be asked, naturally, 'Why do you want us to make any new decrees? The Church does not

---

[1] Pusey, IV, 95.

[2] Pusey calls the *Eirenicon* "a reawakening of Tract 90, which, though its principles have sunk deep, is not much known by the rising generation." Ibid. 99.

[3] Vicar Apostolic of the Midland District in the early nineteenth century, and author of The End of Controversy.

make decrees on matters of faith without a reason; what reason have you to give for what you ask?' Now if, as I believe, the system in regard to the Blessed Virgin is the chief hindrance to reunion, and if a declaration by authority that something which does not necessarily involve this ... is alone of faith, would remove that chief hindrance to reunion, then an intelligible ground is given for the request."[4]

Pusey was expecting too much in demanding that the Church declare what was not of faith, particularly as such a course would limit the future guidance of the Church in matters as yet undefined. He expressed in a subsequent letter what he had expected from Rome, to facilitate the acceptance of the Tridentine Council and consequent reunion with the English Church. "I certainly did think that in a subject which had long been before the Church, as Purgatory, the Cultus of the Blessed Virgin, Indulgences, she might decide what is not *de fide* as well as what is. Of course, one must always trust God for the future. But, as you know, the practical difficulty of the Church of England is much more as to things not defined to be *de fide* than as to the letter of the Council of Trent. But then, supposing the Church of England to be willing to accept the Council of Trent *provided* the acceptance of it involved no more than its words go, how would she escape accepting all the rest, against which the chief objection lies? I mean, supposing the Council of Trent would be authoritatively so explained ... how could she avoid having the whole system contained in the *Glories of Mary* made her system?"[5]

There were possibilities of reconciliation, Pusey thought, provided limits of the dogmatic teaching of the Roman Church could be explained, but then the power of unlimited future definitions rendered such negative explanations useless. Pusey's projected work would have to be borne in two directions: first to restate the doctrine of the Church of England, as was done in Tract 90, and, secondly, to point out how popular Romanism differed from accepted dogmatic

---

[4] Pusey, IV, 98.

[5] Pusey IV, 100.

standards. Was this not the same position held by Newman twenty years before, when he published the last of the Tracts, which met with so severe a condemnation from the heads of the Anglican Church?

In addressing his *Eirenicon* to Keble, Pusey explains its nature to him: "It is chiefly a defence of ourselves against Manning, explaining our Articles in the old way, excepting against the large Roman Catholic quasi-authoritative system, under the head of Art. XXII, and then speaking hopefully of ourselves, and as we trust, our office of reuniting Christendom. Liddon has seen it, for I wished a second eye to see what I was addressing publicly to you. He wished me to say more about the Immaculate Conception, so I am making an appendix, and am going to town tomorrow to examine the votes which the 500 bishops gave. There were some very remarkable opinions given against making it a dogma—especially the Archbishops of Rouen, Paris, Salzburg. All the Professors at Maynooth were against it, and the R.C. Archbishop of Dublin."[6]

Though he was attempting to revive the mode of conciliation exemplified by Du Pin and Wake, he felt that he had to protest against the exaggerations on Papal Infallibility, sanctioned by the *Dublin Review,* as also against the "large development of the system as to the Blessed Virgin."[7] The ground which Pusey covers in the earlier part of his work is merely a vindication of the Thirty-nine Articles as not being directly opposed to the Tridentine Decrees. Like Newman, Pusey found his great difficulties, not in speculative topics, nor in formal doctrines, but in the practical system of the Roman Church. Pusey remarks that the objections against Rome in the mind of the ordinary Englishman relate to that "vast system as to the Blessed Virgin, which to all of us has been the special *crux* of the Roman system."[8]

It is of no particular importance to examine the general content of the *Eirenicon,* but it is necessary to see what were

---

[6] Pusey, IV, 105.

[7] Ibid. 106.

[8] Pusey IV, 108; Eir. 101 sqq.

Pusey's views on the Blessed Virgin. On this question he found a difference between the Roman and Greek Churches, both of which admit invocation of the Mother of God, but the Orthodox Church did not recognize her as universal mediatrix and refused to accept the definition of the Immaculate Conception.[9]

Pusey did not find any difficulty in the decree of Trent sanctioning the invocation of Mary, but he objected to the fact that an entire system had been developed around the fundamental doctrines concerning her, and this system seemed to make her functions co-extensive with those of Christ; she had become, as it were, indispensable in obtaining access to her divine Son, and in the grant of graces to us. For his purpose, he cites a long list of authors, to some of whom, as Olier, he imputes at least material heresy, in practically denying the mediatorial office of Christ. At every instant Jesus seems to be replaced by His Mother; graces are asked of her directly, which can be granted by God alone. Such are the invocations which Pusey repudiates. He is shocked at the extremes to which spiritual writers run, and among them is Faber, a recent convert from Anglicanism, who ascribes the lack of earnestness in the service of God to a want of devotion to Mary. "Here in England," writes Faber, "Mary is not half enough preached. Devotion to her is low and thin and poor. It is frightened out of its wits by the sneers of heresy. It is always invoking human respect and carnal prudence, wishing to make Mary so little of a Mary, that Protestants may feel at ease about her. ... Hence it is that Jesus is not loved, that heretics are not converted, that the Church is not exalted; that souls which might be saints, wither and dwindle, that the sacraments are not rightly frequented, or souls enthusiastically evangelized. Jesus is obscured because Mary is kept in the background. Thousands of souls perish because Mary is withheld from them."[10] One can imagine the Protestant being startled at such apparently

---

[9] Eir. 101, etc.

[10] Pref. to de Montfort's Treatise *on True Devotion to the Blessed Virgin*. Cf. I Eir. 117–118. Faber had translated this work, which had come to light in 1842.

exaggerated language. What becomes of Jesus, of God, if Mary is to be everything in the life of a Catholic? How far this seems to be from the practice of the early Church and the doctrine of Scripture, Pusey shows by numerous citations, in answer to his question "If devotion to the Blessed Virgin were so essential to salvation, how could it be that God, in His last and final revelation of Himself, is so wholly silent about it?"[11] The silence of the Gospels concerning the Blessed Virgin had struck others as well. Newman as an Anglican, ascribed it to a merciful Providence which wished to preserve us from undue worship of her who is so far above all other creatures. Pusey multiplies Scripture texts to prove that Christ ever testified Himself to be the sole Mediator. Is there room, then, for a Mediatrix; and if there is, why did not the Savior mention it?

The center of Pusey's attack, for such it was, was the dogma of the Immaculate Conception defined eleven years earlier. He had gone to great pains to study the documents favoring or opposing the definition.[12] His main preoccupation, however, was to examine the supposed opposition on the part of a certain number of bishops. In this respect, two arguments weighed particularly with Pusey.

First of all, Pius IX, he claims, acted against the manifest wishes of a minority which based its opposition on solid motives.[13] In some places, it is true, there was no response to the Pope's inquiries. Elsewhere, grave objections were raised, as in parts of France and Austria.[14] Doubts were expressed by many other prelates, and nevertheless the Pope proclaimed the dogma. These objections, however, if carefully examined, do not oppose the dogma as such. Scarcely any bishop maintained that such a definition would be counter to Scripture or

---

[11] I Eir. 119.

[12] For his facts Pusey based himself on the *Pareri dell' Episcopato Cattolico sulla definizione dogmatico dell' immacolato concepimento della B. V. Maria.* He also made a thorough study of the innumerable documents compiled by Torquemada for the Council of Basel. This Dominican was a strong opponent of the doctrine.

[13] I Eir. 126.

[14] Ibid.130–132.

Tradition. Practically all the opponents were ranged against the advisability or opportuneness of the declaration. The number of theologians whose views did not coincide with what was ultimately defined as of faith, was comparatively small. Pusey was of the opinion that the definition should have at least made the distinction between active and passive conception, in order to combat the erroneous notion of a few "that the body might have been conceived in original sin, according to the law of transmission of this inherent sin, but might have been cleansed from its stain before the soul was infused into it by God, so that it should not communicate itself to the soul."[15] Pusey was in accord with the Schoolmen, who taught that only a person can be the subject of sin, and consequently no sin can be present before the soul is infused.

Notwithstanding the hesitations of some bishops, based on mere expedience, in view of the storm that certainly would be aroused among Protestants and bigots and because of the troublous times through which the Church was passing, notwithstanding doubts and silence, the majority of those who answered the Pope's queries were enthusiastically in favor of defining what had so long been closely bound up with Catholic traditions. Some feared, however, that good Catholic folk might be troubled at hearing that what they had always held as of faith, had only then been imposed as such.

The second and more serious argument of Pusey against the dogma was that its consequences were dangerous. One lay in the mode of the definition—no General Council had been convened for the purpose. Pusey thought that such a method was giving the Pope undue power, for even the bishops who had given an adverse decision at once protested their filial submission to any contrary action of the Pope. Thus the Pope could, as Pusey supposed, take any popular belief and elevate it to the dignity of a dogma.

Another consequence would be the fact that the gateway would be opened to an infinite variety of dogmas on the Blessed Virgin. If what had been a pious belief for a long period,

---

[15] I Eir. 147.

could become an article of faith, what would hinder the Assumption, the universal mediation of the Blessed Virgin, and a host of other beliefs from becoming dogmas? In due time, all the titles and prerogatives ascribed to Christ would be handed over to the Blessed Virgin. Such a series of definitions would bring umbrage to other communions and would simply widen the gap already existing between them.[16] What limits could thus be placed to the practical system on the Blessed Virgin if even private revelations were being taken into account, as Pusey supposed had been the case for the Immaculate Conception?[17] Furthermore, the hopes that had been expressed by many Catholics, of great benefits to be derived from the proclamation of the dogma, had by no means been realized to Pusey's satisfaction.

It is very likely that the definition of the Immaculate Conception was the greatest stumbling-block to the non-Catholics of Pusey's time and for this reason he probably signalized it for his attacks. The attitude of being shocked or scandalized arose either from a misunderstanding of the mystery itself, or from an almost innate opposition to the principle of Papal Infallibility, which was implied in the proclamation. Personally, Pusey was not opposed to the doctrine itself, for a little later he writes to Newman: "I have no prejudice against the supposition that Almighty God infused grace into the soul of the Blessed Virgin at the first moment of its creation. On the contrary, considering what He did for Jeremiah and St. John Baptist, it seems the most likely. My only difficulty is the counter-tradition."[18] This decision he thought had given a blow to the "Quod ubique, quod semper" of Vincent of Lerins. Newman, speaking of his friend, could testify to the latter's own personal devotion to our Lady: "For the Fathers' sake who so exalt her, you really do love and venerate her. ...

---

[16] I Eir. 121; 181.

[17] He thought the revelation to St. Bridget had something to do with the definition, though the doctrine seems to be contradicted by another revelation to St. Catherine of Sienna. Cf. Ibid. 174, 172.

[18] Pusey, IV, 164.

If you come short of us, you do not actually go against us in your devotion to her."[19]

The primary difficulty for Pusey, as it had been for Newman, was the delusion that Mary was appropriating the honor due to Jesus. The strongest expressions for him seem to be that "God does not will to give anything except through the Blessed Virgin" and "He has placed her between Christ and the Church."[20] Where the Protestant would go directly to God, the Catholic turns to the Blessed Virgin. There seems to be almost a studied "identification of her, in all but what follows from the Hypostatic Union, with her Divine Son."[21]

The great fault with the Catholic system on the Blessed Virgin lay in its very completeness; it professed to know more than could be verified by Scripture or Tradition. This notion of Pusey had also been shared by Newman before his conversion. Thus, Mary is parallelled throughout with her Divine Son, so that every office or prerogative which belonged to Him by nature and absolutely, is imputed to her also in some measure. Her conception was not in the way of nature but by divine interference. She desired naught but the salvation of mankind; she merited it of congruity; as Jesus died in act, so she died in will.[22] And thus Pusey continues the parallel, citing principally Salazar, de Montfort and Oswald, who are his main authorities whenever he wishes to give a theological exposition of the Catholic view. This assimilation of Mary to Jesus had led some to the conclusion that our Blessed Lady is present with Jesus in the Holy Eucharist. Other writers seemed even to assert that adoration might be given to the Blessed Virgin though only of an inferior and relative kind to that paid to God, because of her close relation with the Hypostatic Union, because "she touched the bounds of the Divinity."[23]

---

[19] Diff. II, 90.

[20] The second expression is found in St. Bernard's sermon on Apoc. 12.

[21] I Eir. 151; Pusey might have discovered a remarkable example to suit his purpose in St. Peter Damian's first Sermon de Nativitate B. V.

[22] I Eir. 162.

[23] Ibid. 184, 185.

Whither this increase of devotion to Mary will lead Catholics, Pusey dares not imagine. "We have been told," says he, "that the devotion of the people to the Blessed Virgin outruns the judgment of the priests; but if the whole weight of Papal authority is added to the popular devotions, and the people are bidden, on what is to them the highest authority, to be still more devoted to the Blessed Virgin ... one sees not where there shall be any pause or bound short of that bold conception that 'every prayer, both of individuals and of the Church should be addressed to St. Mary.' Popular devotion now is already very different from what it was in the time of St. Bernard. St. Bernard has strong passages, grounded on what the Breviary stated to be the language of St. Athanasius, St. Augustine, etc., which Roman Catholic critics have discovered not to be theirs. But the devotion of St. Bernard is concentrated on Christ crucified. In St. Bernard on the Canticles one is in a different atmosphere from that of, e.g., Faber."[24] The day of critical or scrupulous devotees described by de Montfort has passed away, giving place to the silent, or overenthusiastic exaggerating clients of Mary, so thinks Pusey. "If the system should grow, as seems likely, and it should be discovered that this vast range of doctrine which the people have been taught or encouraged in, in the name of the Church, has no foundation in ... either Scripture or Tradition—it is an anxious thought what the result might be."[25] To settle this difficulty in advance, he presumed that the best method would be an authoritative explanation, i.e., a declaration of what is not *de fide,* as he demanded with so much insistence of Newman in private correspondence. He was of the opinion that such an explanation would probably be satisfactory to the Anglicans and Protestants and consequently would redound to the benefit of the Roman Church, though in what way, he does not specify.

Briefly, the *Eirenicon* insofar as it is concerned with devotion to our Lady, is not a peace proposition at all, but rather implies an attack on the definition of the Immaculate

---

[24] I Eir. 186, 187.
[25] Ibid.188.

Conception as well as on Catholic devotion to our Lady in general. Pusey even supposed that the former definition required further explanations as being one-sided, incomplete. As for the devotion of Catholics to the Blessed Virgin, he based himself on exaggerated statements or at least on assertions that give the impression of exaggeration, because they were intended for people of a character different from that of the Englishman. Apart from Faber, all of Pusey's authorities are foreigners, and certain ones like Oswald are on the Index.

The first appearance of the *Eirenicon* was hailed with enthusiasm by many sympathizers, and even by those who were not in full accord with Pusey. Bishop Ellicott did not disapprove of the terms laid down by the latter for reunion with Rome.[26] How differently from Newman Dr. Döllinger judged of this work can be seen from a sentence in a letter to Pusey: "I am convinced, by reading your *Eirenicon,* that inwardly we are united in our religious convictions, although externally we belong to two separated Churches."[27] There was only one whose opinion at this juncture Pusey valued more than any other and that was Newman's, but Newman refused to be drawn into any reply at once.

A letter from Ward gave Pusey the opportunity to sound Newman[28] on his reception of the book. Ward had assured Pusey that he would write strongly against it and that Newman, too, was of the opinion that the *Eirenicon* was in reality the reverse of what it pretended to be. The following day Newman penned his answer, which was evidently a decided disappointment to his friend.

The biographer of Pusey prefaces Newman's letter with a statement of Pusey's purpose in writing the book, a purpose, which, as he claimed, Newman misunderstood, for "he ignored the fact that Pusey had not recklessly quoted extreme Roman statements, but that he had taken, as the basis of his hopes of reunion, a supposed willingness on the part of the Church of

---

[26] Pusey, IV, 117.
[27] Ibid. 118.
[28] Oct. 30, 1865; ibid. 118.

Rome to dissociate herself from such teaching as was clearly not in accordance with her authorized dogmatic standards. If he had felt himself bound to give instances of that teaching it had been only with the hope that they might be disavowed."[29]

Newman's reply contains in substance what afterwards he put into his Letter under the caption of "Anglican Misconceptions and Catholic Excesses in devotion to the Blessed Virgin." He charges Pusey with unfairness in throwing together such names as Suarez, St. Bernardine, Eadmer, and Faber. He had never read Faber's books, nor had he heard such names as de Montfort and Oswald. He simply brands their statements (if the translations are correct) as extravagances and not at all representative of the opinion of the great body of Catholics. He chides his friend for not making a distinction between intercession and invocation and explains how under certain conditions an individual may not be saved without devotion to Mary. He suggests that Pusey ought to have stated the conditions for union in respect to the cultus of the Blessed Virgin.

Pusey was not at all insincere in his propositions, but Roman Catholics could hardly view His *Eirenicon* other than as an attack. He wished to clear himself of such a charge. Let it be remarked that the whole correspondence between Newman and Pusey centers exclusively about devotion to the Blessed Virgin, although the *Eirenicon* treated many other points that were sources of controversy between Anglicans and Roman Catholics. Pusey explains his whole attitude at length in a letter of Nov. 2, 1865:

"I had no idea of attacking anything. I thought that I had avoided everything like declamation. I do not recollect using a single epithet or anything but a statement of what I thought important facts. I meant merely to put out what are our difficulties. I did not as a mere presbyter wish to put down formally what I thought should be the formula of union, nor had I any idea of wishing to interfere with others' devotion or that anything should be condemned. What I wanted, I thought

---

[29] Pusey, IV, 119.

I had explained at the beginning of p. 100,[30] that that should be declared to be alone *de fide* which the Council of Trent had laid down on the subject of Invocation. I mean that if the explanation of Milner, which I quoted in p. 100,[31] were laid down authoritatively, so that all besides should be left as pious opinion, an immense step would be gained.

"I certainly meant to put down nothing except what I thought was taught by writers of weight. In St. Bernardine and Eadmer I took, as I thought, favorite authorities in St. Liguori (*Glories of Mary, The Month of Mary,* etc.) Suarez also I took from Liguori. In fact, I *thought* that I had so far only put together what I found together in a favorite book of one canonized.

"Faber I took as being, I thought, one of the most favorite books (to judge from the sale) of the present day, and, in regard to the Holy Eucharist, he cites St. Ignatius.

"I thought that none of the system of the Blessed Virgin had been *de fide* and this is what I wished to be said by your authorities indirectly. I did not want you to deny her Intercession (which of course I never doubt, or indeed that of any of the Saints) or her Invocation, or the forms of devotion. ... After the doctrine of the Immaculate Conception had been so long a pious opinion, it has been declared to be *de fide,* and many bishops said that it was so held among their people. So, I thought and much more, might any of those points which I set down, because there would be no counter-tradition about them, whereas, on account of the doctrine of the transmission of

---

[30] This is the beginning of his commentary on Art. 22, although he has little to say on the subject of Invocation proper. His views were similar to those exposed in Newman's Tract 90. The greater part of the commentary is, as has been seen, taken up with the exposition of difficulties relative to the Roman practical system on devotion to Mary.

[31] "They (the Saints) do nothing for us mortals in heaven but what they did while they were here on earth, and what all good Christians are bound to do for each other, namely, they help us by their prayers. The only difference is, that as the Saints in heaven are free from every stain of sin and imperfection, and are confirmed in grace and glory, so their prayers are far more efficacious for obtaining what they ask for than are the prayers of us imperfect and sinful mortals."

original sin, there was a good deal on the doctrine of the Immaculate Conception. ... In view of the Synod of next year,[32] I was not sorry, since I wrote at all, to say what are our difficulties, lest any of them should be made matters of faith too. But then, too, I wished to show that our difficulties lay outside the Council of Trent, and as I thought, outside what is *de fide* (the Immaculate Conception is a perplexity), and so I thought it no attack, since I was mostly speaking of things not *de fide,* as I believed, but which, as things stand, individuals of us, if we joined the Roman Church must receive."[33]

Newman had at first no intention whatever of replying to the book, and assured Pusey that if he did finally make up his mind to do so, he would treat the *Eirenicon* according to the mind of the author. Pusey insisted all the more with his friend that his intentions were to smooth over difficulties that hindered union, and that the situation would be the more aggravated if fresh definitions were promulgated. "If you could read through what I wrote," he says, "you will have seen another motive in all that which I wrote about the system as to the Blessed Virgin. It seemed to me that, on the principles and with the object upon which and with which the Immaculate Conception was made matter of faith, any other popular belief might be made matter of faith."[34]

Newman admits that it is necessary to receive the Roman practical system, but it is not required to hold by an author such as St. Liguori in all matters of detail. "I hold by his numerous spiritual books," he writes, "but I do not accept and follow views which he expressed about the Blessed Virgin."[35] Pusey felt that Newman would have been the person most fitted on the Catholic side to draw out in detail what might be offered as terms of union with the English Church, but the

---

[32] The opening of the Vatican Council did not take place until 1869, though it was hoped to begin as early as 1867, but the war between Austria and Italy rendered this impossible.

[33] Pusey, IV, 121–122.

[34] Pusey, IV, 124.

[35] Ibid. 127.

latter demurred on the plea that this would require too much time, thought, and advice.[36] The only points that would really require explanation as well as limitation would be those alluded to in Art. 22, consequently, those pertaining to the practical system. Newman himself, alone could set forth the correct views so as to place the Catholic position on a really unassailable basis.[37] He would also have the opportunity of disclaiming any sanction of the extreme statements of Faber, while at the same time saving himself from the accusation of his fellow-Catholics that he lacked a generous, whole-hearted spirit when the honor of the Mother of God was in question.[38]

The possibility of misunderstandings arising on both sides because of the controversy, impelled Newman at length to prepare a reply. What had been produced thus far on the Catholic side was written in a polemical or Utopian spirit, which served only to irritate either Anglicans or Catholics. Within a short time his answer was ready for the press. On November 3 he stated specifically that thus far he had no intention to write, and on December 7 the answer was completed.

He informed his friend of his final resolution on the feast of the Immaculate Conception, when his work was already prepared: "You must not be made anxious that I am going to publish a letter on your *Eirenicon*. I wish to accept it as such, and shall write in that spirit. And I write, if not to hinder, for that is not in my power, but to balance and neutralize other things which may be written upon it. It will not be of any great length. If I shall say anything which is in the way of remonstrance, it will be because unless I were perfectly honest, I should not only do no good, but carry no one with me; but I am taking the greatest pains not to say a word which I should be sorry for afterward."[39]

Pusey's biographer was under the impression that the line

---

[36] Ibid. 127–128.

[37] Ward, II, 99.

[38] Ibid. 100.

[39] Pusey, IV, 131. Ward, II, 102.

of argument followed in the reply was dictated by the difficulties which arose from the internal dissensions of the Roman Catholics in England, not less than by Pusey's project of reunion, and, besides, that Newman felt himself obliged to answer because of its supposed allusions to him and because it treated Faber and Ward as representative of the English Catholics.[40] Liddon accused Newman of injustice in that famous expression familiar to readers of the *Letter:* "There was one of old time who wreathed his sword in myrtle; excuse me—you discharge your olive branch as if from a catapult." Commenting on this passage, Liddon says in his *Life of Pusey:* "Rarely has rhetorical skill been more ingeniously employed than in this half-playful banter. The expression about the 'catapult' lives in memory more easily than the rest of the controversy, but its injustice is generally overlooked. Pusey had certainly laid bare without reserve the serious defects in popular Romanism; for, as has already been said, it would have been useless to approach the question of Reunion without frankly stating the great obstacles which some Roman teaching had put in its way. But Newman's epigram cleverly diverted attention from the fact that the sting lay in the obstacles themselves and not in their enumeration."[41]

That is the view of an Anglican; granted that such a remark was bound psychologically to produce an almost indelible impression on the memory, it was far from Newman's idea to divert attention from the obstacles to reunion. The whole *Letter* is a refutation of such a supposition. Newman's purpose was broad; rather than merely answer the objections raised, he determined to show that devotion to the Blessed Virgin as in vogue at the present time in the Roman Church has its basis in the Scriptural and patristic view of Mary's dignity and position, and is the necessary consequence of it. Consequently, his attention is directed first to a clear exposition of the *prima facie* view of her in Antiquity, with all the inferences that can be

---

[40] Pusey, IV, 135.

[41] Pusey IV, 136. Pusey did not view it in the same light; for him it was a manifestation on Newman's part not to cause pain. Cf. II Eir. 21.

drawn from it. Devotion must necessarily color the belief of the faithful, who by their human nature may be led into extremes. At this point Newman disowns the excessive statements of some writers who incidentally do not possess much authority in the Church. He met Pusey's demand for some sort of authoritative repudiation of extreme language, but at the same time felt himself compelled to explain in what points he disagreed with the *Eirenicon*.

II. BRIEF ANALYSIS OF THE LETTER

A brief survey of the Letter will show how far Newman acceded to Pusey's wishes and even went beyond, by giving a classical exposé of Catholic belief and devotion to the Blessed Virgin.

The Introduction is a delicate and skilful delineation of Pusey's position in the Anglican Church. He is a leader in whom many place their confidence. His proposals for reunion could not but be welcomed with joy; but conscience was to be followed, for this was Newman's own beacon light in every circumstance of life. Newman could sympathize with Anglicans in their doubts and perplexities; he had known these himself, and, besides, had had very little encouragement from Catholics while he was seeking the light; he and his friends had been accused of treachery and deceit and knew that no mercy was to be expected from the Catholic side; his only refuge lay in the convictions that were gradually strengthened because of fidelity to his conscience.

Newman admits Pusey's difficulties, and is not surprised that conditions for union should be placed, though he cannot concur in them himself. He states frankly that there is much in Pusey's work that is offensive to Catholics; the latter's treatment of the subject gives only a one-sided view of Catholic teaching on the Blessed Virgin, so that a writer in the *Guardian* could affirm: "It is language which, after having often heard it, we still can only hear with horror." Is it more than natural that Catholics should feel anger at such an unjustifiable attack?

Pusey's attention is called to certain statements which are

supposed to be the expression of Newman's mind before his conversion, but which he had repudiated long since. These remarks bear on points such as: the position of Anglicanism in face of infidelity; Scripture as the sole rule of faith; the interpretation of Tract 90 as a basis of union; the consequences of his theory of development; the duty of a convert in going to Rome. Newman claims that he accepted Roman Catholicism as a living system, but this does not oblige him to admit all that is secondary or accidental in the Church's system. His own preferences naturally go towards English habits of belief and devotion, concerning which he found the same teaching among his fellow Catholics. Dr. Griffiths[42] had warned him against Italian books of devotion; at Rome he had been taught by his confessor, a Jesuit, that "we could not love the Blessed Virgin too much if we loved our Lord a great deal more."[43] Even as regards the *Saints' Lives,* though carried away by enthusiasm of younger men for a time, he had soon returned to a safer course. Faber and Ward were not to be considered as spokesmen for English Catholics; "they came to the Church, and have thereby saved their souls," but no prominent English theologian was given to indulge in extravagant statements about the Blessed Virgin or the Infallibility of the Pope. In conclusion to these remarks, Newman explains the method he intends to follow in his exposé. He will take his stand upon the Fathers, who had brought him into the Catholic Church. Their teaching on the Blessed Virgin suffices for him.

Such a procedure is the most natural course to expect in Newman. His whole formation as Anglican was along patristic lines, since it was a necessity for a communion that claims to base itself exclusively on Scripture and Antiquity, and pretends to be the logical and sole continuation of the primitive Church. The Roman Church holds to the same rule of faith, but acknowledges an infallible authority in (its) interpretation. All of Christian doctrine is contained at least in germ in these two fecund sources, and as time goes on there is a development of

---

[42] Vicar General of the London District.

[43] Diff. II, 21.

doctrine, but always in accord with the Vincentian canon.

The difficulty which had been Newman's apropos of the practical system, was the same for others, and hence, with the vivid experience of a long struggle still fresh in his memory[44] though twenty years had passed since he had come to the "blessed vision of peace", he was most capable of writing the "Apologia" of Catholic devotion to the Blessed Virgin. He was also favored with the special gift of throwing himself into the mind of others and of realizing their needs, doubts, and difficulties.[45]

The method, then, that he was to follow, naturally suggests itself. Anglican difficulties centered about the question of Tradition or Antiquity which was their stronghold. Newman strongly asserted as Anglican that though Rome pretended to revere and follow the Fathers it was in reality far from containing their teachings. He had been disillusioned in his views and found that Rome alone and in all truth *was* the *Church of the Fathers.* If such be the case, it is his task to demonstrate that what Catholics hold today concerning the Blessed Mother of God is substantially identical with what the Fathers taught. There lies the thesis that he sets himself to prove.

Newman begins by making a distinction between faith and devotion; the latter is distinct from the former, though it cannot exist without faith. On the other hand, there may be belief without devotion. By several illustrations he conveys the idea that the belief in the Mother of God is ever one and the same though the acknowledgment of her dignity did not always bring with it the same degree of devotion. Devotions in the Catholic Church are multiform and multiplex, adapted to the needs or sentiments of each individual, who may choose one form in preference to another. Such is the liberty allowed him in the Church. Now these devotions or observances did not spring up in a day, but are the slow growth of ages. Some Saints

---

[44] That same year he had written his *Apologia,* which brought before him all the details of his religious career.

[45] He deprecated the lack of this quality in Froude. Apo. 25.

who were very popular at certain times have long since ceased to attract attention. Others again, such as St. Joseph, notwithstanding their high dignity and eminent sanctity, seem to have been left in the background of Catholic devotion and only as time went on, a light was cast upon their personality. They are, as it were, discovered anew and begin to be objects of a very special worship.

With the distinction clearly made between belief and devotion, Newman proceeds to divide his treatise under these two general heads: Catholic belief in the Blessed Virgin, and the coloring of this belief by devotion. The ordinary reader of books on the Blessed Virgin would assume that Newman would begin with a subject such as the Predestination of Mary, or her divine Maternity, or with the first mystery of her life in the order of time, viz., the Immaculate Conception. The divine Maternity is the source from which are derived all the privileges of Mary; it is the foundation of devotion to her. But Newman at first sight seems to relegate it to a secondary place, though he describes it as the "issue of her sanctity and the origin of her greatness."[46] His work is apologetic and he knows full well that in the present instance the divine Maternity is not called into question. He rather wishes to set out upon a new untrodden path and prove that even independently of the consideration of this dignity, Mary held a lofty position in the work of Redemption, and that from earliest times the Christians viewed her in the light of this office.

Although the mere thought would do dishonor to God's wisdom, which disposes all things *fortiter et suaviter*, yet it may be imagined that the Son of God could have chosen a creature as His Mother, making of her merely a physical instrument of the Incarnation, without endowing her with any particular privileges or associating her with Him in the work of the Redemption. Such a mode of procedure would seem wholly unworthy of God's sovereign wisdom. Yet it may be asserted that such in a general way is the notion that some Protestants entertain of the Blessed Virgin, though they may not express

---

[46] Diff. II, 62.

the idea in so bold a fashion. In order to give his argument convincing force, Newman had to show clearly that Mary was more than a mere physical instrument, and that she was so regarded from primitive times. Other inferences would necessarily follow.

The rudimental teaching of Antiquity concerning the Blessed Virgin is that she is the Second Eve,[47] a moral instrument in the Incarnation and fully associated with Jesus in the work of Redemption just as Eve participated with Adam in bringing about the fall of the human race. That Mary is the Second Eve is the center of Newman's Mariology as exposed in the *Letter to Pusey*. He examines the testimony of three of the earliest Fathers, Justin, Tertullian, Irenaeus, and evaluates it as representative of the general belief of the times and places in which they lived. Their testimony almost touches upon Apostolic times; succeeding writers are just as explicit on the same doctrine.

Granted that such is the case, the immediate inferences to be drawn, center about Mary's exaltation or dignity and her sanctity. If she was a Second Eve, then like the first Eve she had to be endowed with grace, with even greater grace. As Eve was created immaculate, free from every taint of sin, one would necessarily infer that her antitype should come into the world unsullied by sin. This leads the writer to an exposition of the mystery of the Immaculate Conception, often wholly misunderstood by Protestants, but which, on closer examination, he proves to be less difficult of comprehension than the mystery of original sin.

Anticipating, however, an objection that might be made on the score of Antiquity, he exposes the statements of Basil, Chrysostom, and Cyril, who seem to give the lie to any belief in Mary's total sinlessness. He does not deny their testimony, but proceeds to lay down criteria on the basis of which any Father's authority has to be adjudged. Then with these

---

[47] This question and the rest that follow are briefly touched upon here in order to give a general outlook over Newman's method. Each is treated in detail in Part II.

standards to guide him, he can attest to the demonstrative value or the lack of it in their statements. Not content with a defensive attitude, Newman takes the offensive and shows that Anglicans hold to many points of faith that they consider fundamental, yet there are Fathers who in no unmistakable terms maintain the contrary.

Anglicans not only demand proofs from Antiquity but their cry is: "Where can this be found in Scripture?" Newman accuses them of failing to search rightly the sacred writings where they could find the reason for Mary's exaltation. Another seemingly bold venture is his finding an explanation and proof in the vision of the Woman and the Child as narrated in the Apocalypse.

Once it is admitted that Mary is the Second Eve, there is little need to ponder long over the title *Theotokos*, which was in use among the Christians almost as long as the former title. Newman finds this a subject rather for pious contemplation than for mere speculation, but nevertheless cites a galaxy of Fathers who witnessed to this sublime prerogative. Faith must soon be transmuted into devotion. "No wonder if their language should be unmeasured, when so great a term as 'Mother of God' had been formally set down as the safe limit of it. No wonder if it should be stronger and stronger as time went on, since only in a long period could the fulness of its import be exhausted."[48]

Pusey had admitted the Tridentine Decree declaring that "it is good and useful suppliantly to invoke the Saints and to have recourse to their prayers;" he also admitted the singular exaltation of Mary. With these two principles to direct him, Newman explains the efficacy of prayer in general and the undoubted power of intercession that must be ascribed to the Mother of God.

In kind yet forceful language Newman goes on to explain Catholic devotion to the Blessed Virgin, prefacing his exposition with a few remarks on the faulty method pursued by Pusey when treating of this subject. Pusey is a first-rate

---

[48] Diff. II, 65, 66.

authority on the Fathers, whom he had studied, whom he knew and revered. As for Newman, their times had been for him the *beau-idéal* of Christianity. Yet the author of the *Eirenicon* seems to lose sight of their teachings to attack medieval and modern writers; had their statements been included in his work, most people would hardly have been able to see where the difference lay between what he accepted with them, and what he ascribed to Roman Catholics. It cannot be ignored, however, that the principal object of Pusey's protest differs basically from what the Fathers held. With these preliminary notions disposed of, Newman gives one of the finest psychological analyses of devotion to Mary ever penned by Catholic writer.

The last part of the treatise is devoted to removing the false notions of Anglicans, and in no unequivocal terms denouncing Catholic excesses in devotion to our Lady. To Newman it is perfectly unintelligible that anything doubtful should be said in our Lady's praise when what is certainly true of her supplies such large material for her laudation. The condemnation of Newman on exaggerated statements ascribed to Catholic writers by Pusey is forceful in the extreme: "Sentiments such as these I freely surrender to your animadversion; I never knew of them till I read your book, nor as I think, do the vast majority of English Catholics know them. They seem to me like a bad dream. I could not have conceived them to be said. I know not to what authority to go for them, to Scripture, or to the Fathers, or to the decrees of Councils, or to the consent of schools, or to the tradition of the faithful, or to the Holy See, or to reason. They defy all the *loci theologici*. There is nothing of them in the Missal, in the *Roman Catechism,* in the *Roman Raccolta,* in the *Imitation of Christ,* in Gother, Challoner, Milner, or Wiseman as far as I am aware. They do but scare and confuse me ... I do not, however, speak of these statements as they are found in their authors, for I know nothing of the originals and cannot believe that they have meant what you say; but I take them as they lie in your pages. Were any of them the sayings of Saints in ecstasy, I should know they had a good meaning, still I should not repeat them myself; but I am looking at them, not as spoken by the tongues of Angels, but according to that literal sense which they bear in the mouths of English men and English women. And as spoken by man to man in England in the nineteenth century, I consider them calculated to prejudice inquirers, to frighten the unlearned, to unsettle consciences, to provoke blasphemy, and to work the loss of souls."[49]

After explaining to Pusey that his hopes for reunion are futile unless the Anglican Church makes its entire submission to Rome and accepts the practical system of Rome as he described it, because the honor of our Lady is dearer to Catholics than the conversion of a country, Newman closes his work with a most pathetic supplication to the Immaculate Mother of God, on the eve of whose feast he was terminating the *Letter*:[50]

"So far concerning the Blessed Virgin, the chief but not the only subject of your Volume. And now when I could wish to proceed, she seems to stop all controversy, for the Feast of her Immaculate Conception is upon us, and close upon its Octave, which is kept with special solemnities in the churches of this town, come the great Antiphons, the heralds of Christmas. That joyful season, joyful for all of us, while it centres in Him who then came on earth, also brings before us in peculiar prominence that Virgin Mother who bore and nursed Him. Here she is not in the background as at Easter-tide, but she brings Him to us in her arms. Two great Festivals dedicated mark out and keep the ground, and, like the towers to her honor, tomorrow's and the Purification, of David, open the way, to and fro, for the high holiday season of the Prince of Peace. And all along it, her image is upon it, such as we see it in the typical representation of the Catacombs. May the sacred influences of this tide bring us all together in unity! May it destroy all bitterness on your side and ours! May it quench all jealous, sour, proud, fierce antagonism on our side, and dissipate all captious, carping, fastidious refinements of reasoning on yours! May that bright and gentle Lady, the Blessed Virgin Mary, overcome you with her sweetness, and

---

[49] Diff. II, 114–115.

[50] Dec. 7, 1865.

revenge herself on her foes by interceding effectually for their conversion!"[51]

Newman was not too sanguine as to the effect which his book would produce on his fellow-Catholics. He himself said: "Pusey's work is on too many subjects not to allow of a dozen answers, and since I am only giving one, every reader will be expecting one or other of the eleven which I don't give."[52] Dean Church dedicated a lengthy article in the *Times*[53] to a review of the work. Although not admitting the full force of Newman's arguments, he nevertheless pays a fine tribute to the only one "whose reflections on Pusey's pamphlet English readers in general would much care to know."[54]

Of this article Newman writes in a letter to Pusey, indicating at the same time that some opposition had been aroused: "I hail (it) with great satisfaction as being the widest possible advertisement of me. I never should be surprised at its comments being sent by some people to Pome, as authoritative explanations of my meaning, wherever they are favorable to me. The truth is that certain views have been suffered without a word, till their maintainers have begun to fancy that they are *de fide*—and they are astonished and angry beyond measure, when they find that silence on the part of others was not acquiescence, indifference, or timidity, but patience. My own Bishop[55] and Dr. Clifford[56] and I believe most of the other Bishops are with me. And I have had letters from the most important centers of theology and of education through the country taking part with me."[57]

He informs the Dominican Sisters of Stone, who expressed their appreciation of this beautiful work, that he had done his very best, and that he found it particularly difficult to praise the

---

[51] Diff. II, 117, 118.

[52] Ward, II, 108.

[53] Ibid. 109 sqq.

[54] Ibid.

[55] Dr. Ullathorne.

[56] Bishop of Clifton.

[57] Pusey, IV, 137–138.

Blessed Virgin while at the same time dispraising some of her imprudent votaries. In spite of a modicum of criticism aroused by his pamphlet, the general consensus of opinion was in his favor.[58] The denunciation of some of Mary's "imprudent votaries" could not but irritate some members of the London school of Ward and Manning. The criticisms of Faber and Ward were too justified to allow of a rejoinder.[59] Msgr. Talbot characterized the spirit of the *Letter* as "most offensive."[60]

The opposition to Newman's treatise was, however, insignificant in Catholic circles; on all hands it received a friendly reception. Here at least, on a small scale, Newman had demonstrated the possibility of placing every point of Catholic doctrine on an unassailable basis. When he came to the Catholic Church, he had deprecated the absence of a historico-dogmatic school,[61] and at first thought of devoting his life to this important work, but his plans were not to be realized. Catholics, fully confident in the absolute soundness of their beliefs, had practically lost contact with the non-Catholic world round about them. Scholastic or positive theology as taught in the Catholic universities, seminaries, etc., was excellent for those who accepted the first principles of an infallible authority. Men such as Bossuet, Bellarmine, Canisius and others were alive to the needs of Catholic Apologetics, since the so-called Reformation had estranged so many from the true fold. Newman, too, wished to give a new impulse to Catholic studies so as to enable the Catholic to meet the Protestant on the common footing of Antiquity. His small work, priceless for its profundity, solidity, and conformity to all the canons of historical criticism, was the forerunner of considerable subsequent research on similar lines and in other domains of theology. Newman was not an innovator in his method as such, nor did he pretend to be one, for he was simply continuing the work done as an Anglican. The efforts of Rationalists to

---

[58] Ward, II, 113.

[59] Ward, II, 108.

[60] To Abp. Manning, April 19, 1866. Pusey, IV, 137.

[61] Ward, I, 123.

overthrow all the foundations of the supernatural on the grounds of historical criticism, would have eventually forced Catholics to defend the grounds of their faith from a historical point of view.

The value of the *Letter* in the field of Apologetics was at once recognized in other than English circles. Within a year after its appearance it was translated into German and French.[62] A greater tribute of praise could hardly be given to this work than the one rendered by the renowned Benedictine Rottmanner, who takes the occasion in reviewing a *Summa Mariana* to call attention to the merits of the *Letter to Pusey*.[63] "Unfortunately," he writes in his criticism of the book, "the author seems to be unacquainted with just the work that is most faithful in practically every detail to the rules of critical research. I refer to Newman's *Letter addressed to the Rev. E. B. Pusey, D.D., on occasion of his "Eirenicon."* I consider this little book superior to any other Mariological work with which I am acquainted, not excluding even the work of Terrien, which is designated as 'classical, invaluable.'[64] This latter does not, it is true, contain any false passages from the Fathers, but neither does it treat any question with any degree of profundity."[65] The learned reviewer identified his own wishes with those of Newman when he expressed the desire that in the future no uncritical Mariology should appear, but only such a one as speaks "w*eise über die weiseste Jungfrau."* Scheeben had good reason also to complain of the lack of scholarship in so many works on the Blessed Virgin. As he puts it: "It is to be deplored that even today, in nearly all Mariological writings, even those that claim a certain scientific value, there are to be found

---

[62] The German translation is by Schündelen under the title, *Die heilige Maria*, (Cologne, 1866); the French is by G. Du Pré de Saint-Maur, Paris 1866. A new French translation was undertaken by the Benedictines of Farnborough Abbey (Tequi, Paris, 1908). Its title is Du culte de la Ste. Vierge dans l'Église Catholique.

[63] The author of the *Summa Mariana* is Schütz.

[64] The work referred to is *La Mère de Dieu et la Mère des Hommes* (Paris, 1900).

[65] *Theologische Revue, 1903, XIX, p. 578.*

quotations cited from the Fathers in a perfectly unscientific fashion; that is to say, these authors refer to the early Fathers certain works which belong doubtlessly or at least apparently to a later period and to a less important author."[66]

Newman has acted as guide to the many that have made an attempt to delve into the early history of Marian doctrine and devotion. He has given an impetus to the study of the great Fathers in their teachings on the Blessed Virgin.[67] His greatest merit is, perhaps, the reinsistence on the doctrine of the Spiritual Maternity of Mary, since she is the Second Eve, and the psychological investigation of devotion to our Lady.

---

[66] Scheeben, *Handbuch der kath. Dogmatik*, III, 476.

[67] Among the principal works on Mariology are to be mentioned: Neubert, *Marie dan l'Église Anténicéenne* (Paris, 1908). Friedrich, *Die Mariologie des h. Augustinus* (Cologne, 1907). Niessen, *Die Mariologie des hl. Hieronymus* (Münster, 1913). Eberle, *Die Mariologie des hl. Cyrillus von Alexandrien* (Freiburg, 1921). Morgott, *Die Mariologie des hl. Thomas v. Aquin* (Cologne, 1878).

PART II
Newman's Marian Doctrine

CHAPTER I
Mary, Mother of God

I. Newman's Interest in the Incarnation.

THE great struggle of Newman during the Tractarian Movement, as has already been remarked, was against the liberalizing tendencies so shockingly rampant in the Anglican Church. Dogma was the fundamental principle of his religion. Of all the mysteries of faith, his attention was mostly concentrated on the central truth of the Gospel—the Incarnation,[1] which he considered the standing or falling article of the Church.[2] Without a clear perception of the divine and human natures in Christ, Christianity indeed tumbles into ruins; it becomes a mere man-made religion, with no more convincing force than Buddhism or Mohammedanism.

Newman's great endeavor as an Anglican was to uphold firmly a right belief in the Incarnation. He was particularly capable of so important a task because of his studies of the Fathers, whose polemical writings, discourses, and doctrinal treatises were centered upon clarifying the notions connected with the Word made flesh, and become the "sign which shall be contradicted."[3] Heresiarchs had arisen, the one denying our

---

[1] Dev. 324.
[2] U. S. 35.
[3] Luke 2:34.

Lord's divinity, the other His humanity, another declaring Him a mere phantom, etc.[4] To combat them, God had raised up holy men, mighty in word and deed, all of whom utilized their talents to the full in defending the sacred mystery of the Incarnation. These Saints were Newman's masters and models.

II. Purpose of the Incarnation

When, after a long period of waiting, the Son of God determined to come to earth, He sent the Angel Gabriel to the Virgin of Nazareth to announce that she was to be His Mother. At her *fiat* the Holy Ghost came upon her and overshadowed her with the power of the Most High. "The Word was made flesh and dwelt among us." In Mary "was now to be fulfilled that promise which the world had been looking out for during thousands of years. The Seed of the woman announced to guilty Eve, after long delay, was at length appearing upon earth, and was to be born of her. In her the destinies of the world were to be reversed, and the serpent's head bruised."[5] Newman hereby expresses the purpose of the Incarnation, placing himself with the Fathers. Throughout Scripture it is stated that Christ came to redeem from sin; had man not sinned it would seem improbable that the Word would have been made flesh. Athanasius expresses himself clearly on this point: "Our cause was the occasion of His descent, and our transgression called forth the Word's love of man. Of His Incarnation, we became the ground."[6] However, there are some theologians who hold that this sacred mystery would have come to pass independently of man's fall, and that its principal object was the excellence of Christ Himself and the exaltation of human nature.[7] It is true that the Incarnation was not

---

[4] P. S. II, 36.

[5] P. S. II, 128.

[6] Cf. Ath. II, 188.

[7] Ibid. 187. Newman himself seems to admit that Christ would have come even if man had not sinned, for he says: "He (Christ) once had meant to come on earth in heavenly glory, but we sinned." Mix. 358.

absolutely necessary for the atonement of sin; God could have chosen some other manner in order that satisfaction for sin might have been rendered to Him. But, in view of God's decree, the Incarnation was the most suitable manner. Since Christ had come to appease the wrath of the Almighty offended by the sin of Adam and his posterity, it was most fitting that He should be God, for thus His merits had an infinite value and could satisfy the infinite Majesty of God; it was also fitting that He should at the same time be man, since man had been guilty, and by His atonement would overcome Satan, who had first vanquished man.

A word might have sufficed for the redemption of man; God might have abolished original sin and restored Adam immediately after the fall; but no, He willed otherwise. In His infinite wisdom He saw that it was fitting and expedient to take a ransom. For this reason the coming of the Word was necessary; "for if a true satisfaction was to be made, then nothing could accomplish this short of the incarnation of the All-holy."[8]

Pardon could have been bestowed without the Atonement as made by our Lord, but the second reason of the Incarnation would not have been realized, namely, the renovation of our human nature.[9] By becoming man, our Lord wished to sanctify that nature of which His own manhood is the pattern. Atonement was to have its complement in the restoration of God's favor forfeited by sin. The Incarnate Word by taking upon Himself human nature hallowed it. His humanity, when it had been offered upon the Cross, became the first-fruits of a new man; it became a divine leaven of holiness for the new birth and spiritual life to as many as wish to receive it. Christ dwells in us personally; He becomes the principle of spiritual life for each of His elect individually.[10]

Sects had taught that matter was evil; though not intrinsically such, it had been corrupted by the fall, and so the

---

[8] Mix. 306.

[9] Ath. II, 62.

[10] Ath. II, 193; P. S. VI, 79.

Most High "had taken a portion of the corrupt mass upon Himself in order to the sanctification of the whole; He had purified from all sin that very portion of it which He took into His Eternal Person, and thereunto had taken it from a Virgin Womb, which He had filled with the abundance of His Spirit."[11] Hence, since the Son of God was to make atonement for sin and at the same time renew human nature in holiness, it was no more than fitting that He should have come to us through the Virgin Mary.

III. Nature of the Incarnation

The statement of the dogma of the Incarnation is easier than the comprehension of so great a mystery. "Two natures," says St. Leo, "met together in our Redeemer, and, while what belonged to each respectively remained, so great a unity was made of either substance, that from the time that the Word was made flesh in the Blessed Virgin's womb, we may neither think of Him as God without that which is man, nor as man without that which is God."[12]

Two natures, the divine and human, are hypostatically united in the Divine Person of the Word; the divine nature is from God—Jesus is God; the human nature is from the Blessed Virgin Mary.[13] From all eternity Christ is the living and true God.[14] He clearly disclosed His eternal pre-existence in the bosom of the Father to the Jews when He said: "Before Abraham was, I am."[15] St. John states the case categorically in the prologue of his Gospel: "In the beginning was the Word, and the Word was with God, and the Word was God."[16] The inspired text further testifies abundantly to His divinity.[17]

---

[11] Dev. 401.

[12] Sermon 54. Cf. Ath. II, 223, 191.

[13] T. T. 46–48, 108–109.

[14] P. S. VI, 55; I, 209, 210.

[15] John 8:58.

[16] Ibid. 1:1.

[17] Phil. 2:6, 7; John 20:28; Rom. 9:5; Is. 9:6; Tit. 2:13, etc.

Newman never seems to weary of insisting on the idea that Christ is true God as well as true man. He was obliged to do so during his Anglican days because of the incorrect notions entertained by so many Protestants, unwilling to admit unhesitatingly the full import of the fact that Jesus is God. He explains why He is God; because He is the Son of God. "We are apt at first hearing, to say that He is God though He is the Son of God, marvelling at the mystery. But what to man is a mystery, to God is a cause. He is God, not *though*, but *because* He is the Son of God. 'That which is born of the flesh is flesh, that which is born of the spirit is spirit,' and that which is born of God is God." Reason stands aghast at the profundity of such thoughts, and though unable by itself to comprehend these mysteries, yet, aided by the light of revelation, it is able to understand in a feeble manner that if God should have a Son, this son must be God because He is Son. The doctrine of our Lord's eternal Sonship is of supreme importance, because they who give up this truth are in the way to give up or have already given up belief in the divinity of Christ. "The great safeguard to the doctrine of our Lord's Divinity is the doctrine of His Sonship."[18]

Our Lord's Sonship is not only the guarantee of His Divinity, it is also the condition of the Incarnation. Newman finds in it a reason for the propriety of the Incarnation.[19] Though the Father is God, and the Son is God and the Holy Ghost is God, yet each Person has certain characteristics special to Him. The Son of God became the Son a second time, though not a second Son,[20] by becoming the Son of the Virgin Mary. He was a Son both before His Incarnation, and, by a second mystery, after it.[21]

Now this Eternal Word, the Wisdom of the Father put off His glory and came down upon earth to raise us up to heaven.[22]

---

[18] P. S. VI, 57, 58; Cf. P. S. II, Serm. 3; Arians, 158 sqq.
[19] P. S. VI, 58.
[20] T. T. 367.
[21] P. S. VI, 58.
[22] Mix. 284.

Who can conceive the immense mercy that induced Him to take upon Himself our fallen nature? But He made for Himself a "greater and more perfect tabernacle," a body pure and sinless formed from the substance of the Blessed Virgin.[23] "This was the new and perfect tabernacle into which He entered, entered but not to be confined, not to be circumscribed by it."[24] We might almost be tempted to speak of our Lord as incarnate indeed, come in human flesh, human, and the like, but not simply as man. St. Paul, however, reminds us that we have a Mediator, "the man Christ Jesus". He was perfect man because He had a perfect nature derived from Mary, but His Person is divine. As He had no earthly Father, so He has no human personality.[25]

Newman applies himself to solve the problem created by the formula of St. Cyril: Μια φυσις του Θεου λογου σεσαρκωμενη which is frequently cited and was so used by Eutyches to prove that the Alexandrian was a Monophysite. In the first centuries there were no exact terms and formularies and only as controversies arose, did precision follow in their wake. The Fathers had to develop a terminology that would express exactly the nature of the various mysteries of faith. So in the question of the Incarnation the terms ουσια, υποστασις and φυσις were frequently interchanged, as referring to the Divine Nature and connoting personality. When applied to the Second Person, they meant that that same Divine Being is "Deus singularis et unicus in persona Filii." The question next arises: Since the word is an ουσια, υποστασις or φυσις, can the man, ανθρωπος—the manhood, humanity, human nature, flesh, be designated by these terms in a parallel full sense, as meaning that He became all that "a human being" is, man with all the attributes and characteristics of man? The formula denies that the Word is, in as unrestricted a sense, man as we are, for it calls Him Μια φυσις σεσαρκωμενη not δυο φυσεις.[26]

---

[23] Ibid. 300.

[24] P. S. VI, 61; II, 135.

[25] P. S. VI, 62–66.

[26] T. T. 354.

The three terms spoken of are nevertheless applied by the Fathers to the Word's humanity. Thus υποστασις is substance as opposed to appearance, ουσια is essence, and φυσις is nature.[27] But the terms were not used indiscriminately in the same sense or with the same fulness of meaning for divinity and humanity. For even as regards His manhood our Lord differed from us in certain respects: He had no human father; He was sinless; His knowledge, sanctity, etc., surpass that of all creatures; His body was incorruptible and after the resurrection had transcendent qualities.[28] Scripture affirms these differences.

Furthermore, if the two natures, divine and human, were to be united, this could not be done without some infringement of one upon the other. Heretics escaped the difficulty by simply denying the union; Catholic faith, illumined by divine revelation, teaches that the Word was not absorbed into the man, but the humanity was taken up into the Word. Hence, the Fathers called the Incarnation a sort of Deification of the human element.[29] The divinity remains unchanged, but there is a change in the humanity insofar as it is extricated from the common ουσια or φυσις to which under other circumstances, it would have belonged. Since it was grafted, as it were, upon the Word, it existed from the first in a *super*-natural state. If such be the case, how could it be properly called nature? Thus Newman explains Cyril's position and concludes his reasoning on the question by assigning the meaning of the formula as follows: "It means first, that when the Divine Word became man, He remained one and the same in essence, attributes and personality; in all respects the same as before, and therefore, μια φυσις. It means secondly, that the manhood, on the contrary, which He assumed, was not in all respects the same nature as that *massa, usia, physis,* etc., out of which it was taken, 1) from the very circumstance that it was only an addition or supplement to what He was already, not a being complete in itself; and 2) because in the act of assuming it, He

---

[27] Ibid. 355–357.

[28] Ibid. 357, 358.

[29] A Theosis or Theopoiesis of the anthropinon. T. T. 361.

changed it in its qualities. This added nature, then, was best expressed not by a second substantive, as if collateral in its position, but by an adjective or particle, as σεσαρκωμενη. The three words answered to St. John's 'And the Word was made flesh'."[30]

Cyril's great endeavor was to combat the error of making two sons, one before and one upon the Incarnation—one divine, the other human, or of lowering the divine nature by making it subject to the human. He was under the impression that in this expression he was using what had been sanctioned by Athanasius, though in reality it seems to have been adopted by the Apollinarists.

Nevertheless, he makes his meaning clear in innumerable other passages. Newman shows that the formula as used by Cyril, clearly shields him from the accusations of Apollinarism as well as Nestorianism. There was no absorption of the humanity by the divinity nor were there two persons after the Incarnation. Nestorius spoke of δυο φυσεις and so Cyril had to speak of μια φυσις in the sense of one person.[31] He insists with his adversary: "It is at once ignorant and impious even to imagine that the Word of the Father should be called to a second beginning of being, or to have taken flesh of the Holy Virgin, as some kind of root of His own existence." And again: "There is one Son, one Lord before the Incarnation and after; the Word was not one Son and the child of the Virgin another."[32]

Christ, according to St. Cyril, is a single individual, a single hypostasis. When the humanity was assumed by the Word, though there was a perfect union, it remained intact but lacked

---

[30] Ibid. 362, cf. 380.

[31] Cf. Eberle, *Die Mariologie des hl. Cyrillus von Alexandrien*, p. 100. The method of this author differs from Newman's in explaining the expression insofar as he substitutes for this passage others that clearly indicate the Alexandrian's meaning. Newman is rather concerned with explaining the passage in itself and showing its suitability, though he does not ignore others that indicate Cyril's meaning.

[32] Cf. T. T. 368.

a human personality.[33] The qualities which it had received from its union with the Word were accidental and did not in the least impair its essence.

IV. THE DIVINE MATERNITY

Since it was most fitting that the Word should become incarnate in order to effect man's redemption, He might have come into the world in divers manners. Though he did not wish to have an earthly father, yet He wished to come by the way of generation lest He should miss the participation of our nature. As at the creation the Almighty formed woman out of man, so now by a like mystery but in a reverse order the new Adam was to be fashioned from the woman. The Word set apart Mary as His mother, "to yield a created nature to Him who was her Creator. Thus He came into this world, not in the clouds of heaven, but born into it, born of a woman; He, the Son of Mary, and she ... the Mother of God. Thus He came, selecting and setting apart for Himself the elements of body and soul; then uniting them to Himself from their first origin of existence, pervading them, hallowing them by His own Divinity, spiritualizing them and filling them with light and purity, the while they continued to be human."[34] God chose a daughter of man to become the Mother of God.[35] He was taking upon Him her flesh, and "humbling Himself to be called her offspring."[36] Thereby He conferred upon her the greatest honor ever put upon any individual of our fallen race, so that it is difficult to say which is the more wonderful to admire—the unspeakable grace bestowed upon Mary or the great condescension of the Word, who though Son of God wished also to become the Son of Mary.[37]

When treating of the sublime prerogative of Mary, Newman seems arrested in contemplation of "this most highly favored,

---

[33] Eberle, op. cit. p. 104.

[34] P. S. II, 32.

[35] P. S. VIII, 252; VI, 314.

[36] Ibid. II, 128.

[37] Ibid. VIII, 233, III, 128, 131.

awfully gifted of the children of men."[38] The mere thought that she may be called the Mother of the Creator seems almost impossible to admit, though it is a necessary deduction from her title of Mother of God. Can a creature possess it?

"At first sight we might be tempted to say that it throws into confusion our primary ideas of the Creator and the creature, the Eternal and the temporal, the Self-subsisting and the dependent; and yet, on further consideration, we shall see that we cannot refuse the title to Mary without denying the Divine Incarnation."[39] But there is something more wonderful than that Mary should be called and should be indeed, the Mother of God. It is that God, without ceasing to be God, should become man. Yet this is an elementary truth of revelation; Prophets, Evangelists, and Apostles all testify that the Eternal Word had decreed to come to earth and become a man like any of us, to take a human soul and body and to make them His own.[40]

Faith teaches that the Blessed Virgin Mary is truly the Mother of God, the *Theotokos, Deipara*.[41] The Council of Ephesus defined it in clear, unmistakable terms: "If anyone doth not confess that God is in all truth Emmanuel, and that because of this the Holy Virgin is Mother of God ... let him be anathema."[42] The Council of Chalcedon confirmed it.[43] Newman calls this sanctioning of the *Theotokos* "an addition greater, perhaps, than any before or since to the letter of the primitive faith."[44] Elsewhere he says of this word: "It carries with it no admixture of rhetoric, no taint of extravagant affection—it has nothing else but a well-weighed, grave, dogmatic sense, which corresponds and is adequate to its sound. It intends to express

---

[38] P. S. II, 128.

[39] M. D. I, 38, 39.

[40] Mix. 344.

[41] Diff. II, 62.

[42] Denz. 113.

[43] Denz. 148; Dev. 310.

[44] Dev. 303. For Newman's use of the term *addition* cf. above, pp. 59-60 and note.

that God is Mary's Son, as truly as any of us is the son of his mother."[45]

V. THEOTOKOS, SAFEGUARD OF THE INCARNATION

Since the Incarnation was according to the will of God, it was the most suitable manner for accomplishing the work of Redemption.[46] The Son of God might have taken a body like Adam and Eve, or else formed some celestial body for Himself.[47] In either case men might have refused to believe that He was a real man, because this mystery of one person in two natures is so marvellous and so difficult that mere reason is unable to comprehend it; the natural man evades it, rebels against it.[48] In order to seal this doctrine, to leave no room for evasion or hesitation, God took a human mother, who by the fact becomes the Mother of God. Thus, from the earliest times the Blessed Virgin has been the greatest bulwark of Christ's divinity. Newman, who had so long hesitated about devotion to Mary, fearful lest any honor paid to her should detract from the worship of God, was led by his studies of primitive times to the conclusion that the *Theotokos* is in truth, as he calls her, the *Turris Davidica,* the defence of the true doctrine of the Incarnation. He discovered, in fact, that it sufficed merely to call her the Mother of God to thereby destroy all heresies. This view is particular to Newman, whom succeeding writers have in general followed. For him it was most important that the Blessed Virgin should have a positive role in the Church throughout the ages, and by her title of Mother of God should secure right faith in her Divine Son. At the same time that these heresies were destroyed by the declaration of her divine

---

[45] Diff. II, 62. Petavius makes a distinction in the use of the Latin term *Deipara* as not connoting all that the Greek *Theotokos* implies. Cf. his *de Ino.* V, 15.

[46] P. S. II, 30. Cf. T. T. 180 sqq. Newman develops at length the suitability of the Incarnation; he draws his doctrine largely from Thomassin.

[47] S. N. 22.

[48] Mix. 345.

maternity, they also tended to exalt her and ultimately led to the strong devotion by which succeeding ages of the Church were characterized.

Not long after the mystery of the Redemption had been accomplished, heretics arose to explain, or rather to explain away, the nature of the Incarnation. Thereby they denied that Mary is, in all truth, Mother of God.

1. The Docetes, Gnostics, and Manicheans pretended that our Lord's body had come down from heaven and had merely the appearance of man. Therefore, He had no real body at all. They could not conceive how a born man should be called God. Yet the Creed says expressly, "conceived by the Holy Ghost, born of the Virgin Mary." He was the "immaculate seed of the woman," deriving His manhood from the substance of Mary.[49] He was true man, mortal, heir to our infirmities though not to our guilt;[50] He was born into the world, "made of a woman."[51] The Gnostics as well as the Manicheans held that matter was intrinsically evil, and so necessarily had to deny that Christ was really man, taking upon himself a material body.[52] "Perish the thought," asserted Manes, "that our Lord Jesus Christ should have descended through the womb of a woman."[53] Marcion admitted that Christ dwelt in the womb of Mary, but claimed that He merely passed through her, without touching her or taking aught of her.[54] All these heresies are overthrown by affirming simply that Christ was born of the Virgin Mary, and was truly her son, deriving His manhood from her.

2. Newman places the source of Arianism and subsequent heresies centering about Christ, in the Antiochene School, which he calls the "fount of primitive rationalism."[55] In the latter part of the third century Paul of Samosata was deposed

---

[49] P. S. II, 128–130.

[50] S. N. 22.

[51] Gal. 4:4.

[52] Dev. 402.

[53] Ibid. 403.

[54] Ibid.

[55] Ibid. 145.

for his Sabellian teachings, *i.e.,* declaring that there is no distinction of Persons in the Trinity.[56] His heresy is in turn connected with Gnosticism.[57] Lucian, his successor and later a martyr, was master of the Arian leaders.[58] Arianism and Nestorianism are connected insofar as the latter supplied the subject of the proposition for which the former had already provided the predicate. It was the Antiochene School which "led the Church to determine, first, the conceivable greatness of a creature, and then the incommunicable dignity of the Blessed Virgin."[59] The first took place at Nice when the divinity was defined; the second when the nature of Christ's humanity was clearly explained and secured against misconception by officially ascribing to Mary the title of Mother of God. This point merits clarification according to the mind of Newman.

Arians refused to our Lord the name of God except in the sense in which they called Him Word and Wisdom, not as pertaining directly to His nature or essence, but as being transferred to Him as a creature by grace or privilege. In this sense could He be called God.[60] They even boasted of giving the divine name and authority to our Lord, and there are some modern authors who even wish to assert that the name *Theotokos* is of Arian origin.[61] Evidently these heretics would have no difficulty in admitting the latter term if they held such views of Christ's divinity. Their main argument was that our Lord was a son and therefore not eternal, but of a substance which had a beginning, because He had an origin of existence from the Father. If He was a son, then He was inferior and distinct and consequently not God; if He was not God, then He must have been created. However, Arius, though calling Him

---

[56] Arians, 6.

[57] Ibid. 117.

[58] Ibid. 7; Lucian seems to have denied a human soul to our Lord. This error would be identical with Apollinarianism. St. Epiphanius accuses Lucian of this teaching. Cf. P. G. 43:77a.

[59] Dev. 145.

[60] Ath. II, 35.

[61] T. T. 123.

a creature, said that He was not "as one of the creatures."[62]

Once Arians had denied our Lord's divinity, it mattered little what high titles they bestowed upon Him. They could call Him the first of creatures, the primeval and sole work of God, the Creator, created in order to create, the Mystical Word and Wisdom of the Highest, etc.[63] They had left Him a creature, and so fell short of the truth.

The Arian controversy caused the Fathers gradually to change their position in the interpretation of certain texts of Scripture. Certain accounts of apparitions that had been referred to the Divine Son came to be ascribed to Angels.[64] Further, when there was question of our Lord's exaltation, the texts misapplied by heretics in reference to His divinity were referred to human nature, which was raised and glorified in Christ. "Intimate indeed must be the connection between Christ and His brethren, and high their glory, if the language which seemed to belong to the Incarnate Word really belonged to them."[65] By reason of this exaltation of their nature, they too become objects of worship.

Texts that speak of our Lord's subordination were explained of His humanity. Those that did not admit of such an interpretation were applied to mere creatures. But such an ascription did not come of a sudden; the controversy had opened the question but did not settle it.[66] The Arians maintained that just because our Lord was true Son, He could not be true God. They said that to be a true Son it sufficed for Him to *partake* of the Father's nature, that is, to have a certain portion of divinity—a μετουσια. All holy beings had this participation of the divine nature, but this does not make the possessor God. Creatures have a μετουσια of divinity, but do not thereby have the divine ουσια as did our Lord.[67] Arians,

---

[62] Ath. II, 36, 37; Arians, 205–209.

[63] Ath. II, 38; Arians 210.

[64] Dev. 138.

[65] Ibid. 140.

[66] Dev. 143.

[67] Ath. II, 39–40.

therefore, had reduced our Lord to the level of the supernatural adoption which has been accorded by the Creator first to the whole world, first on its creation and then at the Redemption.[68]

Though the Arians had placed our Lord high above all creatures, they had not done enough, for "between all and anything short of all, there was an infinite interval. The highest of creatures is levelled with the lowest in comparison of the One Creator Himself."[69] They left our Lord a creature, and if they admitted, as they did, the worship of our Lord, they could with reason be charged with idolatry.[70]

Thus the Nicene Council, which condemned the heresy of the Arians, first determined the conceivable greatness of a creature, and by its definition of Christ's divinity led to an ultimate glorification of the Blessed Virgin.[71] If Christ could not be that creature of which Scripture speaks, for He was God, then the Fathers would be induced to recognize in Mary, the "Mother of fair love, and fear and holy hope created from the beginning before the world."[72] And so Arianism helped to emphasize the ineffable dignity of her who was Mother of the Word made flesh, for He was of the substance of the Father, and therefore God, and His humanity was of her own pure substance.

3. Heresies are not mere isolated opinions, but are easily connected with one another.[73] Arianism was a reaction against Sabellianism, yet in reality, it admitted only one Person. In like manner Apollinaris, opposing the Arians, denied that Christ had a human soul, and was eventually led to deny a body to Christ as did the Manicheans and the Docetes.[74] Newman thinks it is doubtful whether Eusebius, one of the Arian leaders, held that Our Lord, on becoming incarnate, took on Him a

---

[68] Ibid. 136.

[69] Ath. II, 159.

[70] Dev. 143; P. S. VI, 56.

[71] Dev. 145.

[72] Eccli. 24:24, 14.

[73] Ath. II, 143; T. T. 304.

[74] Ath. II, 143.

human soul as well as a body.⁷⁵ In case of denial, his heresy would accord with that of Apollinaris as well. He speaks of our Lord's taking a body, almost to the prejudice of the doctrine of His taking a perfect manhood.⁷⁶ So with Apollinaris. The Personality of Christ was divine, he admitted, but His manhood was merely an adjunct to it, an instrument or a manifestation.⁷⁷ His human nature was as a garment or instrument and therefore had to be adjusted for union with the divine; it could not have a personality of its own, therefore it could not in all respects be similar to that of other men. If our Lord had no human personality, then He had no mind or ψυχη which for him was the seat of personality. Hence the Divinity would be obliged to act as a soul for the body.⁷⁸ The outcome was, that the heretic spoke of our Lord merely as θεος σαρκοφορος, God Incarnate, and to call Him perfect man would be considering Him as ανθρωπος θεοφορος, man deified. Consequently, he had to accuse the orthodox of holding two sons, the Son of God and the son of Mary, instead of the one Person of Emmanuel.⁷⁹ In order to escape the assertion of two sons, he had to hold with Arians that the Word merely assumed a body, that Mary gave birth to a body which had God for its inhabitant.⁸⁰ The Fathers such as Amphilochius and Proclus, in inveighing against the ομοουσιον Θεοτητι (consubstantial with the divinity) which Appolinarians were misusing, substituted ομοουσιον Μαρια and not ομοουσιον ημιν.⁸¹

The conclusion to which Apollinarians were forced, was that by the union of Word with the body as soul and body, the divine nature became something new, underwent a change, and so in turn the body of our Lord no longer remained human, but

---

⁷⁵ Ath. II, 106.

⁷⁶ Ibid. 145.

⁷⁷ P. S. VI, 61, sqq.

⁷⁸ T. T. 307–309.

⁷⁹ Ibid. 311.

⁸⁰ Ibid. 113.

⁸¹ Ibid. 43, 377.

became of a celestial nature.[82] For as they said, His body was not consubstantial with ours (ομοουσιον ημιν) but consubstantial with the Divinity (ομοουσιον Θεοτητι). The further conclusion was that our Lord's body became nothing more than a phantom,[83] and so in truth there was no Passion at all, but merely a manifestation of the Word.[84]

However, the Apollinarians confessed that our Lord's body was originally human; if they thereby meant that it existed before its union with the Word, they necessarily fell into the heresy of the later Nestorians.[85] To escape this difficulty, some simply maintained that it was of a divine nature from the first, being taken, "not from the Blessed Virgin, but from the internal essence of the Word Himself, a celestial development, for the purpose of a manifestation."[86] The consequent danger was Sabellianism.

Here it is seen that Apollinarianism was ever on one of two paths, either leading to Manicheism and kindred errors, or to Nestorianism, which it was trying to avoid, though accusing the orthodox of this heresy. Against such false notions, the Church had but to set up the Virgin Mother of God, as a secure defence. Scripture says that Jesus Christ really came in the flesh, and the Athanasian Creed calls Him "man of the substance of His Mother, born in the world, perfect man," lest we should think of Him as not come in the flesh, as a mere vision or phantom.[87]

4. The heresy which formally denied to Mary the title of *Theotokos*, was Nestorianism. Its principal doctrine lay in the ascription of a human as well as a divine personality to our Lord.[88] The whole controversy between Catholics and Nestorians seemed to be a question of words and the meaning

---

[82] T. T. 317

[83] Ibid. 318.

[84] Ibid. 323.

[85] Ibid. 325.

[86] Ibid. 326.

[87] P. S. II, 37; VI, 66.

[88] Dev. 294.

to be attached to them.[89] But it was precisely in attaching a certain meaning to words that Nestorians declared their heresy. They made a distinction between *Person* and *Prosopon*, which Catholics held were identical. They were satisfied to admit one Prosopon, but held that there were two Persons. For them, *Prosopon* merely meant the aspect or character of a thing, which is not the sole meaning attached to the Greek term.[90] If their assertion is drawn to its logical consequence, the personality to which they ascribed unity must have been in our Lord's manhood and not in the Divinity, since the former is what really made an impression upon the beholder.[91]

The whole Nestorian controversy seems to have begun with the denial of the *Theotokos*[92] though, as Newman points out,[93] the denial was but a manifestation of the heretical tendency to ascribe a twofold personality to our Lord. According to Nestorius, the Word placed at the disposition of the man Christ His "Personality," dignity, right to worship, etc.—all that He could exteriorly communicate to man, except His being; and this, not all at once, but gradually according as Christ disposed Himself for further communications of the Divinity, until the subjection of humanity to Divinity became so complete that there seemed to be but one Person, though in reality there were two.[94] Nestorius could then make use of the comparison to which Newman alludes,[95] namely, that the Word dwells in Christ as in a temple or as God in the burning bush. The presence of God in the Jewish Temple might be a symbol of the

---

[89] The Emperor Constantine had thought that the controversy between Athanasius and Arius was also a quarrel about words.

[90] Dev. 294. Cf. Junglas, "Die Irrlehre des Nestorius,"*Katholik*, 1913, p. 445. The author attached the same meaning to the term as Newman, calling it Form, *Erscheinung der Natur*, but later receded from his position and called it Individualität.

[91] Ibid. 295.

[92] Rauschen, *Theol. Revue*, 1912, p. 545; Junglas, op. cit. 226.

[93] Dev. 294. Cf. Eberle, op. cit. 27.

[94] Schultes, *Katholik*, 1913, p. 238.

[95] P. S. II, 34 sqq.

Word's dwelling in the manhood, but there is this essential difference, that the divine Presence could recede from the Temple; the two were separable, whereas the unity between the Godhead and the manhood in Christ was such that there could be no dissolution.[96] Nor did this union resemble the Christian's participation of the divine nature, of which there is question in Arianism.[97] Nestorius could have also said that Christ was God for His great spiritual perfections and that He gradually attained them by long practice.[98] Just because of his assertion that Christ possessed all by communication, Nestorius could use language that on the face of it is orthodox: *non duas personas unam facimus, sed una appellatione Christi duas naturas simul significamus.*[99]

Nestorius, following the Antiochene system of literal interpretation of Scripture, based himself upon St. Paul's Epistle to the Philippians[100] for his *Prosopon* theory, saying that the Word had made use of the human *prosopon* in order to manifest Himself to the world, since the *prosopon* is the aspect or the form by which an essence becomes manifest.[101] It is again to Scripture Nestorius appeals when he denies the title of *Theotokos*, for St. Paul,[102] referring to Melchisedech says, "Without father, without mother, without genealogy, having neither beginning of days, nor end of life, but likened unto the Son of God, continueth a priest for ever." Hence the title for the Blessed Virgin, he claimed, was contrary to Scripture. Nestorius had allowed Bishop Dorotheus to declare publicly in the Church of Constantinople, "Anathema to him who calls Mary the Mother of God." When the Alexandrians opposed

---

[96] Ibid. "They have said that the Word of God dwelt in the man Christ Jesus as the Shechinah in the Temple, having no real union with the Son of Mary," Ibid. 36.

[97] Cf. above, p. 93.

[98] P. S. II, 37.

[99] Cf. *Katholik*, 1913, p. 23.

[100] Phil. 2:6-8.

[101] Eberle, op. Cit. 28.

[102] Heb. 7:3.

such assertions, Nestorius took up the offensive against the use of the title. "Has God a mother?" he demanded. "How can she be the mother of a nature that is entirely different from hers? Therefore she would be made a goddess."[103] Mary gave birth only to the man, who was the instrument of the divinity; therefore she should be called the *Anthropotokos.* Such was the language of Nestorius, but St. Cyril could easily retort to this: All human mothers are called mothers of a certain person, yet they give birth only to a body; it is God who creates the soul to inform the body.[104]

Therefore, Mary was to be considered as mother of Christ's humanity solely[105] and not of the Word. However, it can readily be seen that there was not such a great difficulty for Nestorians to admit even the *Theotokos,* considering the view they held of Christ's humanity. But they insisted that *Anthropotokos* was perfectly admissible and ought to be used simultaneously with the other term. Their obstinacy in refusing unreserved adhesion to the *Theotokos,* was based upon the authority of the Nicene Creed, which contained no such expression. The Council of Ephesus put an end to all controversy on the subject by condemning Nestorius and declaring the title *Theotokos* an article of faith.[106]

5. The Eutychians went to the opposite extreme and asserted a unity of nature in the Incarnate Word. The heresy was substantially a reassertion of Apollinarianism.[107] The two principal tenets of Eutyches were: "Before the Incarnation there were two natures, after their union, one; secondly, our Lord's flesh was not consubstantial with ours, that is, not of the substance of the Blessed Virgin." Eutyches allowed that the Blessed Virgin was consubstantial with us, and that God was incarnate of her, but he would not admit that Christ's nature

---

[103] Cf. Eberle, op. Cit. 33.
[104] Ibid. 34.
[105] Dev. 295.
[106] Dev. 303; S. N. 23.
[107] Ibid. 297.

was consubstantial with ours.[108] At the Council of Chalcedon, which finally condemned Monophysitism, the bishops declared that "it is the faith of the Fathers, let it be set down that Mary is the Mother of God."[109]

The *Theotokos,* though framed as a test against the Nestorians, was equally effective against Apollinarians and Eutychians, who denied that our Lord had taken human flesh at all. Newman aptly cites the statement of St. Cyril on the question: "Let it be carefully observed that nearly this whole contest about the faith has been created against us for our maintaining that the Holy Virgin is Mother of God; now, if we held, as was the calumny, that the Holy Body of Christ our common Savior was from heaven, and not born of her, how can she be considered as Mother of God?"[110] The *Theotokos,* in fact, is the shibboleth of the pure, unadulterated doctrine of Christianity; to deny the title is to fabricate an entire system of false conceptions. There no longer remains any internal union; it is only something external, a mere juxtaposition. Any one could thus be united with God, since no real unity is required. Christ becomes two hypostases, two persons, two sons; the being to which Mary gave birth then, is not God. Thus, Nestorianism was not far from Arianism.

6. All these heresies which have in the past attacked the honor of God's Mother by denying Christ, find their counterpart in modern times as well, for Socinians, Sabellians, Nestorians, and others abound even now, and more than ever.[111] These heretics pretended to safeguard Christ's divinity, and so abolished the honor due to our Lady, claiming that Catholic worship of her was outright idolatry.[112] Modern error, though claiming to reverence the divinity of Christ, really stands on a level with Arianism insofar as it does not rise

---

[108] Ibid. 298.

[109] Ibid. 300. For a summary account of the Eutychian controversy cf. Dev. 297 sqq.

[110] Cf. Ath. II, 212.

[111] Dev. 144.

[112] S. N. 23.

higher in its notions of our Lord than to consider Him a man singularly inhabited by a divine Presence, that is, He is regarded simply as a Catholic Saint.[113]

Newman has left a very remarkable analysis of the Protestant notion about Christ. "Mere Protestants," he says, "have seldom any real perception of the doctrine of God and man in one Person. They speak in a dreamy, shadowy way of Christ's divinity, but when their meaning is sifted, you will find them very slow to commit themselves to any statement sufficient to express the Catholic dogma. They will tell you at once that the subject is not to be inquired into, for that it is impossible to inquire into it at all without being technical and subtile. Then ... they will speak of Christ, not simply and consistently as God, but as a being made up of God and man, partly one and partly the other, or between both, or as a man inhabited by a special Divine Presence. Sometimes they even go on to deny that He was in heaven the Son of God, saying that He became the Son when He was conceived of the Holy Ghost, and they are shocked, and think it a mark both of reverence and good sense to be shocked, when they hear the Man spoken of simply and plainly as God. They cannot bear to have it said except as a figure or mode of speaking, that God had a human body, or that God suffered."[114] These words, pronounced in a sermon in 1849, were not mere rhetorical exaggeration, calculated to produce an effect on the hearers. Newman's own experiences had already justified all of these statements;[115] they are confirmed in a still more forceful manner, if that be possible, in these last years. The Rationalist School has about completed its work among Protestants, by stripping the character of our Blessed Savior of everything that suggests the Divinity, denying His virginal birth, explaining away all His miracles and, to put the climax to all its nefarious endeavors, even attempting to prove the non-historicity of such a

---

[113] Dev. 144.

[114] Mix. 345 eqq.

[115] "We have well-nigh forgotten the sacred truth ... that Christ is the Son of God, in His divine nature as well as human." P. S. II, 170.

personage as Jesus.

The doctrine about our Lady prevents a dreamy, unreal way of regarding the whole mystery of the Incarnation.[116] It protects the doctrine and keeps the faith of Catholics far from a specious humanitarianism. The declaration of St. John that "the Word became flesh" expresses distinctly the Catholic idea; to show this more emphatically and unequivocally, it suffices to declare that God was born a man, or that He had a mother.[117] For if He had no mother, one would be tempted to ask how He came here; the natural supposition would be, then, that He had no real body and therefore was not really man.

Protestants may not shrink at saying that God is man, for they admit that God is everywhere, and frequently say (for Pantheists are no rarity) that God is everything; but they will certainly recoil from saying that God is the son of Mary. "The confession that Mary is *Deipara* or the Mother of God, is that safeguard wherewith we seal up and secure the doctrine of the Apostle from all evasion, and that test whereby we detect all the pretences of those bad spirits of 'Antichrist which have gone out into the world.' It declares that He is God; it implies that He is man; it suggests that He is God still, though He has become man, and that He is true man though He is God. ... If Mary is the Mother of God, Christ must be literally Emmanuel, God with us."[118] The most effectual means the Church had of expelling false prophets from its bosom was by using the word *Theotokos* against them. Heretics of the sixteenth century knew full well that if once they could get men to revile the prerogatives of Mary, there would be but a short step to dishonoring the Son. Newman expresses this thought most beautifully when he says: "The Church and Satan agreed together on this, that Son and Mother went together; and the experience of three centuries has confirmed their testimony, for Catholics who have honored the Mother still worship the Son, while Protestants, who now have ceased to confess the Son,

---

[116] S. N. 23.

[117] Mix. 346.

[118] Mix. 347.

began then by scoffing at the Mother."[119]

Mary's special office now in the Church is to protect the doctrine concerning her Divine Son. She reminds us ever that there was one who, on becoming her Son, "did not abhor the Virgin's womb."[120] She is the *Turris Davidica,* the high and strong defence of the King of Israel. With good reason, then, can the Church say of her that she alone destroyed all heresies in the whole world.[121]

This conception of Mary's special function is not peculiar to Newman, though hardly another writer before him has brought out the point more forcibly. St. John Damascene had already suggested the idea when he wrote: "It is with good reason that we give St. Mary the name of Mother of God, for this title suffices to establish in all its integrity the mystery of the Word made flesh."[122]

Thus, as Arianism caused the Church to declare the sublime condition of the creature, Nestorianism and the other heresies have helped to bear witness to the incommunicable dignity of the Mother of God; and all of them in a most wondrous manner combined to effect her elevation and glorification in the minds and devotions of the faithful.

VI. HISTORY OF THE TITLE

As is evident in most of the investigations concerning the Divine Maternity, Newman places himself in a position that is partly dogmatic and partly historical. Nor did he overlook the historical aspect of the title of the *Theotokos* itself, which had already been considered briefly by such writers as Petavius and Canisius. He places his thesis in general by holding that the

---

[119] Ibid. 348; cf. Dev. 426, M. D. I,

[120] Mix. 349.

[121] I Ant. III Noct. Commune Fest. B. V.

[122] Migne P. G. 94:1029. In a homily attributed to St. Epiphanius, Mary is called the incomparable book in which the Word is read. Terrien op. cit. develops this thought in a chapter speaking of her as the *Livre de la Foi.* Vol. I, p. 37 sqq.

Christians from the first were accustomed to call the Blessed Virgin Mother of God because they saw that it was impossible to deny her that title without denying the statement of St. John in the Prologue of his Gospel. If the term itself was not used from the first, it was implied.

As regards the origin of this title, Newman holds that it may be traced to a time not far distant from the period when the Fathers are found calling her the Second Eve.[123] The spontaneous or traditional feelings of Christians had anticipated by a long time the formal ecclesiastical decision.[124] Newman places the first recognized utterance of the term in Origen, i.e., in the first half of the third century.[125] The authority accepted for this affirmation is Socrates, who in his *History*[126] says that Origen treated largely of the word, "interpreting how *Theotokos* is used, he discussed the question at length." From this it is inferred that the term was already in use. But Socrates cites Origen's *Commentary on the Epistle to the Romans,* the original of which no longer exists. There is a Latin translation by Rufinus and only an equivalent expression for the *Theotokos* is to be found. However, Rufinus did not attempt a literal translation and, consequently, it may be possible that Origen did actually use the title. Furthermore Socrates, who wrote in the fifth century, was inveighing against the Nestorians for not knowing the early Fathers who had spoken of the Mother of God. Hence he would not have been inclined to invent. If we bear in mind that Rufinus did not hold himself slavishly to the original text and that the more conscientious Socrates is precise in his description of the passage, we cannot reject Origen's testimony without very

---

[123] Diff. II, 63, i.e., in the middle of the second century.

[124] Dev. 145.

[125] Neander puts the origin at the end of the fourth century; Harnack at the beginning of the fourth; Reitzenstein admits its use in the third. Cf. Schweitzer, "Alter des Titels Theotokos," in *Katholik* 1903, p. 97 sqq. Ath. II, 211; Diff. II, 63; Dev. 145.

[126] VII, 32.

strong arguments to the contrary.¹²⁷

Furthermore, the expression could coincide perfectly with the Christological views of Origen, who frequently makes use of the *communicatio idiomatum*. He used the term God-man Θεανθρωπος; the logical conclusion is that he may also have used *Theotokos*. The term found its origin at any rate with the Alexandrian school,¹²⁸ and though there is no absolute certainty on the point, it is very probable that Origen is the first writer to make use of it.¹²⁹ Newman does not examine into the details connected with the ascription of *Theotokos* to Origen, but simply contents himself with accepting the testimony of Socrates. Nor does he investigate the use of the title or its equivalent in chronological order, but cites the Fathers rather according to the nature of their testimony. However, these citations when grouped serve to give an accurate historical conspectus of early Catholic belief concerning the Blessed Virgin's Divine Maternity. We shall follow Newman's guidance, beginning with the times closest to the Apostolical period, down to the fifth and sixth centuries.

St. Ignatius of Antioch, whose career touches upon apostolic times, expresses the equivalent of Mother of God when he says: "Our God was carried in the womb of Mary":¹³⁰ and, again, "There is one Physician, fleshly and spiritual, generate and ingenerate, God come in the flesh, in death true life, both from Mary and from God, first passible, then impassible, Jesus Christ our Lord."¹³¹

Hippolytus and Archelaus are also quoted by Newman as giving equivalent expressions for the Divine Maternity. "The Word of God," says Hippolytus, "was carried in that Virgin

---

¹²⁷ Cf. Schweitzer, loc. cit. p. 108.

¹²⁸ Eusebius refers to the title. He was opposed to the new Alexandrian school represented by Alexander and Athanasius, but was favorable to the old school of that city.

¹²⁹ Schweitzer, loc. cit. p. 112–113.

¹³⁰ Ad Eph. n. 18; P. G. 5:660.

¹³¹ Ibid. n. 7. P. G. 5:662

frame."¹³² The work ascribed to Archelaus is not really his; his name was employed as a literary device to expose and refute the Manichean doctrines. The composition really must be placed at the earliest between 300 and 350. Heraclius of Chalcedon ascribes the authorship to Hegemonius.¹³³

By the time the Arian controversies had arisen, the title of *Theotokos* was in common use. Thus Athanasius says: "As Gabriel confessed to Zachary and Mary, the Mother of God"; "His flesh was assumed from Mary, the Virgin Mother of God."¹³⁴

Alexander, Patriarch of Alexandria likewise professed the same doctrine: "And after these things we admit the resurrection of the dead, whose first-fruits was our Lord Jesus Christ, who took His body really and not merely in appearance from Mary, the Mother of God."¹³⁵

Eusebius of Caesarea (338), adherent to semi-Arianism, calls Mary the "most beloved and august Virgin, Mother of God."¹³⁶

The Emperor Constantine himself, though merely a catechumen, draws a rather unpleasant parallel by an allusion to pagan mythology, but expresses the idea of the divine maternity: "When He had to draw near to a body of this world and to tarry on earth, the need so requiring, He contrived a sort of irregular birth for Himself, for without marriage was there conception and childbirth, from a pure Virgin and a maid, the Mother of God."¹³⁷

Julian the Apostate (363), certainly not inclined to be partial to Christians, uses the very title as an argument against them: "But if the Word is God from God as you think, and proceeds from the substance of the Father, why do you call the virgin, Mother of God? How could she bring forth God, since He is a

---

[132] Cf. Diff. II, 65.

[133] Cf. Cath. Enc. art. Manicheans; Harnack, *Gesch. der altchr. Lit.*, p. 540.

[134] P. G. 26:350; ibid, 386.

[135] Cf. Theod. Hist. I, 3; P. G. 82:908.

[136] Vita Const. III, 43; P. G. 20:1103; cf. also in Ps. 119:4; P. G. 23:1343.

[137] Ad sanct. Coet. 11. P. L. 8:432.

man like us?"[138]

Hilary of Poitiers (367) also contributes his testimony when he affirms: "The One God only- begotten is introduced into the womb of a Virgin."[139]

Cyril of Alexandria, the great defender of the *Theotokos*, could well say that the whole contest about the faith had been created because of the belief in Mary's Divine Maternity. In his *De Recta Fide* he called various Fathers of the fourth century as witnesses against the Nestorians. Thus Atticus, for example, writes: "The fleshless becomes flesh, the impalpable is handled, the perfect grows, the unalterable advances, the rich is brought forth in an inn, the coverer of heaven with clouds is swathed, the king is laid in a manger." Ammonius of Thrace is none the less explicit: "It is manifest into what impiety the Arians have fallen who assert that Mary, the Mother of God, stood in need of the purification prescribed by law for women after childbirth."[140]

Gregory of Nazianzen, his namesake of Nyssa, as well as Cyril of Jerusalem, also speak expressly of the *Theotokos*.[141]

Amphilochius (400) says: "The Maker of all is born to us of a Virgin."[142] Antiochus, also cited by Cyril, speaks of our Savior, "with whom yesterday in an immaculate bearing, Mary travailed, the Mother of Life, etc."[143]

We come then to the period when the Nestorian controversy was rife. In order to ground the argument more forcibly, Newman appeals to Theodoret, bishop of Cyrus, John of Antioch, and Alexander of Hierapolis, all of whom from party connections would hardly be partial to the term. Theodoret maintains "that the most ancient heralds of the orthodox faith taught the faithful to name and believe the Mother of the Lord *Theotokos* according to the Apostolical

---

[138] Cyrill. Alex. c. Jul. 8; P. G. 76:923–926.

[139] De Trin. II, 25; P. L. 10:66.

[140] P. G. 76:1214.

[141] P. G. 36:80; 37:178; 46:647; 33:686.

[142] P. G. 76:1214.

[143] Ibid.

tradition."[144] John of Antioch (441), who befriended Nestorius and strongly opposed Cyril, writes to the heresiarch: "This title no ecclesiastical teacher has put aside; those who have used it are many and eminent; those who did not use it, never attacked those who did."[145] Alexander of Hierapolis, fierce partisan of Nestorius, allowed the use of the term for mere rhetorical effect, since no dogmatic meaning was implied in it. "It as well as *anthropotokos* was used by the great Doctors of the Church."[146]

The East does not alone bear witness to the *Theotokos*. Though Pearson affirms that the term originated with St. Leo,[147] Western Fathers before his time show the contrary. Ambrose (397) asks:

"What is nobler than the Mother of God?"[148] One could hardly be more precise in this regard than Cassian (450) when he says: "If He is God, then she who bore Him is *Theotokos*, i.e., Mother of God."[149] Vincent of Lerins insists that Mary is to be confessed Mother of God, not merely by simple appellation, but in the full sense of the word.[150]

Newman's citation from St. Jerome, found in the *Letter to Pusey* is an abbreviation of the text, quoted at length in his *Notes on Athanasius*. It reads: "Happily do some understand by the closed gate by which the Lord God of Israel enters, that Prince on whom the gate is closed to be the Virgin Mary, who both before and after her bearing remained a Virgin.[151]

---

[144] Haer. IV, 12; P. G. 83:435.

[145] Ep. I ad Nest. P. G. 77:1455.

[146] Mansi V, col. 875.

[147] P. L. 54:191; ibid. col. 486.

[148] De virg. II, cap. I, 7; P. L. 16:220, 296.

[149] De Inc. II, 5; P. L. 50:43, 32.

[150] Common. m. 15; P. L. 50:658.

[151] Cf. Diff. II, 65 In Ezeeh. 44; P. L. 25:786. The French version of Newman's Letter (p. 248) attributes the quotation to Origen. This would be true if the reference given corresponded to Newman's citation. The editor claims it to be drawn from Hom. 14 on Ezech. 44. This homily, with the preceding ones, is translated from Origen. (Cf. Bardenhewer, Gesch.

Capriolus and Augustine[152] close the list of illustrious witnesses to the belief in the Blessed Mother of God.

In the *Essay on Development* as well as in the Letter to Pusey are encountered numerous titles of the Blessed Virgin attributed by Newman to St. Proclus of Constantinople. These are taken from Oratio Sexta: "Laudatio S. Dei Genitricis Mariae." This sermon is of unusual length and is intended to portray the Annunciation scene, which is interspersed with long dialogues between Mary and Joseph, and between Mary and Gabriel. The whole sermon presents certain peculiarities that cause it to differ from other works of Proclus, believed to be authentic. This sermon is probably to be rejected as an interpolation and as belonging to a considerably later period. The dialogues may be referred to the *Kontakia* of Romanus or some other personage. In general the sermons of Proclus still require a good deal of critical examination to test their authenticity.[153]

The text in the *Essay on Development* does not lose its value, for Newman is not there strictly limiting himself to any period in particular though, as a rule, he confines himself to the first five centuries. These beautiful invocations of our Lady may perhaps be placed in the sixth century.[154]

Newman quotes Theodotus of Ancyra twice; the first time without any comment,[155] the second time with an added remark. In the *Essay* he puts it thus: "Theodotus too, one of the Fathers at Ephesus, or whoever it is whose Homilies are given

---

der Altchr. Lit. III, 612). On closer investigation it will be found that the text in question has no direct reference to the Blessed Virgin, whereas Newman's citation is from Jerome's Commentary on Ezechiel (P. L. 25:430); cf. Niessen, op. cit. p. 124. The second quotation of a similar nature is to be found in the Comm. on Isaias as well as in the work against Pelagius.

[152] "That man from heaven is God conceived in the womb." "He is made in thee who made thee." P. L. 53:851; 38:1318.

[153] Bardenhewer, op. cit. IV, 205.

[154] Ibid. 203. The other citation from Proclus is authentic. P. G. 65:682.

[155] Diff. II, 65.

to St. Amphilochius."[156] In the Letter he cites Theodotus, or "some one else at Ephesus."[157] The former citation is taken from the bishop's homily *"in Die Nativitatis Domini"* where he asks "When thou hearest that God speaks from the bush, in the bush seest thou not the Virgin?"[158] The second is from Homily 4, "Homilia in Deiparam et Simeonem" in which he addresses the Mother of God thus: "Hail, Mother, clad in light, of the light which sets not; hail, all- undefiled Mother of holiness; hail, most pellucid fountain of the life-giving stream."[159] Two other homilies ascribed to Theodotus are, however, spurious. It may be because of this fact that Newman expressed his doubts.

VII. Conclusion

After having shown what the faith of the Fathers was concerning the Mother of God, Newman remarks justly that it should cause no wonder that they should have transmuted their belief speedily into devotion.[160] Indeed, what limit could be set to it, when once the full import of Mary's glorious title was realized? As time went on, there was a tendency to increase her honors rather than limit them. Could there be a limit, this side of the infinite, since the great title of Mother of God is hers by right? No attempt was made to circumscribe the honors due to her; on the contrary, the Fathers became almost violent in their zealous indignation against any one who attempted to belittle her grandeurs or deny her prerogatives. Instances of this are met with in St. Jerome against Helvidius, who denied Mary's virginity. Ambrose combatted Bonosus for the same reason; St. Epiphanius denounced Apollinaris, and St. Cyril refuted Nestorius.

In fact when once the controversies concerning Christ her Son had been settled, the Fathers naturally turned their

---

[156] Dev. 147.

[157] Diff. II, 67.

[158] P. G. 77:1371.

[159] Ibid. 1394.

[160] Diff. II, 65.

attention more to the person and office of the Blessed Mary. The Nestorian controversies particularly drew forth panegyrics of the Blessed Virgin, which became more and more exalted in their language.[161] St. Cyril, in one of his sermons, manifests the deep devotion that had already taken its roots in the hearts of the faithful, when he cries out: "Hail, Mary, Mother of God, majestic common-treasure of the world, the lamp unquenchable, the crown of virginity, the sceptre of orthodoxy, the indissoluble temple, the dwelling of the Illimitable, Mother and Virgin! Through thee, He in the holy gospels is called blessed who cometh in the name of the Lord. ... Through thee the Holy Trinity is praised and adored ... the cross is honored in the whole world ... heaven rejoices ... evil spirits are driven out ... idolaters are brought to the truth ... churches are raised... . Through thee went the Son of God as light to those who sat in darkness and in the shadow of death. ..."[162]

---

[161] Diff. II, 66–67.
[162] Hom. ex div. 4; P. G. 77:992–993.

CHAPTER II
Mary, Second Eve

I. Importance of this Doctrine in Newman's Mariology

HEN Newman wrote his *Letter to Pusey* he had no intention to attempt a systematic doctrinal explanation of Mariology, since this, in a certain way, was unnecessary for the class of people to whom he was addressing his treatise. Pusey and his followers accepted the Catholic doctrine on the divine maternity, her perpetual virginity, and her sanctity. Pusey himself found no difficulty in the Immaculate Conception itself, though he protested against the mode of its proclamation. The whole difficulty lay with the devotion of Catholics to our Lady; the objectors in the Anglican camp based their attitude on the claim that Catholics were departing from primitive doctrine in the matter. Had not Newman had the very same difficulty in Anglican days? His greatest charge at that time was that Catholics had supplanted the Fathers by mere papal authority which, he held, enforced absolute submission and contradicted Antiquity. The outcome, as he thought, was corruptions of primitive truth, additions to the deposit of faith confided to the Apostles. Pusey's difficulties were identical; hence the solution that had served for himself would be beneficial to Pusey and other Anglicans.

When he worked at his *Essay on Development,* he had discovered a *prima facie* view of the Blessed Virgin in Antiquity from which he could deduce numerous other inferences that are to be found in the system on the Blessed Virgin. This view was but the primitive basis for that devotion which naturally sprang from it and which eventually led to the forms presently in use among Catholics. These devotional manifestations against which Newman, Pusey, and others had protested, were legitimate developments, and not corruptions.

Aware of his own difficulties, Newman was able to combat the notion that the Fathers were relegated to an inferior position in the estimation of Catholics. He took the weapon, which Pusey thought most powerful, out of his hands by proving that Rome does not stand against the Fathers; that, on the contrary, the Fathers themselves testify to the present beliefs held by Roman Catholics in regard to the Blessed Mother of God. These are all witnesses to the primitive admission of Mary's incomparable dignity.

II. Scripture View of Blessed Virgin

From the very earliest times, Christians had recognized that Mary was the Mother of Jesus the Savior. She is inseparable from Jesus whenever she is introduced in Scripture. Thus, the Mother of the Lord is present when the Precursor is sanctified in the womb of Elizabeth;[1] the shepherds and the Magi find the "Child and His Mother,"[2] and so on through the infancy of Jesus. At the marriage feast of Cana, Mary "the Mother of Jesus" is there.[3] There stood by the cross "Mary the Mother of Jesus."[4] After the Ascension, while the disciples were preparing for the reception of the Paraclete, they persevered "with one mind in prayer with the women and Mary the Mother of Jesus."[5] The sacred writers seem to take a special care to introduce Mary always in the role which is pre-eminently hers by a special providence; consciously or unconsciously, they were proving the truth of the humanity of Jesus, by merely

---

[1] Luke 1:43.

[2] Ibid. 2:16; Matt. 2:11.

[3] John 2:1.

[4] Ibid. 19:25.

[5] Acts 1:14.

referring to His Blessed Mother. We may say, then, that the Gospel view of our Blessed Lady is her motherhood of our Lord's human nature.[6] Controversies about the divinity of Jesus would in due time bring out in bold relief the ineffable dignity of her Divine Maternity. Hence, it is not this prerogative that first arrests the attention of the faithful, though implicitly and even explicitly they held it, for they admitted that Jesus was both God and man, and that Mary was the mother of Jesus. The great rudimentary teaching of Antiquity concerning her, the *prima facie* view of her as Newman calls it,[7] bears on her relation to Christ in the redemption of mankind. That she was mother of Jesus and therefore mother of God, was taken for granted; no need to emphasize it for the moment; only when the belief of the faithful was called into doubt by heretics would there be an imperative demand for accentuating her intimate relations with the Blessed Trinity in the work of the Incarnation.

III. *PRIMA FACIE* OF HER IN ANTIQUITY; ITS SCRIPTURAL BASIS

Now this *prima facie* view of Mary is that she is the Second Eve. It has its foundation in the Scriptures, which, with the Fathers, never ceases to affirm that Christ came to redeem mankind from the heavy burden of sin, from the legacy of crime bequeathed by our first parents to their unfortunate posterity. Adam and Eve, in whose hands lay the fate of the whole human race, succumbed to the machinations of the evil one, who wished man to share the miserable lot that was his own as the result of his rebellion against the Almighty. When Satan was cast out of heaven into the infernal abyss, no opportunity for repentance was given him; but for man, less endowed with gifts of intellect and will, a means of reparation was provided. At the very moment when Adam and Eve were cast out of Paradise, a gleam of hope was held out to them. They could once more possess the title of children of God and

---

[6] Neubert, op. cit. p. 1.

[7] Diff. II, 31. Cf. Ess. II, 15, note.

heirs of heaven. A Savior would one day come, who would be the Seed of the Woman, and would vanquish the Serpent.

For four thousand years Patriarchs and Prophets were to keep alive the hope, and renew the promise of a future Redeemer. At a moment when idolatry seemed to have reduced man to the lowest level, when the idea of the true God had all but disappeared save among a small chosen people, the Savior appeared and by His Passion and death effaced the handwriting against mankind. The Apostles were commissioned by Christ to publish the "glad tidings" to the whole world, telling all creatures that now they were once more free, that the kingdom of Satan was overthrown and that the gate of heaven was once more open to receive those who had completed their term of exile upon earth and had lived in accord with God's holy precepts.

The fall and the reparation were not to be two isolated facts; man had been vanquished; by man, God wished to conquer Satan. Hence the mystery of the Incarnation, by which God became man. As Adam had fallen and had brought upon the human race a host of misfortunes, a new Adam arose who, in an inverse order, had reinstated man to his lost dignity. As the tree in the garden became the occasion of ruin, the tree of the cross became the instrument of restoration.

This idea of Jesus as the new Adam is encountered in Scripture, and was strongly impressed on the minds of the faithful. In fact, it was the theme of all the apostolic preaching and writing—this was the glad tidings which they were to announce to the world. The most complete and original picture which St. Paul draws of Christ's mission of redemption is that of the new Adam.[8] The term first Adam, as used by the Jews, rather signified the first man, but it was left to St. Paul to express the doctrinal value contained in it and to demonstrate the harmonious relations established in Christian soteriology. Adam and Christ epitomize the two great periods of the human race; they do not merely symbolize them, but realize them by a mysterious identification. A few texts from the Apostle suffice

---

[8] Prat, Théologie de S. Paul, II, p. 249–256; 261–265.

to bring out the point in a strong light: "The first man Adam was made into a living soul, the last Adam into a quickening spirit ... (Yet that was not first which is spiritual, but that which is natural, afterwards that which is spiritual). The first man was of the earth, earthly, the second man, from heaven, heavenly.[9] ..." "For by a man came death, and by a man the resurrection of the dead. And as in Adam all die, so also in Christ all shall be made alive."[10]

Here everything is antithesis. In the Epistle to the Romans,[11] the contrast is united with the parallelism; there Adam is expressly called a figure of Him who was to come. The disobedience, the offense of the first man finds its counterpoise in the obedience and grace conferred by Christ the new Adam, so that "where sin abounded, grace did more abound." Christ, the second Adam, had as His special role the reparation of sin by the gift of His justice, and the victory over death, by making us partakers of His immortality.

Consequently, it is most natural to find the early Christians all impregnated with the idea of Christ's role; the parallelism between the fall and the restoration could not long remain incomplete. Instinctively the Christians would seek the woman who was instrumental in man's redemption, as the first Eve was the occasion of man's ruin. Where would they look if not to Jesus, the second Adam, to find associated with Him, Mary the second Eve.

This doctrine is the central point of Newman's Mariology as exposed in his *Letter to Pusey*. From it he derives the doctrines of Mary's dignity, her sanctity, her Immaculate Conception, and Assumption. His treatment of Mary's position as Second Eve really merits the designation of *"magistrale"* as given it by Terrien.[12] His method is not merely historical; the

---

[9] I Cor. 15:45.

[10] I Cor. 15:21-22.

[11] I Cor. 5:14-21.

[12] Terrien, op. cit. III, 10. The author bases his two volumes on the spiritual maternity of Mary on the principle that she is the second Eve. His basic exposition is borrowed from Newman.

foundation for the belief is indirectly placed in Scripture. He explains it and then strengthens it by the testimony of the Fathers.

Adam as head of the human race was really responsible for the fate of posterity;[13] he was our representative. By his fall, all men forfeited the privileges conferred originally upon him by God; had he not fallen, though Eve had yielded to the tempter's wiles, yet grace would not have been lost.[14] Eve was not head of the race as Adam was; still, she had a definite, essential position in the First Covenant. Adam named her the "Mother of all the living" to show not only her relation to the human race, but also her dignity. She had her own place as regards its trial and fall in Adam; she had an integral share in the primeval events. She listened to the serpent, ate of the forbidden fruit, and offered it to her husband. "She co-operated, not as an irresponsible instrument, but intimately and personally in the sin; she brought it about. As the history stands, she was a *sine qua non*, a positive, active cause of it. And she had her share in the punishment; in the sentence pronounced on her, she was recognized as a real agent in the temptation and its issue, and she suffered accordingly."[15] Satan had suggested to Eve that by eating of the fruit she would become like unto God; she fell into his snares. She sinned and in turn tempted Adam.[16]

Three actors are represented in this tragic scene of the Proto-Gospel—a scene fraught with so many consequences for the billions of human beings that would people the globe in future ages. There was the serpent, the woman, and the man. When the sentence was pronounced on each of these three individually, an event was announced for some distant future when the three same parties would meet again,—the serpent, the woman, and the man; but it was to be a second Adam and a second Eve, and the new Eve was to be the mother of the new

---

[13] Diff. II, 31 sqq.

[14] This is the opinion of St. Thomas; cf. Summa I, II, q. 81 a. 5.

[15] Diff. II, 32.

[16] M. D. I, 35.

Adam,[17] for the Lord had said: "I will put enmities between thee and the woman, and between thy seed and her seed."[18]

With the fall was promised the remedy; and when the time had come, the Redeemer was at hand. Mary was to be the Gate of Heaven through which the Word might pass to earth as was foretold by the Prophet Ezechiel: "The gate shall be closed; it shall not be opened, and no man shall pass through it, since the Lord God of Israel has entered through it—and it shall be closed for the Prince, the Prince Himself shall sit in it."[19] The Seed of the Woman foretold in Genesis was the Word Incarnate, and the Woman, whose seed or son He is, is the Virgin Mary.

Jesus was not merely to take flesh of the Blessed Mary by becoming her Son. As Adam primarily brought about the fall, so the new Adam would be the principal and absolutely essential cause of Redemption. However, Eve had her share in the first sin; in like manner, Mary was to have her place in the economy of Redemption. Eve was responsible and instrumental in Adam's sin; Mary, too, was to bear a part; she was to be a voluntary agent;[20] she was to be united with her divine Son in spirit and in will, as she was associated with Him in body, by furnishing Him the elements of His human nature. "As Eve opened the way for the fatal deed of the first Adam, so it was fitting that Mary should open the way for the great achievement of the second Adam, even our Lord Jesus Christ."[21]

Mary is the second and better Eve, as taking the initial part in the world's restoration. God ever demands a reasonable service and the voluntary co-operation of creatures in His works; He forces no will, but requires acquiescence in His designs. Though the Incarnation was to be of such tremendous significance for the whole human race, nevertheless as for man's fall, so for the restoration, He allowed the accomplishment or non-accomplishment of His will to rest

---

[17] Diff. II, 32.

[18] Gen. 3:15.

[19] Ezech. 44:2, 3.

[20] Dev. 415; M. D. I, *35;* Diff. II, 35.

[21] M. D. I, 36.

solely on the *fiat* of a young maiden. When God sent the Angel to announce the great dignity that was to be Mary's portion, He wished that she should enter upon her function as Mother of the Redeemer knowingly and willingly. Had she not believed or obeyed, the Divine Economy would have been frustrated.[22] We dare not think of what might have been the outcome had she refused the awful responsibility given her; nor need we conjecture what other plan the Divine Mercy might have devised for our salvation in case of Mary's refusal. Mary pondered the full import of the Angel's message and, with the consent of a heart full of God's love to her and her own lowliness, she answered: "Behold the handmaid of the Lord, be it done unto me according to thy word."

It is at once evident from the mere Gospel narrative that Mary was not only the physical instrument of our Lord's taking flesh, but also an instrumental, responsible cause. This is also the view of the Fathers. Protestants seem to lose sight of this important fact. Newman was obliged to call Pusey to task for his assertion in the *Eirenicon* that "the Fathers speak of the Blessed Virgin as the instrument of our salvation in that she gave birth to the Redeemer, and apply personally to her the title of chosen vessel of the Incarnation."[23] Newman, as an Anglican, did not share this view of his friend, though he speaks of her as an instrument, as in every Saint, working towards an end appointed by God.[24] But he does not consider her exclusively as such, although he was obliged to emphasize the point at that time, lest "extreme" honors be paid her in consequence of her great dignity. He had already remarked the parallelism between Eve and Mary: "Jesus is the seed of the woman announced to guilty Eve ... in her (Mary) the destinies of the world were to be reversed and the serpent's head bruised ... in her the curse pronounced on Eve was changed to a

---

[22] Dev. 415.

[23] I Eir. 155–156; 151. Pusey afterwards affirmed that he had never intended to consider Mary merely as a physical instrument. Cf. II, Eir. 22 sqq.

[24] P. S. II, 134.

blessing ... in bearing our Lord, she has taken off or lightened the peculiar disgrace which the woman inherited for seducing Adam, in that she was ruled over by man."[25]

Newman teaches clearly that the Fathers in reality saw more in Mary than a mere physical instrument. "They declare," says he, "that she was *not* a mere instrument in the Incarnation, such as David or Judah may be considered; she co-operated in our salvation not merely by the descent of the Holy Ghost upon her body, but by specific holy acts, the effects of the Holy Ghost within her soul; but as Eve forfeited privileges by sin, so Mary earned privileges by the fruits of grace: as Eve was disobedient and unbelieving, so Mary was obedient and believing; that as Eve was a cause of ruin to all, Mary was a cause of salvation to all; that as Eve made room for Adam's fall, so Mary made room for our Lord's reparation of it; and thus, whereas the free gift was not as the offense, but much greater, it follows that, as Eve co-operated in effecting a great evil, Mary co-operated in effecting a much greater good."[26]

IV. Testimony of Justin, Irenaeus, Tertullian

In order to prove that the Fathers regarded Mary as something more than a physical instrument of our salvation, Newman adduces the testimony of the three Fathers, Justin, Irenaeus, and Tertullian, who say in various ways what has just been stated of the resemblance between Eve and the Blessed Virgin. Justin was converted about A.D. 120 and died about the year 165; Irenaeus lived from about 120–200, and Tertullian from about 160 to after 220. Hence these authors witness to the belief of the second century. Justin almost touches upon the Apostolic times, having embraced Christianity about twenty years after the death of the Apostle St. John. Irenaeus is connected with the same Apostle through the latter's disciple

---

[25] P. S. II, 128–131.

[26] Diff. II, 36.

St. Polycarp.[27] Nothing can be brought forward to prove a contrary view of the Blessed Virgin at this early period. After the Council of Nice, the current of testimony in favor of the Mother of God and of the Second Eve becomes stronger as time advances. In exposing this matter, Newman limits himself merely to the Fathers from the second to the fifth centuries. By the time the period of St. Jerome and St. Augustine is reached, the parallelism between Eve and Mary has entered so deeply into the consciousness of the faithful that they seem to be quoting a proverb when they say "death by Eve, life by Mary."[28] All of these Fathers express the same thought, most of them in a severe dogmatic style, others, such as St. Peter Chrysologus and Fulgentius, in oratorical form, which does not in the least diminish the value of their statements, for as Newman justly remarks: "After all, men use oratory on great subjects, not on small."[29]

Before proceeding to the examination of the doctrinal question, and the value of patristic testimony in favor of the Second Eve, it may be serviceable to indicate here the assertions of the three Fathers upon whom Newman lays so much stress.

St. Justin writes in his *Dialogue with Trypho:* "And since we read of Him as Son of God in the commentaries of the Apostles, we say and know that He is a Son and, before all creatures, proceeded from the Father by His power and will (and indeed in the books of the prophets is called Wisdom, the Day, the Orient, the Sword, the Stone, the Rod, Jacob, and Israel, etc.) and by means of the Virgin became man, that by what way the disobedience arising from the serpent had its beginning, by that way also it might have an undoing. For Eve, being a virgin and undefiled, conceiving the word that was from the serpent, brought forth disobedience and death; but the Virgin Mary, taking faith and joy, when the Angel told her the good tidings,

---

[27] Cf. Ehrhard, *Die altchr. Lit. und ihre Erforschung von 1884–1900*, (Freiburg in. Br. 1900), p. 264.

[28] Diff. II, 39–44.

[29] Ibid. 44.

that the Spirit of the Lord should come upon her and the power of the Most High overshadow her, and therefore the Holy One that was born of her was the Son of God, answered, 'Be it to me according to thy word.' "[30]

Irenaeus has several remarkable passages on the subject: "With a fitness Mary the Virgin is found obedient.... But Eve was disobedient; for she obeyed not, while she was yet a virgin. As she having indeed Adam for a husband, but as yet being a virgin ... becoming disobedient, became the cause of death both to herself and to the whole human race, so also Mary, having the predestined man, and being yet a Virgin, being obedient, became both to herself and to the whole human race the cause of salvation. ... For, whereas the Lord, when born, was the first-begotten of the dead, and received into His bosom the primitive fathers, He regenerated them into the life of God, He Himself becoming the beginning of the living, since Adam became the beginning of the dying. Therefore also Luke, commencing the line of generations from the Lord, referred it back to Adam, signifying that He regenerated the old fathers, not they Him, into the Gospel of life. And so the knot of Eve's disobedience received its unloosing through the obedience of Mary; for what Eve, a virgin, bound by incredulity, that Mary, a virgin, unloosed by faith."[31]

Again, he says: "As Eve by the speech of an Angel was seduced, so as to flee God, transgressing His word, so also Mary received the good tidings by means of the Angel's speech, so as to bear God within her, being obedient to His word. And, though the one had disobeyed God, yet the other was drawn to obey God; that of the virgin Eve the Virgin Mary might become the advocate. And, as by a virgin the human race had been bound to death, by a Virgin it is saved, the balance being preserved, a virgin's disobedience by a Virgin's obedience."[32]

In recent years a work of Irenaeus, previously known only by name, has come to light. It is entitled *The Apostolical*

---

[30] Dial. cum Tryph. 100; P. G. 6:709.

[31] Adv. Haer. III, 22, 34; P. G. 7:958 sqq.

[32] Ibid. V, 19; P. G. 7:1175.

Preaching and serves to sum up Christian doctrine as contained in the teaching of the Apostles. In this particular work the parallel between Mary and Eve is again developed. Evidently Newman did not know of this treatise, otherwise he would certainly have made use of it to prove his argument. Irenaeus says: "And just as through a disobedient virgin, man was stricken down and fell into death, so through the Virgin who was obedient to the word of God, man was reanimated and received life. ... For it was necessary that Adam should be summed up in Christ, that mortality might be swallowed up and overwhelmed by immortality; and Eve summed up in Mary, that a Virgin should be a virgin's intercessor and by a Virgin's obedience undo and put away the disobedience of a virgin."[33]

Tertullian in his *De Carne Christi* writes: "God recovered His image and likeness, which the devil had seized by a rival operation. For into Eve, as yet a virgin, had crept the word which was the framer of death. Equally into a Virgin was to be introduced the Word of God, which was the builder-up of life; that, what by that sex had gone into perdition, by the same sex might be brought back to salvation. Eve had believed the serpent; Mary believed Gabriel; the fault which the one committed by believing, the other by believing has blotted out."[34]

V. Value of Their Testimony

What value does Newman attach to the testimony of these three Fathers? That their words have a great worth insofar as they are witnesses to a pretty general belief is unquestioned, for these men lived in what is called the sub-Apostolic age.

Newman leaves aside for the moment, the testimony of Irenaeus and considers only Justin and Tertullian. As he adds: "I think I may assume that the doctrine of these two Fathers about the Blessed Virgin was the received doctrine of their own respective times and places; for writers, after all, are but

---

[33] Cf. Robinson, *Irenaeus, the Apostolical Preaching*, n. 33, pp. 99, 100.

[34] De Carne Christi, 17; P. L. 2:782.

witnesses of facts and beliefs, and as such they are treated by all parties in controversial discussion. Moreover, the coincidence of doctrine which they exhibit and, again, the antithetical completeness of it, show that they themselves did not originate it. The next question is, Who did? for from one definite organ or source, place or person, it must have come. Then we must inquire what length of time would it take for such a doctrine to have extended and to be received in the second century over so wide an area; that is, to be received before the year 200 in Palestine, Africa, and Rome."[35]

Two questions present themselves to us in the investigation of Newman's reasoning: Are these writers as independent of each other as he supposes? What is the common source?

To answer the first of these two questions, it must be recalled that the foundation of Anglicanism is its claim of adhering steadfastly to Antiquity; a tradition, then, to be valid must justify itself as apostolical. Newman lays down the principles for determining the Apostolicity of a tradition:[36] first, when credible witnesses declare that it is apostolical; secondly, when, in various places, independent witnesses enunciate one and the same doctrine. There is hardly a possibility of proving that any early writer taught the apostolicity of the doctrine on the Second Eve, and Newman admits it. Consequently the second criterion must be applied, and Newman maintains that the writers in question are really independent witnesses, because in three distinct parts of the Christian world they expose one and the same doctrine. He calls attention to the fact that they witness just for the three great seats of Catholic teaching, where the truth in this matter was likely to be established. St. Justin, he holds, speaks for Jerusalem, Irenaeus for Ephesus, and Tertullian for Rome. Newman places Tertullian as representative of Africa and Rome, Justin of Palestine, and Irenaeus of Asia Minor and Gaul. Of the latter, he adds: "Rather, he represents St. John the Evangelist, for he had been taught by the martyr St. Polycarp, who was the intimate

---

[35] Diff. II, 37–38.

[36] Ibid. 140, 141.

associate of St. John and also of other Apostles."[37]

It will be at once observed that Newman bases his entire argument of the independence of these Fathers on their separation in place. The mere coincidence that one Father is in the East and another in the West would not prove that one was not subject to the influence of the other. Each one of these three spent some time in Rome, particularly Justin and Tertullian.

Furthermore, each of these three is separated from his predecessor by an interval of several years. Thus, the date of Irenaeus' death (about 200) occurred some 35 years after that of Justin. Tertullian died some time after the year 220. Considering the esteem in which these Fathers were held, as well as their prominent positions in the Church, it would be no more than likely that their writings should he known to their contemporaries and successors though living in different parts of the Church. And, especially, since all three had been in Rome for some time, there is a still greater likelihood that they should have become acquainted with each other's writings.

Justin's *Dialogue with Trypho* is thought to have been composed between 150 and 160.[38] Irenaeus was born about the year 120.[39] Thus, there would be no *a priori* difficulty in admitting the latter's knowledge and possession of this work. As for many other subjects, it is very possible that Irenaeus borrowed the comparison of Mary and Eve from Justin.

---

[37] Ibid. 33. (Jerusalem was the see of St. James; Ephesus the seat and burial place of St. John; Rome the city of St. Peter and Paul.)

[38] Bardenhewer, op. cit. I, p. 230.

[39] In this matter Zahn and Chapman are in accord with Newman; Harnack places his birth ca. 142. Zahn places it as early as 115, Chapman about 120. The latter concludes this from Irenaeus' use of the term ἡλικία when he refers to his acquaintance with Polycarp. Elsewhere Irenaeus (Adv. Haer. III, 3, 3) when alluding to our Lord uses the same word to signify manhood, i.e., between the ages of 30 and 35. According to Harnack's calculation Irenaeus would have been 44 when he wrote his great work, but he seems rather to be writing as an old man, giving his recollections of a past now in danger of being forgotten. Cf. Ehrhard, op. cit. 262 sqq., also *Journal of Theol. Studies*, IX, 1908, p. 61.

Robinson[40] points out the dependence of Irenaeus upon Justin Martyr by a comparative study of texts. The First and Second Apologies, besides the *Dialogue*, seem to have been in Irenaeus' hands and must have been familiar to him, for ever and anon he uses expressions that occur in Justin; this is particularly evident when texts of Scripture are combined or peculiar constructions occur.

If, then, Irenaeus was acquainted with Justin's work, it is not difficult to suppose that he borrowed the comparison from Justin and elaborated what he found; if he did not borrow it, two alternatives lie before us, either to suppose that this idea had already become a preacher's commonplace, or that both used a common source. Newman inclines to the notion of a common source and at the same time rejects an interdependence.[41]

As for Tertullian, he seems to have derived his theology concerning Christ from Irenaeus. Chapman does not hesitate to state that Irenaeus is unquestionably the authority for Tertullian in the passage from *De Carne Christi*.[42]

If the case is such as has been exposed, Newman seems to give too much importance to the independence of his witnesses. He wishes thereby to infer the apostolicity of the doctrine. He, however, insists that they must have received their doctrine from a common source and were simply testifying to a belief rather universally held. Even though they were not independent, they could have derived the doctrine from some common source. Newman finds in the very fact of the coincidence of the doctrine and its completeness a reason to show that they themselves did not originate it.

The next question resolves itself to this: Did Justin originate this doctrine, or did he receive it from some one else? Certainty

---

[40] Cf. Introduction to his *Irenaeus, Apostolical Preaching*.

[41] Diff. II, 37–38. Cf. Chapman, "The Age of Christ according to Papias," *Journ. of Theol. St.* IX, 1908, p. 51. Both Irenaeus and Tertullian borrowed from Justin. Bardenhewer, op. cit. I, 211.

[42] Cf. Chapman, loc. cit. also Harnack, *Lehrbuch der Dogmengeschichte*, I, p. 515. Neubert, op. cit. p. 247 says: "Here, his role limits itself to that of witness of a tradition of which he had not grasped the full import."

here is out of the question. Newman puts his conclusion thus:

"Can we refer the common source of these local traditions to a date much later than that of the Apostles, since St. John died within twenty years of St. Justin's conversion, and sixty of Tertullian's birth?" And, besides, he holds that the testimony of Irenaeus is so close upon that of the school of St. John himself in Asia Minor. Of course, Newman here bases himself upon the fact of the independence of the Fathers.

It is not impossible to accept the notion that Justin originated the idea, since in some respects he was original in his exposition of certain Christian doctrines, as for example the virginal birth.[43] However, there are some patristic students who contend that Justin was not sufficiently original to have developed the comparison between Eve and Mary.[44] It is true, however, that the suggestion for the comparison has already been given, as was noted, when St. Paul calls Christ the second Adam. It required only a single influential writer to take up the hint and elaborate it in the form in which it is to be found.

Chapman suggests that the common source might be found in Papias, of whose works only fragments remain. From the fact that Justin's development is so complete, it would seem that he could have received the teaching from another, but it is by no means certain that he knew and used Papias' work. There is no doubt that Irenaeus knew of it.[45] The entire argument of Father Chapman rests upon a text of Victorinus, who was martyred during the reign of Diocletian. This text is claimed to be drawn from Papias.[46] In it are to be found the words "ea die Gabrihel angelum Mariae virgini evangelizasse, qua die draco Aevam

---

[43] Neubert, op. cit. p. 90.

[44] Cf. Cath. Enc. art. Justin.

[45] "That Irenaeus used Papias in Bk. IV, chap. 25–36, is quite obvious, not only from the chiliastic matter, but from actual citations of the presbyters, and in one place (V, 33, 3) he appeals to Papias by name. Besides, Eusebius implies (III, 39) that Irenaeus followed Papias, while the fragment of Philip of Side ... asserts it." Chapman, loc. cit. p. 47. Cf. *Expositor*, Fifth Series, Vol. I, (1895), p. 334.

[46] Born about A.D. 80; wrote his work probably after 138. Cf. Ehrhard, op. cit. 111–112.

seduxit." This may have served as a suggestion to Justin, who developed the thought in detail. Victorinus did not, like Justin, emphasize the virginity of Eve when she fell, but he mentions that of Mary. The parallel is between the speech of the angel and that of the serpent. It may be that Justin was developing the same passage of Papias which Victorinus has used. The sentence of Victorinus is so short that he could not parallel the whole of Justin's passage; one would, then, suppose that the simpler and shorter one is nearer the original thought.

Thus, one would be rather inclined to Newman's view, which affirms some common source from which all of these Fathers drew, a source not far removed from apostolic times. Though the three Fathers, of whom Newman treats, are not quite so independent of each other as he supposes, still they would not have exposed the subject as a commonly accepted doctrine. Had this doctrine been contrary to the Christian sense, there would have been some opposition to its acceptance, or divergence of views on it, but there is no evidence of such an attitude. Consequently, it must be supposed that the doctrine of the Second Eve was generally accepted by the faithful of the second century.

VI. Mary's Merit of This Position

A point that is drawn out by Newman from the testimony of the early Fathers, is her meriting the position which she held in the restoration of the human race, since she is an active responsible cause. The Saints of the Old Covenant might have merited the Incarnation *de congruo*, as some authors hold, or, at least, might have merited certain circumstances connected with this mystery.[47] As to the Blessed Virgin, the liturgy seems to indicate that she merited her dignity, for we pray: "Ut dignum Filii tui habitaculum effici mereretur, Spiritu Sancto cooperante praeparasti,"[48] and elsewhere: "Regina coeli, laetare ... quia quem meruisti portare."

---

[47] Cf. Dictionnaire de la Théol. Cath. Fasc. 54–55, col. 1529.

[48] Orison following the "Salve Regina."

St. Thomas explains in a few words how Mary could have merited her divine maternity: "by the grace conferred on her she merited that degree of purity and holiness in order that she might become a fit mother of God."[49] Newman held that her faith, obedience and virginity were "accessories" to the Incarnation and gained it as her reward.[50] As Eve had failed in faith and obedience and thereby brought on the fall of the race, so Mary by the practice of these virtues had a part in its restoration. Mary in reality, "co-operated in our salvation by specific holy acts," as Newman declares.

Evidently, by her mere personal endeavor, she could not have merited the divine maternity and her association in the work of the Redemption; but her virtues enter into the divine economy in such a manner as to draw down upon herself this favor. First she is singled out by the Divine Majesty from all eternity to be the Mother of the Incarnate Word. In order to make her a worthy Mother for His Divine Son, God bestowed upon her a plenitude of grace commensurate with her great dignity. No one could estimate her holiness and perfection. Holiness and divine favor go together, for so it is expressly told us in Scripture: "to him that hath, more is given." We cannot conceive what must have been the transcendent purity of her whom the Creator Spirit condescended to overshadow with His miraculous presence; nor can we imagine what must have been the gifts of her "who was chosen to be the only earthly relative of the Son of God, the only one whom He was bound by nature to revere and look up to; the one appointed to train and educate Him, to instruct Him day by day, as He grew in wisdom and stature."[51]

As Newman points out, it was first of all by *faith* that Mary gained the rewards of the Incarnation. Eve had believed the serpent, but Mary believed the angel; by her faith she blotted out the fault committed through Eve's belief in the words of the

---

[49] In IV Sent. 1. III, dist. 4, q. 3, a. 1 ad 6. "Quia meruit ex gratia sibi data illum puritatis et sanctitatis gradum, ut congrue posset esse mater Dei."

[50] Diff. II, 35, 41.

[51] P. S. II, 132.

tempter.[52] The serpent had deceived the one, while to the other the angel brings good tidings,[53] and Mary answers his message with a sublime faith: "Behold the handmaid of the Lord, be it done unto me according to thy word." She acquiesced in the manifestation of God's will.[54]

Newman develops this thought in showing how Mary not only became a model of faith at the moment of the Incarnation, but all through her life as well, so that in her person she symbolizes both the faith of the unlearned and that of the doctors of the Church.[55]

Mary *obeyed* besides believing, and here again she stands in contrast with Eve, who "brought forth disobedience and death," as St. Justin says.[56] St. Irenaeus is still more explicit when he says that as Eve by her disobedience "became the cause of death both to herself and to the whole human race, so also Mary ... being obedient, became both to herself and to the whole human race the cause of salvation. ... And so the knot of Eve's disobedience received its unloosing through the obedience of Mary."[57] The same Father makes a picturesque comparison when he demonstrates how Eve's disobedience is balanced by Mary's obedience.

Another virtue that won for Mary her position of Second Eve was her virginity.[58] St. Jerome expressly adds this virtue to her faith and obedience; however, the earlier Fathers as well love to insist on the fact that it was a virgin who was the occasion of death, and a Virgin who brought us forth anew to life. Justin recalls that it is by a Virgin that the Son of God became man; by a virgin undefiled, disobedience and death were brought forth, and by the Virgin Mary, the mystery of the Incarnation was brought to pass. Tertullian explains how the

---

[52] Diff. II, 34.
[53] Ibid. 39.
[54] U. S. 312.
[55] U. S. 313.
[56] Diff. II, 33.
[57] Ibid. 34–35.
[58] Ibid. 41

order by which mankind fell, was reversed, and both operations take place through the instrumentality of virgins. "For into Eve, as yet a virgin, had crept the word which was the framer of death. Equally into a Virgin was to be introduced the Word of God which was the builder-up of life." Irenaeus calls the Virgin Mary the Advocate, the Intercessor, the Παράκλητος, of the virgin Eve.[59]

God, then, had prepared the soul of Mary so that at the moment of the Incarnation the Angel could salute her as "full of grace." The mere fact of her conception without sin, (and Newman considered this, even as Anglican, a necessary predisposition for the divine maternity) implies a superabundance of grace, which augmented continuously to an extent beyond what the feeble intellect of man could ever measure. Catholic as well as Protestant theologians hold that Adam and Eve were created in grace; can it be possible to deny that Mary should have had even greater grace than her prototype?[60]

It seems the most natural thing to expect that she who was to receive the greatest possible dignity that could ever be conferred on a creature, should also possess the grace, holiness, and perfection proportionate to such a position.[61] Besides, she was in such close contact with Jesus, the Author of all grace, that she ought necessarily to be filled with an abundance of grace and virtue.[62]

Newman does not content himself with showing how Mary co-operated in the Incarnation and Redemption and merited this position insofar as it is possible for a creature. He points out, further, how the Fathers describe her office, and that in terms which might very readily have shocked Pusey and others had these expression been found in later writers. Mary "blotted out" Eve's fault and brought forth the human race to salvation; by her the human race is saved; she is Eve's advocate. In this

---

[59] Diff. II, 34.

[60] Ibid. 45.

[61] P. S. II, 131; Mix. 364.

[62] Diff. II, 140.

connection, Newman makes the profound remark: "It is supposed by critics, Protestants as well as Catholics, that the Greek word for Advocate in the original was Paraclete; it should be borne in mind, then, when we are accused of giving our Lady the titles and offices of her Son, that St. Irenaeus bestows on her the special Name and Office proper to the Holy Ghost."[63]

From her co-operation with the Redeemer, Catholics have come to style Mary co-Redemptress, an appellation against which Pusey protests, in his *Eirenicon* especially as numerous bishops had used it in their replies to Pius IX. These prelates used such titles as "Companion of the Redeemer," "co-Redemptress," "Authoress of everlasting salvation" and refer to them as "ancient, well-known, traditionary."[64] Pusey sums up Catholic doctrine on this question by a series of long extracts from de Salazar, whom Newman designates as too "ruthlessly logical to be a safe or pleasant guide in the matter of devotion."[65] Why should there be any objection to calling her co-Redemptress, when the Fathers themselves call her by such names as Mother of God, Second Eve, Mother of all living, the Mother of Life, the Morning Star, the mystical new heaven, the Sceptre of Orthodoxy?[66]

She does not usurp the place of her Divine Son in the work of redemption. She is not the cause of grace. Jesus alone is the life of the soul; He alone regenerates us; Mary is our mother by divine appointment, her office is external to us. She does not enter into the distribution of the sacraments; her power is indirect, she is of avail to us through her prayers.[67] This is elementary dogma known by the simplest Catholic. No matter

---

[63] Diff. II, 37.

[64] Eir. I, 153.

[65] Diff. II, 98.

[66] Ibid. 78. Pusey later acknowledged these expressions as weaker forms for *Theotokos*, as so "many colors evolved out of that central light." She was the Mother of our Redeemer and so, from her, as the fountain of His Human Birth, came all which He did and was to us. II Eir. 27.

[67] Diff. II, 84.

how high we elevate Mary—and we may raise her to a height short of the infinite—she remains ever a creature as one of us, though a very privileged one.

Her function of Mediatrix or co-Redemptress was not absolutely necessary *necessitate medii,* as the Schoolmen would say; yet it was necessary according to the designs of Divine Providence. He willed that she should have a real share in the work of the Redemption. The Fathers manifest this clearly[68] when they speak of her as the cause of salvation to the human race. From the doctrine of the Second Eve, springs that of the spiritual maternity. She is truly the Mother of men; like Eve, she has become the Mother of all the living.[69] By becoming the Mother of God and therefore instrument of the Incarnation, she has entered into an intimate relationship with us in what concerns the spiritual life, for through the Incarnation we become brethren of Christ and heirs of heaven.[70] Grace was restored by the coming of Christ, human nature is sanctified. Christ dwells in His elect personally; He is the immediate source or principle of the spiritual life in them.[71] This Physician, as St. Ignatius calls Him, is from Mary; He gave Himself first through Mary; she was associated with Him in the first act that led on to our Redemption; she became thus the cause of our salvation; should she not, then, participate also in the fruits of the Redemption by becoming the Mother of all the living, the Mother of "fair love and fear and knowledge and holy hope," the health of the weak, the Refuge of sinners, the Comforter of the afflicted?[72]

Newman hardly draws out this doctrine of Mary's spiritual maternity as he could have done, from the central doctrine on the Second Eve. The prophecy uttered in the Garden of Paradise applies to her. The Messias, Jesus, is the predestined posterity of the woman, but since the race of the demon is

---

[68] Ibid. 37.

[69] Mix. 363.

[70] M. D. 39.

[71] Ath. II, 193 sqq.

[72] Mix. 363.

collective, the race of the woman can be understood in the same manner. Hence, her offspring is principally Christ, but likewise the multitudes who, being born children of God, also combat the infernal serpent. This is easily understood, for these men belong to Christ as members to the head; they form part of His fulness; they are included in His mystical body; they are, too, according to the measure of their sanctity, the Christ victorious over Satan. How well these considerations coincide with and are borne out by the text of the Apocalypse[73] which describes the war with Satan: "And the dragon was angry against the woman; and went to make war with the rest of her seed who keep the commandments of God and have the testimony of Jesus Christ."

For Newman, the texts of Genesis and the Apocalypse must complete each other; with the Fathers, he discourses on Mary's role in the conquest of Satan and in the salvation of the human race. As Eve is the mother of the living from the corporal point of view, Mary, too, becomes the spiritual mother of the human race. But this basis for Mary's spiritual maternity does not seem to have struck Newman with all the force that really underlies it. He laid down the principle without drawing the conclusion;[74] it is true, he was merely developing an apologetic argument.

---

[73] 12:17.

[74] Terrien, op. cit. III, 24–25, has used this exposition of Newman on the Second Eve as the groundwork of his treatise on the Spiritual Maternity of Mary. He draws the conclusion from this principle:
"La chute et la réparation ne seront pas deux faits isolés. La rédemption, dans les desseins de Dieu, est une revanchée. L'homme avait été vaincu ; c'est par l'homme que Dieu prétend vaincre. De là, cette sollicitude divine a faire servir tous les instruments de notre malheur au ministère de notre salut. Ou, parce que la femme avait eu sa grande part dans la déchéance de l'humanité coupable, il fallait que Dieu prédestinât une nouvelle Eve aussi bien qu'un nouvel Adam. Faute de cela, la revanche divine n'aurait pas été parfaite, et ses desseins auraient manqué de leur meilleur complément...
. Donc et ce sera le couronnement de l'antithèse, si la première Eve est, en toute verité, la mère des morts en Adam, la seconde, c'est-à-dire, la divine Marie, doit être en Jésus-Christ la mère des vivants: car c'est le rôle propre à la mère de communiquer la vie."

He rather looks elsewhere for the origin of Mary's spiritual maternity by associating the words of Christ "Behold thy Mother" to the texts of Genesis and the Apocalypse.[75] He sees in Mary, our Mother by divine appointment, given us from the Cross. The words of Jesus addressed to the beloved disciple apply to all of us. Jesus wished to supply us with all the relations, in a spiritual way, which we have in nature, and so He gave us also a mother.[76] There, at the foot of the Cross, she brings us forth in pain. But, we may rather say that she had already brought us forth to the spiritual life at the moment of the Incarnation, when by her obedience and faith the Eternal Word took up His abode in her chaste womb. Then she became rather the Mother of the living, for then she fulfilled more particularly the role of Second Eve. The words of Jesus on Calvary were but the explicit declaration of what had taken place more than thirty years before.[77]

---

[75] S. N. 93.

[76] S. N. 81.

[77] M. D. I, 55. Of the mode of interpreting the passage of St. John, Pusey has this to say: "The interpretation of the passage, upon which Roman Catholics now generally rest the title of the Blessed Virgin, 'our mother' is, of course, much graver. For this introduces a new personal relation of the Blessed Virgin to us, not indirectly through our Lord, but directly as given to her by Him. It is a great change. In the two ancient passages (of Origen and St. Augustine) where alone, as I believe, she is spoken of as hypothetically the mother of any Christian, or mother of Christians, it is because we are members of Christ. Our relation to Christ is immediate; she is the Mother of Him our Head, of whom we have been made the members. She has not, in this aspect, been assigned to men as a Mother to bring them to Christ by her intercessions; her only relation to us is in that we are already Christ's. ... I myself (cannot) think otherwise than that they (the Fathers) did not introduce it, because they were unacquainted with the doctrine, that they did not look upon St. John as a type of Christians, or think of any thing beyond the bare literal meaning." II Eir. 45 sqq.

Because of her relation to us, Mary's affection for us, like a mother's love, is unwearied; nothing can ever extinguish it. Hence, we pray to her to assist us in the hour of our death, for she will never leave us.[78] She has become for us the fount of mercy, though she does not displace Jesus, the primary source of all mercy.[79]

---

[78] S. N. 137, 138.

[79] Ibid. 93.

CHAPTER III
Mary Ever-Virgin

I. Newman and the Virginal Birth

IN HIS classic description of Froude, Newman says: "He had a high severe idea of the intrinsic excellence of virginity; and he considered the Blessed Virgin its great pattern."[1] This same esteem for celibacy was held by Newman himself. At the age of fifteen, he had the firm conviction that God called him to lead a single life. "This anticipation," he tells us, "which has held its ground almost continually ever since ... was more or less connected in my mind with the notion that my calling in life would require such a sacrifice as celibacy involved. ... It also strengthened my feeling of separation from the visible world."[2]

The church of which he was minister in his Anglican days was dedicated to Mary the Virgin. He too, like Froude, must have delighted to look upon Mary as the great type of virginity, the *Virgo Virginum*. Thoroughly grounded in the doctrine of the Incarnation, he could not imagine Christ in any other way than "conceived by the Holy Ghost, born of the Virgin Mary." The mere suggestion of the contrary shocked him. The Creed was a sufficient argument for his belief in the miraculous conception of Christ. As an Anglican, already he summed up the doctrine thus: "Christ came by a miracle. He came as the Son of Man, but not as the son of sinful Adam. He had no

---

[1] Apo. 24.
[2] Ibid. 7.

earthly father; He abhorred to have one. The thought may not be suffered that He should have been the son of shame and guilt. He came by a new and living way; not, indeed, formed out of the ground as Adam was at the first, lest He should miss the participation of our nature, but selecting and purifying unto Himself a tabernacle out of that which existed. As in the beginning, woman was formed out of man by Almighty power, so now, by a like mystery but in reverse order, the new Adam was fashioned from the woman. He was, as had been foretold, the immaculate 'seed of the woman,' deriving His manhood from the substance of the Virgin Mary."[3]

Mary's special prerogatives are intimately involved in the doctrine of the Incarnation itself.[4] In consequence, those who reject the true nature of this ineffable mystery, find it the most natural thing to repudiate the Virginity of Mary. The historical fact of the supernatural birth of Christ is asserted in the Gospels and in the Creed, but for Rationalists, neither Creeds nor Gospels have any value. Heresies centering about the miraculous conception of Jesus are as old as Christianity itself. In Newman's time the doctrine was not singled out for special attack, though it was not necessarily accepted by the Liberal element. Shortly after the death of the great English Cardinal, Harnack published a dissertation, maintaining the thesis that many articles of the Apostles' Creed are of late origin and some of them distinctly go beyond Apostolic teaching.[5] Among these articles was, he claimed, that of the Virginal Birth, which he called a "Gnostic invention".[6] In 1924 a bitter controversy was waged in the Anglican Church and in the American Episcopal branch on that very question. The Modernists, as they were styled, maintained the natural birth of Jesus against the Fundamentalists, who adhered to the Christian dogma. It can be seen at a glance that this dispute, as well as those that have gone before, has a deeper root than the mere denial of a given

---

[3] P. S. II, 31. This was preached in 1832.

[4] Dev. 415.

[5] *Expositor*, 1895, I, p. 401.

[6] *Lehrbuch der Dogmengeschichte*, I, p. 551, note.

mystery of faith. The Rationalists start out with *a priori* principles that Christ is not God, that the supernatural, and hence the miraculous, does not exist. Scripture is not to be explained, but explained away.

Newman treats the question though rather succinctly, as he found no particular need of insisting on this dogma, rather generally accepted by those whom he intended his *Letter to Pusey* and his sermons. Pusey, for example, never for a moment doubted about the mystery of the Incarnation, nor the manner in which it was brought about. Consequently, the *Letter* carries no exposition of the Divine Maternity as such nor of the Virginity of the Blessed Virgin. The *Notes on Athanasius*, however, give an exposition of the perpetual Virginity of Mary, the comparison between her flesh and the earth of Paradise from which Adam was formed. Before investigating the doctrine of Newman, a few preliminary considerations on the nature and importance of the dogma are inserted.

II. Nature and Importance of the Dogma

Frequently false ideas arise on what is meant by the Virginal Birth. Some identify it with a special meaning attached to the Immaculate Conception; in ignorance, they apply it to the Blessed Virgin instead of to our Lord, thinking that she was conceived in a miraculous manner. The Virginal Birth is proper to our Lord alone. The term means simply that Christ had no human father, that up to His birth, Mary remained a virgin. Further, the birth of Christ was miraculous, Mary remaining a Virgin *in partu* and continuing thus to the end of her life. Hence, the doctrine of Mary's Virginity contains really three distinct dogmas: Mary was *Virgo ante partum, in partu,* and *post partum.*[7]

Every dogma taken in itself is fundamental, and the mere fact of its denial overthrows the whole structure of Christianity. The doctrine of Mary's virginity is not necessarily connected with the divine maternity, though it is a most

---

[7] Cf. *America,* Jan. 5, 1924, p. 273.

suitable concomitant. It has had a determining and often far-reaching influence on Christological teaching; nevertheless, it may be admitted that the divinity of Christ does not stand or fall with His virginal birth.[8] In fact, Suarez is of the opinion that Christ could have been born of the natural union of man and woman and still be God; generation has as its end that of a person and not merely that of a nature. Through this co-operation it could never have terminated in the production of a divine Person.[9] However, mere Christian sense recoils from such a thought as being unsuitable to the infinite purity and sanctity of God. We may now proceed to examine Newman's doctrine.

III. Preparation for the Virgin Birth

From age to age the Jews looked out for the coming of the Messias, who was to set all things right. It matters little in the present study what role He was expected to play in this capacity, whether He was to be a great temporal ruler who would restore the ancient splendor of Israel, or a Judge who would destroy the world by fire and then repeople it with a new race of Israel, dominating over all other nations. Few really had a correct notion of the spiritual kingdom which He would establish. All of the Jews were occupied by the two great questions: *When* was He to come, and *Who* would be His Mother? "It had been told them from the first, not that He should come from heaven, but that He should be born of a woman. At the time of the fall of Adam, God had said that the seed of the Woman should bruise the serpent's head. Who, then, was to be that Woman thus significantly pointed out to the fallen race of Adam? At the end of many centuries, it was further revealed to the Jews that the great Messias, or Christ, ... should be horn of their race, and of one particular tribe. ... From that time every woman of the tribe hoped to have the

---

[8] Cf. McCormick, "The Doctrine of the Virginal Birth and Some of Its Consequences," *Eccl. Review,* May 1924, p. 497.

[9] Suarez, *Opera Omnia,* Ed. Vives, 1860, xix, p. 172–173.

privilege of herself being the Mother of the Messias, or Christ; for it stood to reason, since He was so great, the Mother must be great and good and blessed too. Hence it was, among other reasons, that they thought so highly of the marriage state; because, not knowing the mystery of the miraculous conception of the Christ when He was actually to come, they thought that the marriage rite was the ordinance necessary for His coming."[10]

Such were the ideas of the Jews concerning the coming of the Messias and the mode of His coming. It may be objected to this exposition that the Jews had the prophecy of Isaias concerning the Virgin Birth of Christ. That may be true, but it cannot be presumed that all seized the full significance of it, for the sign promised to Achaz was indeed so wonderful, that only after the accomplishment of the prophecy was its meaning grasped by faithful souls. A parallel of that may be found in St. John, who calls attention to the fact that Christ's triumphal entry into Jerusalem had been foretold, but the disciples did not realize its accomplishment until after the Resurrection of Jesus. "These things His disciples did not know at the first; but when Jesus was glorified, then they remembered that these things were written of Him, and that they had done these things to Him."[11] So, in like manner, the Jews easily overlooked the significance of the oracle.

She who in reality had been chosen to become Mother of the great King was too humble and too pure to entertain the desire of the divine maternity. She had been inspired to serve God in the state of virginity, a condition practically unknown to the Jews and considered almost a dishonor.[12] She prized her virginity more than the dignity of Mother of God, and accepted the latter only when she had been assured by the angel that she would not be obliged to revoke her purpose of leading a virginal life. Declining the grace of maternity, she gained it by means of a higher grace. It is in this sense that Newman

---

[10] M. D. I, 42–43; cf. P. S. V, 89–90.

[11] John 12:16.

[12] M. D. I, 43; Mix. 352.

interprets the words of Elizabeth: "Blessed art thou among women, and blessed is the fruit of thy womb," for she had become the Mother of God in a way far different from that in which pious women for so many ages had expected Him.[13] Following the suggestions of St. Jerome, Newman sets the Blessed Mary as the model of the virginal life. Her virginity, added to her faith and obedience, had merited for her the divine maternity.[14]

IV. THE FACT OF THE VIRGIN BIRTH: VIRGO ANTE PARTUM

The fact of the miraculous birth of Christ is sufficiently attested to by Scripture. St. Luke states explicitly that Mary was a virgin when the Angel appeared to her and announced the designs of God upon her. "And the Virgin's name was Mary. ... The Holy Ghost shall come upon thee, and the power of the Most High shall overshadow thee. And therefore also the Holy which shall be born of thee shall be called the Son of God."[15] It is not at all unlikely that Luke should have received this account as well as others from the Virgin Mother herself, in whom these things were accomplished, or at least he may have derived it from some secondary source received from Mary's own relation.[16]

In Matthew the explanation is given to St. Joseph, who was troubled, not knowing what to do, when he found his holy spouse with child. The Angel said to him: "That which is conceived of her is of the Holy Ghost. She shall bring forth a son and thou shalt call his name Jesus."[17] For Newman, the authority of Matthew is sufficient to demonstrate the meaning of Isaias' prophecy, no matter what the interpretation of the Hebrew word is that conveys this doctrine. Scripture for him was the highest authority while he was an Anglican, and here

---

[13] Ibid.

[14] Diff. II, 41.

[15] Luke 1:27–35.

[16] Cf. *Expositor*, Fifth Series, 1895, Vol. I, pp. 404–405.

[17] Matt. 1:20–21.

he found an explicit interpretation of a text that offered difficulties for others. The version of the text in St. Matthew leaves no doubt that it is a virgin who should be with child and should bear Him who is Emmanuel. Though the Hebrew expression as it occurs in Isaias[18] may mean any young woman whether married or not, it matters little, for the context is clear that God was announcing something very special. He was going to give Achaz a sign; evidently there is nothing extraordinary in that a young woman should conceive and bring forth a son. But it had never been heard that a virgin should be with child and should bring forth a son who is the Son of God. Only by Almighty power could such a wonder be wrought; this, in truth, would be a sign.[19]

The Prophet then had predicted that a Virgin was to be Mother of the promised Messias. She was to be a Virgin also when she gave birth to Him, for the act of parturition was no more contradictory to virginity than the act of conception.[20]

V. Its Propriety

Newman emphasizes the propriety of the miraculous conception of Christ, as becoming the holiness and purity of God. By one man sin entered into the world, and not a human being comes into existence without the taint of original sin upon him. Two exceptions alone are to be found: Jesus, and Mary for the sake of Jesus. When the Word of Life was to come into the world, the Holy Ghost was to display the creative power by which in the beginning Eve was formed; the Holy Child thus conceived by the power of the Most High was to be clear from all infection of the forbidden fruit; He was to be

---

[18] Is. 7:14. V. M. I, 112. For a discussion of this text cf. Morgott, op. cit. p. 203 sqq.

[19] Some wish to assert that the son spoken of is either the son of Achaz or of the prophet. How could that be a sign? In what manner would it have been fulfilled? Cf. Morgott, op. cit. pp. 208, 209; *America*, Jan. 5, 1924, p. 274.

[20] Ath. II, 204.

sinless and incorruptible.[21] The Incarnate Word was to be the "immaculate Son of a Virgin Mother."[22]

Because He was the All-holy Son of God, He had to come to us in a manner suitable to the All-holy. He condescended to be born, but He would be born in a manner different from other men. "He took our nature upon Him, but not our sin; taking our nature in a way above nature. Did He, then, come from heaven in the clouds? did He frame a body for Himself out of the dust of the earth? No, He was as other men, made of a woman, that He might take on Him not another nature, but the nature of man."[23]

Apart from the authority of Scripture, Newman seeks for the suitableness of the Virgin Birth and finds it primarily in the holiness of God, who loves purity and therefore chose for His divine Son a Virgin-Mother.[24]

But a still more cogent reason for Newman lay in its practical necessity. As an Anglican, he could not have reconciled himself to the thought that the mere fact of the hypostatic union itself would have precluded the contraction of original sin. Had Christ been born in the ordinary way, He would have been unclean. Newman develops this argument at length:[25] "It was ordained, indeed, that the Eternal Word should come into the world by the ministration of a woman; but born in the way of the flesh He could not be. Mankind is a fallen race; ever since the fall there has been a 'fault and corruption of the nature of every man that naturally is engendered of the offspring of Adam; ... so that the flesh lusteth always contrary to the spirit, and therefore in every person born into this world it deserveth God's wrath and damnation.' And the Apostle says that concupiscence and lust hath of itself the nature of sin. 'That which is born of the flesh, is flesh.' 'Who can bring a clean thing out of an unclean?' 'How can he be clean that is

---

[21] P. S. II, 141.

[22] Ibid. V, 104.

[23] P. S. V, 89.

[24] Ibid. VI, 187.

[25] Ibid. V, 90.

Mary Ever-Virgin

born of a woman?' No one is born into the world without sin, or can rid himself of the sin of his birth except by a second birth through the Spirit. How, then, could the Son of God have come a Holy Savior had He come as other men? How could He have atoned for our sins, who Himself had guilt? or cleansed our hearts who was impure Himself? or raised up our heads who was Himself the son of shame? Surely, any such messenger had needed a Savior for his own disease, and to such a one would apply the proverb, 'Physician, heal thyself.' Priests among men are they who 'have to offer' first for their own sins, and then for the people's, but He, coming as the immaculate Lamb of God, and the all-prevailing Priest ... came by a new and living way, by which He alone has come, and which alone became Him."[26]

The Prophet Isaias had been the first to announce this great event. "The Lord Himself shall give you a sign; Behold a Virgin shall conceive and bear a Son and shall call His name Emmanuel." And accordingly St. Matthew, after citing this text, declares its fulfillment in the case of the Blessed Mary. "All this was done that it might be fulfilled which was spoken by the prophet." And, further, two Angels, one to Mary, the other to Joseph, declare who the adorable Agent was by whom this miracle was wrought. Because He was incarnate by the Holy Ghost of the Virgin Mary, therefore He was Jesus, a "Savior from sin." Because God the Holy Ghost wrought miraculously, therefore was her Son a "Holy Thing", the Son of God, Jesus, the heir of an everlasting kingdom.

"Since the body of Jesus is the fruit of a miraculous conception, He could cleanse us from corruption, make us partakers of His divine nature and raise us up to that immaculate purity and the fulness of grace that are in Him."[27]

The text of St. Paul to the Hebrews, "But Christ, being come a high priest of the good things to come, by a greater and more

---

[26] Had Christ come in the ordinary way, the hypostatic union would have precluded the contraction of original sin, though Newman seems to imply the contrary.

[27] P. S. V, 93.

perfect tabernacle not made with hands, that is, not of this creation,"[28] serves Newman also as a proof of Mary's virginity. This tabernacle, greater than anything earthly, is Christ's pure and sinless flesh, miraculously formed of the substance of the Virgin Mary and therefore called "not of this building" or, as Newman puts it with the Catholic version, "not of this creation," for it was a new creation by which He was formed, by the descent of the Holy Ghost. This was the new and perfect tabernacle into which Christ entered.[29]

Elsewhere Newman expresses the same thought of Christ's freedom from sin, in taking upon Himself human nature. "He had not fellowship with sin. It was impossible that He should. Therefore, since our nature was corrupt since Adam's fall, He did not come in the way of nature. He did not clothe Himself in that corrupt flesh which Adam's race inherits. He came by a miracle, so as to take on Him our imperfections without having any share in our sinfulness. He was not born as other men are. All Adam's children are children of wrath; so our Lord came as the Son of Man, but not the son of sinful Adam. He had no earthly father; He abhorred to have one. The thought may not be suffered that He should have been the son of shame and guilt. He came by a new and living way."[30]

From this it must not be assumed that Newman held that Christ would have been subjected to original sin had he not been born of a virgin. Such a thing is clearly impossible, for any sin, even original, is wholly incompatible with the hypostatic union. Mary herself by an extraordinary grace of God was conceived without original sin. Had it not been for a special preservation, she who was conceived according to the common law of nature, would have borne the curse inherited by every child of Adam. Should the human nature of Christ, conceived and formed in the womb of Mary, have borne the same curse pronounced on man? was it preserved sinless only by the grace of the hypostatic union? Such would have been the case had

---

[28] Hebr. 9:11.

[29] P. S. VI, 61.

[30] P. S. II, 31.

His conception not been virginal. It is impossible that there be any sin to taint the purity and holiness of the God-Man, and yet, had He been born in the ordinary manner, only the union of the divinity with the humanity would have prevented the contraction of the sinful stain.

Newman grants the possibility of Christ's being born in the ordinary way, but hastens to add that it would not have been fitting.[31] From this disposition of Providence, he deduces in the same place the propriety of the Immaculate Conception, so that He who was to take away the sin of man, should be far removed from every sin and every shadow of sin.

Heretics had assumed from St. Paul's declaration of Christ's being in the "likeness of sinful flesh"[32] that Christ did not have a human nature like ours, but something unsubstantial and hence, of course, not liable to contract original sin. Newman repeats that Christ did not come in the clouds, or derive His body from celestial matter, but that He was true man, that had really taken unto Himself sinful flesh, the flesh of Adam's race, but that His Mother was set apart, and He had selected and set apart for Himself the elements of body and soul which He united to Himself from the first origin of their existence, "hallowing them by His divinity, spiritualizing them, filling them with light and purity."[33]

It was fitting that He should thus come in the likeness of the fallen creature whom He was coming to restore, suffering all the infirmities of our nature, but having no relation with its guilt; the offspring of the old race, but the beginning of the new creation of God.[34] And so, separated from all defilement, the human nature could become a divine leaven of holiness for the new birth and spiritual life of those who would wish to profit by the Redemption.[35]

---

[31] S. N. 300; P. S. VI, 79.

[32] Rom. 8:3.

[33] P. S. II, 32.

[34] Ibid. 30–31.

[35] Ibid. VI, 79.

VI. VIRGO IN PARTU

Mary was a virgin also in the birth of Jesus. If the conception of Christ was miraculous, there is no difficulty in admitting that His birth should have been the same. Newman does not consider this question independently of Mary's virginity *ante partum* except to explain its consequences in the Blessed Virgin and the rest of womankind.

She had not contracted original sin nor did Jesus have aught to do with sin; hence it was but proper that Mary should not inherit the curse pronounced upon the first Eve in the garden. Eve and all other women were to bring forth their children in sorrow, but Mary was to be spared this suffering. Hence, she is represented as kneeling at the manger, adoring her divine Child.[36]

Through Mary, the curse pronounced on Eve is turned into a blessing; the very act of child-bearing becomes the means by which salvation is conveyed to the world. The very taint of the birth-sin admitted of a cure. God could have cast us forever from Him and had other creatures to serve Him, but instead, He sent us His Son, who transforms us and sanctifies all that belongs to us, our reason, our affections, pursuits, and relations in life.[37]

In bearing our Lord, the Blessed Virgin removed or at least lightened the special disgrace which woman inherited for seducing Adam. God had told Eve that her husband would rule over her, and down through the centuries until the coming of Christ, this prediction was strikingly fulfilled. Even under the patriarchal and Jewish dispensations, polygamy and divorce were tolerated.[38] Woman's condition was infinitely worse among the heathens. Man always utilized his strength to tyrannize over the weaker sex and debased himself, making it the slave of every cruel or evil purpose. Thus, man degraded

---

[36] S. N. 300; Cf. Ess. II, 440.

[37] P. S. II, 129.

[38] Ibid. VI, 187.

himself by her who originally tempted him, and she had to suffer from him who was seduced.

But Christ, born of a woman, vindicated the rights and honor of His Mother. Woman remains inferior and subject to man, yet she is no longer his slave, but his companion and helpmate. On her was bestowed a special blessing insofar as woman was the way appointed for the entrance of the Savior into the world. The "woman shall be saved through the Childbearing."[39] Hence the union of man and woman is restored to its original dignity, elevated to the rank of a sacrament and becomes the symbol of the mystic union of Christ and His Church.[40]

VII. VIRGO POST PARTUM

The third dogma connected with Mary's virginity concerns the period after the birth of Jesus. Mary was for ever the immaculate and blessed Virgin, the "ever-Virgin." The Church has been persuaded in all ages that she continued in the same virginity and must be regarded as the ever-Virgin.[41] Heretics attempted at various times to reject the perpetual virginity of Mary, because as they claimed there was no record of it in Holy Writ, but this idea of her virginity seems so directly conformable to elementary Christian sentiment that the mere suggestion of the contrary is repulsive. Two expressions in Scripture, however, seem to militate against this dogma. There is question in no less than ten places of the "brethren of our Lord."[42] The *Proto-Evangelium* speaks of these as sons of Joseph by a first marriage; Hegesippus explains that they are in reality cousins of our Lord, but according to Jewish usage were called brethren; this is the explanation generally accepted.[43]

---

[39] I Tim. 2:15.

[40] P. S. II, 130–131.

[41] Ath. II, 205.

[42] Matt. 12:46–50; 13:55; Mark 3:31–35; 6:3; Luke 8:19–21; John 2:12; 7:3–10; Acts 1:14; I Cor. 9:5; Gal. 1:19.

[43] Cf. Niessen, op. cit. p. 161 sqq.; Neubert, op. cit. p. 198 sqq.

Newman does not concern himself with this phase of the question, but confines his attention to the text of St. Matthew[44] adduced by adversaries of the Catholic dogma. The evangelist says of St. Joseph, "And he knew her not till she brought forth her first-born son." The point of contention is the word "till." After the birth of Jesus, as Newman sees it, intercourse became, as it were, morally impossible, and hence there would be no room for denial. If we suppose the Evangelist to have said that Joseph knew her not "till her death", this would certainly imply that he never knew her.[45] Newman explains that the word "till" need not imply a termination at a certain point of time, but may be given as information up to a certain point, and after that there can be no doubt. "Supposing the Evangelist thought the very notion shocking that Joseph should have considered the Blessed Virgin as his wife, *after* he was witness of her bearing the Son of God, he would only say that the vision had its effect upon him up to that moment when the idea was monstrous."[46] If a sinner prayed every day up to the time of his conversion, one could not conclude that he left off prayer once he was converted.

The argument may be further confirmed from passages in Scripture with a similar expression.

Thus, in Genesis,[47] the Lord, speaking to Jacob, says: "I will be thy keeper whithersoever thou goest, and will bring thee back into this land; neither will I leave thee, till I shall have accomplished all that I have said." Did God forsake His servant after He had restored him to his home? In Deuteronomy we read of the place where Moses was buried, "and no man hath known of this sepulcher to this day."[48] Elsewhere, "And Samuel saw Saul no more till the day of his death."[49] and "Therefore

---

[44] Matt. 1:25.
[45] Ath. II, 272.
[46] Ath. II, 206.
[47] 28:15.
[48] 34:6
[49] I Sam. 15:35.

MARY EVER-VIRGIN

Michol ... had no child to the day of her death."[50] Again, in St. Matthew: "Behold, I am with you all days to the consummation of the world."[51] The words of Psalm 109, "The Lord said to my Lord: Sit thou at my right hand: until I make thy enemies thy footstool," likewise serve as evidence on the point under consideration. Newman considers this last citation as particularly remarkable because the school of Marcellus wished thereby to prove that our Lord's kingdom would have an end.[52] If our Lord is King before He has subdued His enemies, is there not greater reason for presuming that He will be King after His conquest.

These texts, then, serve to bring out the force of the word "till" in Scripture and particularly show that its use in Matthew does not connote the slightest suggestion of infidelity on the part of the virginal St. Joseph.

Furthermore, Newman finds an adequate explanation in the mere fact of the divine maternity. If Mary is the Mother of God, then the Evangelist would instinctively feel that a violation of her virginity is an impossible idea. Pearson, whose authority Newman here follows,[53] gives four reasons, which are those also indicated by St. Thomas.[54]

The pre-eminence and dignity of the Mother of God. The denial of her virginity is an insult offered to Mary's honor and holiness. It is inconceivable that the noblest of creatures should have shown herself ungrateful for having her virginity preserved in giving birth to Jesus, that she could have ever renounced it. How could she, the purest, the holiest of creatures, inundated with all graces, preserved from original sin and inclination to sin—how could she have yielded to a love other than that of God?

The special honor and reverence due to her Son required

---

[50] II Sam. 6:23.

[51] Matt. 28:20.

[52] Thus Scripture would be made to contradict itself, for the Angel had said "And of His kingdom there shall be no end." Luke 1:33.

[53] Ath. II, 205.

[54] Summa III, q. 28.

that Mary should remain a virgin. He who was the Only-begotten of the Father should also be the only son of His Mother Mary.

The regard of the Holy Ghost, who came upon her and was the active principle in the Incarnation, could not tolerate that the sanctified womb of the Virgin should be outraged by the conception of any mere mortal.

The singular goodness and piety of Joseph, who is called by Scripture a "just man", would fill him with such a respect for his holy spouse, in whom great wonders had been accomplished, that the mere notion of desecrating the sanctuary of the Eternal Word would not even come to his mind.

VIII. Testimony of Antiquity

Apart from Scripture, Antiquity also offers its testimony to the belief of the first Christians in Mary's virginity. Newman gives ample suggestions on the point. The authority of the Fathers readily puts to naught the supposition of Protestants of recent times, when they affirm that the belief of Christians in the virginity of Mary began only towards the second century under the influence of Docetism, as claimed by Herzog,[55] or of Gnosticism, as maintained by Harnack.[56] Unfortunately for the theory of these Rationalists, the first Father to oppose Docetism was also the first to call attention to the mystery by which a Savior was given to the world. Ignatius not merely says that Jesus was truly born of a Virgin,[57] but also affirms three mysteries unknown to the prince of this world, namely, the virginity of Mary, the birth and the death of Jesus Christ.[58] In treating of the Second Eve, Newman calls attention to the testimony of Justin, who particularly insists, in the parallel between Mary and Eve, that Eve, being a virgin, conceives and

---

[55] *Revue de l'histoire et de la littérature religieuse*, T. XVI, (1907) p. 483–496.
[56] *Lehrbuch der Dogmengeschichte*, I, 551.
[57] Ad Smyrn. n. 1. P. G. 5:708.
[58] Ad Magn. n. 19; P. G. 5:660.

brings forth death; Mary, on the other hand, also a virgin, brings forth life.[59] Tertullian uses the same language; Irenaeus, if anything, is still more insistent on the fact that Eve, a virgin, bound by incredulity, what Mary, a virgin, unloosed by faith; the Virgin Mary was to be the advocate of the virgin Eve; a virgin's disobedience is corrected by a Virgin's obedience. Yet these three Fathers also testify to the same belief elsewhere.[60] Irenaeus as well as Tertullian waged war against Docetism.[61] Tertullian, however, seems to find no difficulty in admitting that the Mother of God, who was *Virgo ante partum* and *in partu*, need not have been such *post partum*.

In citing the authority of the Fathers on the perpetual virginity of Mary, Newman emphasizes two aspects, first, that they call her ever-Virgin and, secondly, taken up as they are with the parallelism between Christ and Adam, Mary and Eve, they compare the Virgin's flesh from which Christ's substance was drawn, to the pure earth of Paradise out of which Adam was formed.

The title ever-Virgin occurs for the first time in the fourth century, though in all the preceding centuries the idea was expressed. St. Athanasius associates intimately the divinity of Jesus with the virginity of Mary when he says: "Let those who deny that the Son is from the Father and proper to His substance deny also that He took true human flesh of Mary ever-Virgin."[62] And, again: "She, the Mother of the Lord and ever-Virgin, when she knew what had been accomplished in her, said: Behold, from henceforth all generations shall call me blessed."[63]

St. Epiphanius writes against the heretics who blaspheme the name of the Virgin-Mother: "For indeed I know not whom I perceive contemplating anything against the most holy and

---

[59] Cf. Diff. II, 33.

[60] Cf. Adv. Haer. IV, 33, II; P. G. 7:1080. Also P. G. 7:549, 950–953.

[61] Tert. Adv. Valent. 27; De Carne Christi 20. Cf. Alès, *Théologie de Tertullien*, p. 194–196.

[62] Cf. Orat. II, n. 70. P. G. 26:296.

[63] Fragm. in Luc. P. G. 27:1394.

ever-Virgin Mary and attacking her honor by some shamefnl opinion."⁶⁴ About the time when Jerome was writing his treatise against Helvidius on the perpetual virginity of Mary, Didymus the Blind expresses himself thus: "For He who by an unspeakable light shone from all eternity, in later times, because of His goodness towards men, was born in an ineffable manner from the ever-Virgin."⁶⁵ Rufinus has the same language: "The Word, only-begotten God, became man, taking a body from Mary ever-Virgin, creating a rational soul for Himself, of that same substance as ours, and was born a man of the ever-Virgin."⁶⁶

St. Leo, the champion of the Incarnation, says: "Christ, born of the virginal womb, should have the form of man and the truth of His Mother's body. Perhaps the thought comes to some that our Lord Jesus Christ was not of our nature because the Angel sent to Mary said to the ever-Virgin: The Holy Ghost shall come upon thee, etc."⁶⁷ Cassian is similarly explicit: "We confess the Lord our God, Jesus Christ the only Son of God, who was born of the Father from all eternity, and was born for us of the Holy Spirit and of Mary, ever-Virgin."⁶⁸

The Fathers also love to dwell on the comparison between the Virgin's flesh and the pure earth of Paradise out of which Adam was formed. Thus, St. Athanasius calls Mary the "fallow earth."⁶⁹ Irenaeus, explaining the text of Isaias against Ebionites and Jews, insists on his recapitulation theory. "As Adam was formed from the earth, still virgin ... and had his substance ... so, recapitulating Adam in Himself, the Word existing from Mary, who was still a virgin, rightly undertook the recapitulation of Adam. ... If Adam was taken from the earth, then the Word had to be taken from the Virgin."⁷⁰ Tertullian

---

⁶⁴ Haer. 78 n. 5; P. G. 42:705.

⁶⁵ Trin. I, 27; P. G. 39:405.

⁶⁶ Fid. I, 43; P. L. 21:1146.

⁶⁷ Ep. 28, 2; P. L. 54:76

⁶⁸ Inc. I, 5; P. L. 50:26.

⁶⁹ Orat. II, 7.

⁷⁰ Haer. III, 21; P. G. 7:954, 955.

has the same language: "That virgin earth, not yet watered by rains, nor impregnated by showers, from which man was formed in the beginning, from which Christ is now born according to the flesh a Virgin."[71]

St. Ambrose sums up the idea very tersely: "Adam from the virgin earth, Christ from a Virgin."[72] St. Theodotus cries out: "O earth unsown, yet bearing a salutary fruit, O Virgin, who didst surpass the very Paradise of Eden."[73] Innumerable other passages might be adduced confirming the same doctrine.[74] There is hardly a writer in antiquity who does not simultaneously speak of the divine maternity and the virginity of Mary.

By her sublime purity Mary becomes the model of all virgins. Prom the earliest times down to the present and on to the end of the world, thousands upon thousands follow in the footsteps of the *Virgo Virginum.* "Adducentur Regi virgines post eam." Mary guides them, she draws them by her example, her charms and by the special lights and graces which she obtains for them from her divine Son.[75]

---

[71] Adv. Jud. 13.

[72] In Lucam IV, 7; P. L. 15:1614.

[73] Cf. Ath. II, 206.

[74] Cf. ibid. 204–207.

[75] Cf. Berulle, *Oeuvres* (Migne) col. 451.

CHAPTER IV
Dignity of Mary

THE dignity of a person results from his state of life and the prerogatives attached to it. The loftier such a calling or state, the greater the dignity of the one possessing such an office. All Christians, by their elevation to the supernatural life, have a high dignity, but there is one who is exalted far above any other mere creature. It is the Blessed Virgin, who was given a twofold function on this earth. From this function must be judged her dignity. She was the Mother of God, and by the fact of her co-operation in the Redemption she becomes mother of men, for she is the Second Eve. These are the two great centers of Mary's prerogatives and it is from this fact that Newman shows how Mary's dignity rests on a solid basis: first of all, because of her relations with the Divine Word on this earth; secondly, from the explicit exaltation of her as demonstrated by the Apocalypse.

I. Relation to Eve

Newman transports us to Paradise and by gradual steps leads us to contemplate the lofty position held by the Virgin Mary. Mary had come as the Second Eve to repair the fault of the first and thereby co-operated in the restoration of the human race. But were it possible to suppose that Adam and Eve had remained faithful and had thereby secured for their descendants grace in this life and glory in the world to come, what thanks and honor would have been rendered them from age to age? The story of their steadfastness in obedience, their fidelity, the vigilance and purity of Eve in particular, would ever have been a welcome theme to the generations rendered happy by them. Such sentiments are perfectly natural and legitimate. Every nation has its heroes, celebrated in song and verse. Should not the human race as a whole have its own also?

But, alas! this happy lot was not to be realized. Adam fell, and with him the millions and millions who are born into the world. Newman remarks that if the human race is not continually invoking maledictions on the head of the first man, it is owing "to the exigencies of our penal life, our state of perpetual change, and the ignorance and unbelief incurred by the fall"; besides, though we are fallen, because of the hopefulness of our nature we feel more pride in our national great men, than dejection at our national disasters.[1]

In the Church of God, it is the Saints who by the sanctity of their lives attract our attention more than the misfortunes incidental to the fall of the race. Not only the Saints, but even the ordinary Christian, elevated to the supernatural life, has a high dignity. What, then, must be the dignity of her who was the only near earthly relative of the Son of God?

II. Elevation of Christians in General

If we look to Scripture, we see at once, particularly in the Epistles of St. Paul, a strong insistence on the benefits which came to man as a result of the Incarnation. Christ not merely redeemed from sin, but restored fallen man to his pristine dignity of child of God and heir of heaven, though certain privileges conferred at the creation were not returned with the supernatural gifts. Newman tells us that this truth was held by Christians from the first, but was less perfectly realized and not publicly recognized until the controversies with the Arians brought out the doctrine more precisely. This deification of the human nature is an important phase of St. Athanasius' theology.[2] The Second Person could receive no additional glory by becoming man, but human nature which he assumed, was

---

[1] Diff. II, 51.

[2] Dev. 140.

raised and glorified in Him. Christ becomes the principle of spiritual life for the elect, who become as it were divine sons, gods, for He communicates to them a deified nature.[3]

In proportion to the depth to which Christ descended, in that degree we are elevated above our mere natures. Can any mystery be so great, any grace so overpowering as manifested in the Incarnation and death of the Eternal Son? No consequence is too great to follow from such a marvellous dispensation. In one of his Christmas sermons delivered as an Anglican, Newman is eloquent in describing the heights to which the elect on earth and the Saints have been elevated by this wonderful mystery: "Men we remain, but not mere men, but gifted with a measure of all those perfections which Christ has in fulness, partaking each in his own degree of His Divine Nature so fully, that the only reason (so to speak) why His saints are not really like Him, is that it is impossible—that He is the Creator, and they His creatures, yet still so, that they are all but Divine, all that they can be made without violating the incommunicable majesty of the Most High. Surely in proportion to His glory is His power of glorifying; so that to say that through Him we shall be made all *but* gods—though it is to say, that we are infinitely below the adorable Creator—still is to say, and truly, we shall be higher than every other being in the world ... that is, ... in heaven and in Christ."[4]

Such, then, is the exalted condition to which we, ordinary mortals, regenerated by Christ, have been raised. Who can conceive the glorification in heaven of the Saints who have led such holy lives on earth and whose works follow them? "As we call them by their earthly names, so we contemplate them in their earthly characters and histories. Their acts, callings, and relations below, are types and anticipations of their present mission above." And because of this, they are entitled to a claim on our memories and gratitude.[5]

Shall we say less of the Virgin Mother of God, who is chief

---

[3] Cf. Ath. II, 193 sqq.

[4] P. S. VIII, 253.

[5] Diff. II, 52.

of all the followers of the Lamb, of her who is the first of created beings after the humanity of Christ?⁶ Has she had no part in our redemption to merit our thanks and veneration?

III. MARY'S DIGNITY AS SHOWN BY HER RELATIONS WITH JESUS; HER KNOWLEDGE ALSO A RESULT OF THIS, ACCORDING TO NEWMAN

Following the thought of the spiritual writer Segneri, Newman lays down the principle that God might easily have made a better world, etc., but it was not possible to make a greater Mother than the Virgin Mary.⁷ If Christ is the first-born by nature, Mary is the same by adoption, for all that her divine Son has by nature, she possesses by participation, because of her close proximity to the Incarnate Word. She was chosen of all creatures to be the only one whom the Son of God was bound by nature to revere and obey; she was the one appointed to train Him and educate Him as He grew in wisdom and stature.⁸

Other Saints that are honored in Scripture are presented as mere instruments fulfilling God's designs; they partake mystically of Christ, but Mary is so near to God, for "Christ derived His manhood from her and so had an especial unity of nature with her."⁹ How difficult it is to contemplate this wondrous relationship between God and Mary; though brought so close to the Divinity, she remains a creature. "She seems to lack her fitting place in our limited understanding." An unspeakable grace is hers, that a daughter of man becomes the Mother of God.

The relations of Jesus with His Holy Mother throughout His mortal life are delicately described by Newman: "He took the substance of His human flesh from her, and clothed in it, He lay within her; and He bore it about with Him after birth, as a sort

---

⁶ Dev. 434, 435.

⁷ Ibid. 434.

⁸ P. S. II, 132.

⁹ Ibid. 135.

of badge and witness, that He, though God, was hers. He was nursed and tended by her; He was suckled by her; He lay in her arms. As time went on He ministered to her and obeyed her. He lived with her for thirty years, in one house, with an uninterrupted intercourse, and with only the saintly Joseph to share it with Him. She was the witness of His growth, of His joys, of His sorrows, of His prayers; she was blest with His smile, with the touch of His hand, with the whisper of His affection, with the expression of His thoughts and feelings, for that length of time."[10]

Because she is the Mother of our Lord, she comes nearer to Him than any other creature on earth; more than that, she is nearer than the angels, nearer even than the Seraphim, who surround His throne and cry continually: Holy, Holy, Holy. Nay, these very angels honor her as their Queen; hence, she is superior to them in dignity, though inferior in nature. Newman sees her superiority clearly demonstrated in Holy Writ. Few of the angels are known to us by name, and yet two of them, St. Gabriel and St. Michael, are associated with Mary in the history of the Incarnation. St. Gabriel is the heavenly messenger who salutes her as "full of grace" and "blessed among women." Usually the angels accepted a worship from the men whom they visited to communicate some divine message, but here the case is reversed. Gabriel offers this humble and modest virgin, his tribute of homage and praise, and thereafter makes known to her the mystery in which she was to have a great share.[11]

St. Michael also had a ministry to her on the birth of her divine Son. Scarcely had Jesus been born when Herod sought to take the Child's life. Newman sees Michael and his angels, who fought against the dragon, as the real guardians of Mother and Child; it was they who came to the rescue when the evil spirit persecuted her; it was they who prevailed against the dragon. In heaven as well as on earth, Mary has hosts of angels to do her service, because she is their Queen.[12]

---

[10] Mix. 362.

[11] M. D. I, 28.

[12] Cf. Apoc. XII. M. D. I, 29.

Since Mary's dignity is so great from her relation with the Godhead, Newman concludes that nothing is too high for her to whom God owes His human life; no exuberance of grace, no excess of glory. The fulness of the Godhead ought to flow into her, that she may be a figure of the incommunicable sanctity, beauty, and glory of God Himself; that she may be the Mirror of Justice, the Mystical Rose, the Tower of Ivory, the House of Gold, the Morning Star. She becomes the Queen of Heaven, the Refuge of sinners, the Comforter of the afflicted. Angels and prophets, apostles, martyrs, all the Saints honor her and rejoice in the shadow of her throne. The heavenly King Solomon, Jesus rises up to meet His Mother, and has her sit at His right hand.[13]

Even on this earth, the intimate relation with Jesus produced its effect on her. Not only is she the Mirror of Justice reflecting the sanctity of her Divine Son, but she becomes the Seat of Wisdom, the human throne of Him who reigns in heaven. From her intercourse with Jesus, Newman supposes in her an immense knowledge, proportional to her sanctity, which had to be inconceivably great. That Newman, who carefully avoided anything which might savor of exaggeration in her regard, should have ventured such a conclusion may seem a little strange. Yet, he places in her a wisdom surpassing that of any creature and in this goes beyond what theologians generally would assert. In a sermon, preached in 1853, he maintained only a supernatural knowledge and not a physical.[14] Towards 1874, when he wrote his *Meditations and Devotions*, he went further so as to include both.[15]

Ordinarily theologians classify knowledge as beatific, infused, and acquired. *Beatific* knowledge is associated with the beatific vision, i.e., a knowledge of things as seen in God's essence, by those privileged to behold it in heaven. *Infused* knowledge is that conferred directly by God, while *acquired*, is that obtained through personal endeavor.

---

[13] Mix. 363.

[14] S. N. 107.

[15] M. D. I, 33. He does not, however, maintain a perfect knowledge in her from the first.

Newman does not pronounce himself on the question whether our Lady, while on earth, enjoyed the beatific vision at least at intervals.[16] As for infused knowledge, he places it in her from the first moment of her existence[17] and, furthermore, in a degree superior to that of any creature.[18] Adam, in the state of original justice, possessed it in a high degree; his knowledge far surpassed ours in extent, clearness, and mode of acquisition. But with the fall came ignorance which darkened the intellect. Mary, the Mother of God, by her Immaculate Conception was never deprived of original justice, it is true, but from that it may not be inferred that her intellect should have been as brilliant as that of Adam before the fall. Christ and the Blessed Virgin were free from all sin, yet they were subjected to sufferings and death, which are the consequences of sin. In like manner, it may be that Mary could have been without much of the knowledge that was not requisite to make her a worthy Mother of God. But it was most proper and reasonable that she should have had at the very beginning at least the knowledge to understand what was implied in her becoming the Mother of God.

Mary's extensive knowledge, according to Newman, was derived from her conversations with Jesus during a period of thirty years. He describes it as "so large, so profound, so diversified, and so thorough, that, though she was a poor woman without human advantages, she must, in her knowledge of creation, of the universe, and of history, have excelled the greatest of philosophers, and in her theological knowledge the greatest of theologians, and in her prophetic discernment the most favored of prophets."[19] Jesus must have explained to her the nature, the attributes, the providence and the works of Almighty God; He must have unfolded to her the eternal decrees, the purposes, and the will of God. He would

---

[16] Some authors hold this opinion, as Albert the Great, St. Bernard, Gerson, St. Bernardine of Sienna, St. Thomas of Villanova, Suarez, and others.

[17] S. N. 107.

[18] M. D. I, 33.

[19] M. D. I, 33.

even, in Newman's opinion, have explained to her the doctrines of the Church as they would be discussed and eventually defined by infallible authority. Where the knowledge of revelation would be obscure and fragmentary for the rest of mankind, Jesus would make it as clear to her as is possible to be apprehended by a mere creature. Thus, for example, she could have had a very clear notion of the mystery of the Holy Trinity.[20] Even future events would not remain hidden to her. The prophets were instructed in figures and parables, but she was face to face with Him who is Eternal Truth, who cannot deceive nor be deceived, and so could demand of Him explanations of anything not understood by her.

Most modern writers on the Blessed Virgin, well-known for their sober views, would hardly be inclined to agree with Newman on this question. Though it cannot be denied that Jesus, who is Wisdom itself, could have enlightened her on anything she desired to know, still it need not be inferred that she did inquire about matters which had no importance whatever in the fulfillment of her duty as Mother of God. In general, the principle is laid down that nothing should be presupposed in the Blessed Virgin that is not required by her dignity of Mother of God. However, Newman, even as an Anglican, was very much impressed by the lofty dignity of the Blessed Virgin, and this profound reverence was all the more accentuated when he became a Catholic, that he felt no limit could be placed to her prerogatives provided these left her always subordinate to the Divinity; it is the very same contact with her Divine Son which made her so holy, this same intercourse, he thought, ought to be the cause of the highest degree of knowledge, as well as of grace and glory.

IV. *QUID MIHI ET TIBI?*

Frequently the words of our Blessed Lord to His holy Mother at the marriage feast of Cana are taken by those who decry Catholic devotion to the Blessed Virgin, as a slight upon

---

[20] S. N. 107.

her dignity. "Woman," Jesus said to her, "what is it to Me and to thee? My hour is not yet come." Newman comments on the text, using the Revised Version, which puts it: "What have I to do with thee?" This form is accepted by many as an English rendering of the Greek original.[21] *A priori*, making abstraction entirely of the text and its possible difficulties, it must be affirmed that Mary is above all creatures, that, having the best of sons for her offspring, she should be honored and revered in a manner commensurate with her glorious position.

Newman views the question first in the light of the Fathers. St. Athanasius, with Chrysostom and Theophylact, sees here a rebuke to the Blessed Virgin. Chrysostom even seems to consider the Virgin guilty of a slight sin of vain-glory on this occasion. Athanasius holds the words as a proof of our Lord's humanity, since He appeared to decline a miracle; while other Fathers see there a reminder that He is the Son of God. Irenaeus thinks Mary was rebuked because of her eagerness to drink of His cup. This passage has ever aroused the interest of Scripture students from the days of Augustine and Chrysostom, and various explanations have been offered. Newman derives his from St. Augustine.[22]

The Modernist finds no particular difficulty in the passage, for in his view it is only after an unwonted idealization of Christ and Mary that one can conceive such a tender relationship between them as would make it hard to believe an apparent sternness of Scripture facts. At least one thing must, however, be admitted by them, that the first manifestation of Christ's power was made at the request of the Blessed Virgin.

In one place Newman considers these words, humanly speaking, as "cold and distant,"[23] but in two other passages he

---

[21] John 2:4. Cf. *Ecclesiastical Review*, Feb. 1911, XLIV, No. 2.

[22] Cf. Ath. II, 277. An article on these words provoked some discussion in the pages of the *Eccl. Rev.* during 1911 and 1912. Father Reilly, O.P., the author of the first article, maintains that the second part of the passage should be taken in conjunction with the first. This is the mode of Newman's procedure. (Cf. *Eccl. Rev.*, Vols. 44, Nos. 2, 6; 45, No. 1; 46, No. 6; 47, Nos. 1, 2, 5.)

[23] Ath. II, 277.

makes no reference to this view.[24] All through his sermons Newman makes beautiful *rapprochements* of various Scripture scenes and in this case, the marriage feast of Cana, which marks the opening of Christ's public ministry, is connected with the Last Supper, which marks its close, and in the relation of the two events he finds the solution of the problem. At the feast of Cana Jesus supplied a want miraculously and thereby showed that He was beginning a new life. The feast itself was the last scene of His old life. The expression that He used in answer to His Mother's remarks seems to imply that this change of condition is really in His thoughts. Newman paraphrases Jesus' query thus: "What is between Me and thee, My Mother, any longer? The time is fulfilled and the Kingdom of God is at hand."[25]

This scene was to mark the separation of Jesus from His Mother. "What have I to do with thee?" He asks. He had had to do with her for thirty years. She had borne Him, nursed Him, taught Him. At the age of twelve, He was still more intimately united with her, and remained subject to her until the age of thirty, but now He must part. He had intimated this eighteen years earlier, when He told her that He must be about His Father's business. The time was now come when this was to be fulfilled.

He said to her: "What have I to do with thee? Mine hour is not yet come." This would seem to imply, according to Newman, that *when* His hour was come, then He would have to do with her again as before. " 'What have I to do with thee *now?*' I have had, I shall have; but what have I to do with thee now, as before? what as yet? what *till* my hour is come?" He seems henceforth to put His Mother from His thoughts as being called to the work of a divine ministry. When His Mother and brethren waited to see Him on one occasion,[26] He seemed to answer that henceforth He had no brethren, no mother according to the flesh, that all men were His mother and

---

[24] S. D. 31 sqq., preached Feb. 26, 1843; Diff. II, 149.
[25] S. D. 32.
[26] Matt. 12:48–50.

brother and sister. The same takes place when the woman proclaimed her blessed who had borne Him in the womb. But Jesus declares that there is a greater blessedness in hearing the word of God and keeping it, than in being merely His Mother according to the flesh.[27]

The hour of Jesus is not yet come, but just before the Passion He announced that His hour was at hand.[28] And it was during the Passion that His seeming separation from Mary ended; in these solemn moments He allowed His love to appear once more, just when His Father's work was ending. We all know what were the tender words which almost immediately preceded His "It is finished." In His dying hour He looked upon His beloved Mother, commended the disciple to her and in turn confided her to the keeping of St. John.

Elsewhere in the Gospels, an expression similar to the one used at the marriage feast occurs, when for example the evil spirits cry out: "What have we to do with Thee, Jesus, Son of God?"[29] The time would come when He would reign and they would be punished; they implied that they would have to do with their Judge when the time came, but not yet. So Jesus wishes to tell His Mother that He would have to do with her again, but a temporary separation would first intervene. He seems to turn from her prayers, and still He grants her request. Newman adds the significant remark: "From this we may learn the present influence and power of the Mother of God." When Newman pronounced these words, he was just reaching the term of his doubts and difficulties relative to the Blessed Virgin.[30]

This same interpretation is taken up by Newman in his *Letter to Pusey* when he sets about to explain the Scripture passages which furnish the occasion for certain remarks of the

---

[27] Luke 11:27, 28.

[28] Matt. 26:18, 45.

[29] Mark 1:23–24; Matt. 8:29.

[30] S. D. 31.

Fathers disparaging to the Blessed Virgin.[31] The reason assigned by him is that these Scripture statements were intended to discriminate between our Lord's work as our Teacher and Redeemer and the ministrative office of His Mother.[32] When Jesus began His ministry, and during the entire period of His public life, He separated Himself from all ties of earth in order to fulfill the typical idea of Teacher and Priest. "The separation from her, with whom He had lived thirty years and more, was not to last beyond the time of His ministry. She seems to have been surprised when she first heard of it, for St. Luke says, on the occasion of His staying in the Temple, 'they understood not the word that He spoke to them.' Nay, she seems hardly to have understood it at the marriage-feast; but He, in dwelling on it more distinctly, then implied also that it was not to last long. He said, 'Woman, what have I to do with thee? My hour is not yet come'—that is, the hour of His triumph, when His Mother was to take her predestined place in His kingdom. In saying the hour was not yet come, He implied that the hour would come when He would have to 'do with her' and she might ask and obtain from Him miracles. Accordingly, St. Augustine thinks that that hour had come when He said upon the Cross, 'Consummatum est,' and, after this ceremonial estrangement of years, He recognized His Mother and committed her to the beloved disciple. Thus, by marking out the beginning and the end of the period of exception, during which she could not exert her influence upon Him, He signifies more clearly by the contrast, that her presence with Him, and her power, was to be the rule of His kingdom. In a higher sense than when He spoke to the Apostles, He seems to address her in the words, 'Because I have spoken these things, sorrow hath filled your heart. But I will see you again, and your heart shall rejoice and your joy no man shall take from you'."[33]

---

[31] This question is treated in the following chapter. Sts. Basil, Chrysostom, and Cyril seem to admit at least a small venial sin in Mary.

[32] Diff. II, 148.

[33] Diff. II, 149–150.

St. Augustine, who is Newman's authority here,[34] explained the passage against the Manicheans, who tried to deduce from these words that Mary was not really the Mother of Jesus, for Jesus was actually repudiating her as such, so they claimed. How could she be His Mother, when He said "What have I in common with thee, woman?" Augustine states that Mary was expecting a miracle, and Jesus reminded her that it was not in virtue of His humanity but of His divinity that He would perform one. He had always known her, nay even from all eternity, but the time would come when He would refuse mysteriously to recognize her for a certain period until the moment of His death. And so Augustine proceeds along the lines exposed after him by Newman. The apology of the great African Father and adopted by Newman is equally effective in proving the divine maternity against the Manicheans and defending the dignity of Mary against the Protestants who pretend to find in the words of Jesus a lack of respect and veneration for His holy Mother.[35]

V. SCRIPTURE TESTIFIES TO MARY'S EXALTATION

The argument exposed thus far to show Mary's dignity or exaltation was based upon her relation with her divine Son; in other words, she was considered in her person. The principal argument of Newman, however,[36] which he develops systematically, rests on her historical position in Sacred Scripture. Scripture shows that she is exalted. If she had a real

---

[34] In Joann. Evang. Tract. 8, n. 9. Cf. Friedrich, op. cit. p. 156 sqq.

[35] A beautiful suggestion is made by Father Reilly, *Eccl. Rev.*, Feb., 1901, p. 193: "Would it not seem more plausible to read in St. John a modestly suggested request on the part of our Lord that Mary should solemnly inaugurate His hour, the hour of His personal prestige, by humbly performing a last act of maternal authority over Him?" P. 176: "The term 'hour' should be defined as the period of Christ's independent activity and influence." P. 179: *"Her* hour, *her* day had ended with a glorious sunset. *His* hour, *his* day, the time of His public manifestation and independent activity had in a moment succeeded."

[36] Diff. II, 52–61.

part in the economy of grace, as is proved by her being the Second Eve, then she has a claim on our memories; we may not put her away from us, because she is gone from us. Rather, we ought to look at her still according to the measure of her earthly history, with expectation and gratitude. The conclusion of this is evident: "If, as St. Irenaeus says, she acted the part of an Advocate, a friend in need, even in her mortal life; if, as St. Jerome and St. Ambrose say, she was on earth the great pattern of Virgins, if she had a meritorious share in bringing about our redemption, if her maternity was gained by her faith and obedience, if her Divine Son was subject to her, and if she stood by the cross with a mother's heart and drank in to the full those sufferings which it was her portion to gaze upon, it is impossible that we should not associate these characteristics of her life on earth with her present state of blessedness; and this, surely, she anticipated when she said in her hymn that all generations should call her blessed."[37] What Newman wishes to show here is the dignity Mary now possesses in heaven, how high she has been exalted in consequence of her office exercised on earth.

It may be demanded why men outside the fold should be astonished at Catholic belief in our Lady's present dignity. Newman finds the answer to this in the fact that these individuals, too much engrossed in worldly affairs, have never taken the time to examine calmly her historical position in Scripture, with all that it imports. Many serious Protestants, he holds, expend their devotional energies on abstract doctrines, such as justification by faith, the sufficiency of Holy Scripture, etc. The average Catholic does not reflect much more than his Protestant neighbor; but throughout the ages of the Church, devout and intellectual men have employed their talents in the contemplation of Scripture facts, and have brought out in tangible form the doctrines involved. By their exposition, their less gifted brethren in the faith are influenced; Catholic instinct draws the faithful to accept conclusions to which their own powers of reflection would never have brought them. Even

---

[37] Diff. II, 52.

though disputes arise between various Schools of theology on certain points as yet undefined, the ensemble of the faithful seem to be able, once the question becomes a practical one, to direct themselves towards the view that may be eventually defined. They may not understand all the fine points of a discussion, nor would they see the necessity of great precision in expressing their notions, yet they feel the truth more than they know it. A remarkable instance of this is to be found in the Immaculate Conception, which for centuries had been the center of heated arguments pro and con, yet through all that time the faithful regarded Mary as the all-pure, the all-holy, with whom they could not associate the idea of sin. The sentiment of the faithful had likewise anticipated the formal definition of the divine maternity.[38]

Newman does not hesitate to take a very original step when he looks to Scripture to find the doctrine of our Lady's present position exposed.[39] The vision of the Woman and Child in the Apocalypse furnishes the necessary matter. The Apostle's vision is thus recorded as follows: "A great sign appeared in heaven; a woman clothed with the sun, and the moon under her feet, on her head a crown of twelve stars; and being with child, she cried, travailing in birth, and was in pain to be delivered. And there was seen another sign in heaven; and, behold, a great red dragon..... And the dragon stood before the woman who was ready to be delivered; that, when she should be delivered, he might devour her son. And she brought forth a man child, who was to rule all nations with an iron rod; and her son was taken up to God and to His throne. And the woman fled into the wilderness..... And there was a great battle in heaven, Michael and his angels fought with the dragon ... and that great dragon was cast out, that old serpent, who is called the devil and Satan, who seduceth the whole world ...

---

[38] Dev. 145; cf. Marin-Sola, op. cit. I, 368. Some of the bishops objected to Pius IX that the definition of the Immaculate Conception might unsettle the consciences of certain of the faithful, who had regarded it already as a matter of faith.

[39] Diff. II, 53 sqq.

and he persecuted the woman ... and the dragon was angry against the woman; and went to make war with the rest of her seed, who keep the commandments of God and have the testimony of Jesus Christ."[40]

Who is this woman? Undoubtedly the Church. The constant traditions of the Fathers and Doctors do not allow any doubt on the subject. There are few commentaries on the Apocalypse among the early Christian writers, and practically all of them speak of this Woman as the Church. Among the Greek writers, St. Andrew of Caesarea remarks that several see in this Woman the Blessed Virgin, Mother of God, but Methodius refers the symbol to the Church.[41]

The real or direct sense, as admitted by Newman as well, is that the Woman represents the Church, with its destinies, combats and sufferings. It has the sun for its garment, because the Christians who form it are clothed with Christ, the luminous Sun of Justice, or because it itself is filled with the light of God. The moon under its feet represents the perishable goods of this world, and the twelve stars typify the twelve Apostles. It brings forth its children in sorrow, for it gives them life in the midst of great tribulations; the child is a man-child because it must be armed with strength and fidelity. The demon is there to persecute the Church and pursue its members to the solitude of the wilderness and when some have gone to their reward, persecutes the other followers of Christ. Evidently there can be no reference in the painful child-birth to the joyous and virginal child-bearing of Bethlehem. Still, were this text applied to the Blessed Virgin, her travailings could be interpreted as her "compassion" in the birth of the Church on Calvary.[42] Though the majority of Catholic commentators apply this text directly to the Church, they do not hesitate to see the Blessed Virgin represented here in a secondary sense. Newman goes a step further than they when he inquires into the

---

[40] Chap. XII.

[41] Comment. in loco. P. G. 106:320, 324. For a detailed list of the Fathers who apply this symbol to the Church cf. Terrien, op. cit. IV, 61.

[42] Allo, *L'Apocalypse*, p. 174.

DIGNITY OF MARY

meaning of the symbol under which the direct meaning is conveyed. The Woman and Child are not personifications; they are persons—there lies the nucleus of his argument.[43]

VI. OBJECTION TO NEWMAN'S INTERPRETATION

However, two objections seem to present themselves at once to such an interpretation: first, that it is scarcely held by the Fathers; secondly, that Newman is committing an anachronism by ascribing such a notion of the Blessed Virgin to the Apostolic Age.

As to the first, Newman answers: "Christians have never gone to Scripture for proof of their doctrines till there was actual need from the pressure of the controversy; if in those times the Blessed Virgin's dignity was unchallenged on all hands as a matter of doctrine, Scripture, as far as its argumentative matter was concerned, was likely to remain a sealed book to them."[44]

Was the dignity of the Blessed Virgin really unchallenged in those earliest of Christian times? Were not her virginity and divine maternity denied? Was not even the verity of her human motherhood rejected shortly after Jesus had ascended into heaven, perhaps even in her own lifetime? These doctrines were taught explicitly in the Gospels, and the defenders of the faith were obliged to explain precisely the texts which oppose them. Thus, for example, the Valentinians, taking the words of the angel in St. Matthew's gospel, insist on the single word "in" for the grounds of their heresy. The angel said "that which is born *in* her is of the Holy Ghost."[45] The Fathers insist that Jesus is truly born of Mary, that He is born of a Virgin, that He is truly God, and Mary therefore is the Mother of God. It is true, the definition of the last of these dogmas just mentioned did

---

[43] Diff. II, 58. The maledictions pronounced on Babylon and Tyre have real facts or individuals as types, of which these latter events are the antitype. Evidently the historical literal sense must be considered first.

[44] Diff. II, 54.

[45] Matt. 1:20.

not take place until the fifth century, and was preceded by long discussions on the natures and the Person of Christ. Even though the words "Mother of God" did not appear until the third century, yet the reality of the divine maternity was asserted from the first, for this dogma is simply the affirmation that He who is born of Mary is true God and, at the same time, true man. The angel had foretold to Mary that the Child to be born of her was the Son of the Most High.

Did the Fathers ignore the Scriptures in their struggles with the heretics? Just the contrary, though St. Irenaeus insists on the necessity of adhering to the doctrine preached by Christ and His Apostles and transmitted to their successors in the episcopate and faithfully taught by the Church.[46] They were not at first led to seek for a proof of Mary's present exaltation in heaven. Newman gives us the clue to the *modus agendi* of the Fathers with regard to their appeal to Scripture and precisely when there is question of the Savior and His Blessed Mother, for, as he shows, texts that were at first interpreted of our Lord's divinity gradually were ascribed to His humanity and eventually to the Blessed Virgin and other creatures. He claims that the Arian controversy had as its result that "It discovered a new sphere in the realm of light to which the Church had not found its inhabitant." Christ's position as God had been underestimated; a creature would be found that would correspond to the description given in the Apocalypse: "There was a wonder in heaven; a throne was seen, far above all other created powers, mediatorial, intercessory, a title archetypal; a crown bright as the morning star; a glory issuing from the Eternal Throne; robes pure as the heavens; and a sceptre over all; and who was that predestined heir of that Majesty? Since it was not high enough for the Highest, who was that Wisdom and what was her name? 'the Mother of fair love and fear and holy hope' 'exalted like a palm-tree in Engaddi, and a rose-tree in Jericho'; 'created from the beginning before the world' in God's everlasting counsel, and 'in Jerusalem her power'? The vision is found in the Apocalypse, a Woman clothed with the

---

[46] Neubert, op. cit. 23.

sun, and the moon under her feet, and upon her head a crown of twelve stars."[47]

The early Christians would not have been inclined to look to the Apocalypse for proofs of the virginity of Mary nor of her divine maternity, because nothing was there explicitly taught on these subjects. Besides, this mysterious book was not one to be frequently cited or commented by the ancient Fathers.[48]

Newman brings an *argumentum ad hominem* for the very ones to whom he was addressing the *Letter,* namely, the so-called *Catholic* party in the Anglican Church. These were obliged to have recourse to Scripture in order to find in certain texts support for some of the doctrines which they advanced without any patristic confirmation. The texts have great force and yet the Fathers seem to be silent on these interpretations. Thus, they find a Scriptural proof for maintaining the sacrificial character of the Eucharistic service, and for prayers on behalf of the departed. And yet, Newman, in assigning a special force to the Apocalyptic vision, has to a certain extent the support of the Fathers, who admit that the vision of the Woman may be referred to the Blessed Virgin in a secondary sense. But he goes further than they when he holds that the Blessed Virgin herself is the primary type of the Church. She was the reason why the Woman was chosen to represent the Church.

The second objection against Newman's interpretation implies that his association of Virgin and Child is a comparatively modern idea, but facts show the contrary. From the very outset of the Christian era, as soon as Mary appears in the paintings of the Catacombs, she is represented with the Child. The very earliest of these portray her seated, with the Child Jesus in her arms; to the right stands the prophet Isaias. Jesus has his head turned slightly as though he were listening to some one calling Him. The most common subject is the

---

[47] Dev. 143–144.

[48] The first commentator properly so called is Victorinus, martyred about the beginning of the fourth century. About the same period is Methodius, who sees the Church represented, though others had already referred the text to Mary.

Virgin and Child receiving the gifts of the Magi. De Rossi, upon whose authority Newman bases his assertions, hesitates about attributing to the earliest of these paintings a date as early as the time of the Apostles, but claims that they must be put, at the very latest, before the middle of the second century.[49] Wilpert affirms as the date for the "Adoration of the Magi" the beginning of the second century,[50] and for the "Prophecy of Isaias" the first half of the same century.[51] Already, at the end of the second century, the scene of the Annunciation is represented[52] and from the fourth century on, the Blessed Virgin is pictured as an *Orante* between the Apostles Peter and Paul.[53] The painting which had particularly impressed Newman on his visit to Rome after his conversion[54] represents Mary with her Divine Son in her lap, she with hands extended in prayer, He with His hand raised in the attitude of blessing. To him it seemed that no other representation could more forcibly convey the doctrine of the high dignity of the Mother of God and of her influence with her Son.[55] The Christians seem to have delighted particularly in recalling the period of Christ's subjection to His blessed Mother.

Anglicans, and others as well, must admit that these paintings belong to the period of what they call the "undivided Church"; hence these must be accepted as a valid argument for the interpretation given to the Apostle's vision. It is not necessary that a particular doctrine, to be Scriptural, be contained in the sacred writings in direct categorical terms. The expressions of sacred writers force us to suppose that they held the same opinion concerning certain doctrines as Christians of the present time. Frequently a circumstance from without suggests the appositeness of a certain text.

---

[49] Diff. II, 50.
[50] Wilpert, *Fractio Panis*, Taf. VII.
[51] Wilpert, *Malereien der Katak. Roms.*, Text p. 187; Tafel XXII.
[52] Ibid. 202.
[53] Cf. Call. 26.
[54] Ward, I, 152.
[55] Diff. II, 55.

VII. Justification of His Interpretation

Now to come to Newman's interpretation in particular. There is scarcely any doubt that the man-child represents Christ or the mystical body of Christ, that is, the children of the Church; it is He whom the Woman brings forth and the dragon seeks to devour. The Child here represented may be born either of the Church or of the Virgin, for Mary has a part not only in the work of Redemption but in applying the fruit of Redemption. She gives life to the faithful; she suffered in giving birth to the brethren of Christ.

The Woman seen first in heaven descends upon earth and flees to the desert when she is pursued by the demon. Though this may not seem exactly to apply to Mary, yet Newman finds such an application, for when Mary gave birth to Jesus, enemies sought to kill the Divine Child. Joseph seemed to have been the immediate protector of the Mother and Child when he flees with them into Egypt, but Newman sees Michael and his angels fighting against the infernal dragon to protect these two august beings. But if Mary is regarded in her present position, she is victorious; she reigns in heaven with her divine Son; she is a protectress rather than a Woman persecuted. However, the vision applies easily to the Church. It is first in heaven, then upon the earth, for its origin and its end are heavenly. The earth and the agitated seas spoken of, symbolize this world; the Church descending from heaven wars against the demon; at times apparently on the verge of being swallowed up by the floods of persecution, then again succored by God Himself or earthly powers used as the instruments of God.

Newman's *a priori* argument suggests that we look to St. John of all the Apostles for some teaching on the Blessed Virgin, because she was committed to him by our Lord on the Cross. After the Ascension of Jesus, as tradition informs us, she remained with St. John at Jerusalem and followed him to Ephesus. *A posteriori*, it is Irenaeus, who had been taught by St. Polycarp, a disciple of St. John, and who emphasizes the role of

Mary as second Eve.[56]

Newman saw the relation between Mary and the Church, as others before him, such as St. Caesarius of Arles, who speaks of these "two mothers."[57] St. Augustine has given us in a masterly page the doctrine on the relation between Mary and the Church:[58] "The Church imitates the Mother of Christ, her Spouse and Lord. The Church also is both mother and virgin. Of whose purity do we take such jealous care if she is not a virgin? and to whose children do we speak if she is not a mother? Mary has given corporal birth to the head of this body; the Church brings forth spiritually the members of this head. For both, virginity is no hindrance to fruitfulness; for both, fruitfulness does not tarnish their virginity. ... But to one woman alone, to Mary, belongs the right to be both spiritually and corporally, Mother and Virgin. Spiritually, she is not mother of our Head, of our Savior, from whom she was rather spiritually born, but she is certainly mother of His members, that is, she is our mother; for she has co-operated by her love in giving birth to the faithful in the Church. ... Mary is, then, in body and soul, mother and virgin, Mother of Christ and Virgin of Christ. As for the Church, in the person of the Saints who will possess the kingdom of God, she is in spirit, Mother of Christ (i.e., by doing the will of God according to the expression in St. Matthew) and wholly Virgin of Christ."

By consenting to the Incarnation and becoming the Mother of God, Mary becomes mother of men, since she willed the regeneration of men; the Church is on earth to continue the work in which Mary had co-operated. The superiority, however, lies on the side of Mary. She is united to the Conqueror and triumphs with Him; the Church succeeds to continue the struggle. Mary has her place in the work of Redemption, in the acquisition and distribution of grace; the Church participates only in their distribution. In the acquisition and distribution of grace Mary is associated, though only in a

---

[56] Diff. II, 57 sqq.

[57] Hom. 2; P. L. 67:1048.

[58] *De sancta Virg.* cap. 2 et 6; P. L. 40:397, 399.

secondary manner, to Jesus Christ, principal cause and source of all merit; in the distribution of grace the Church is but an instrument. Mary is mother of the Savior and of the members of His mystical body; the Church is mother of the member only.[59]

This is what is meant by Newman when he maintains that the Apostle would not have spoken of the Church under this particular image unless there had existed a Blessed Virgin Mary. Under the symbol of the Woman, the real sense applies to the Church. But Mary is not an inferior personage taken as symbol of something greater; she is rather taken as the model of all who are to follow her; as a sovereign, she unites in herself all the forces and the will of the whole Church. The thought of the Church and of Mary complete and recall each other. Such is the meaning of the Fathers and theologians as well as of the Church's liturgy, when applying this chapter of the Apocalypse to the Blessed Virgin.[60] Hence, Newman can say that the Woman and Child are more than mere personifications; they are *real persons*. Thus, it is not a mere accommodation of the text to the Blessed Virgin; when St. John contemplated in the heavens the Woman clothed with the sun, he found in her a resemblance to the one whom he could call his own mother.

And besides this, a further reason suggests itself. For the first time in Scripture, we are informed who the serpent is, the enemy of the Woman. There is no doubt possible here. St. John takes very special care to designate the infernal dragon as "that old serpent, who is called the devil and Satan, who seduceth the whole world."[61] Only once before, the serpent is introduced and that in the act of seducing the first Eve. Man, woman, and serpent meet again as they met for the first time in Paradise.[62] Now we are told that this serpent is the evil one, to whom God

---

[59] Cf. de la Broise, "Mulier amicta sole," *Études* t. 71, p. 302.

[60] This chapter is used as the Epistle for the feast of the Miraculous Medal, Nov. 27, and the opening verses occur in the sixth Resp. of Matins and as the *Capitulum* at None for the feast of the Immaculate Conception.

[61] Apoc. 12:9.

[62] Diff. II, 32.

said in the beginning: "I will put enmities between thee and the woman, and thy seed and her seed."[63] When he tries to devour the infant about to be born, when he pursues the Woman into the desert, when he wars against others of her race, he is fulfilling the ancient prophecy. The combat described in the Apocalypse is the one foretold in Genesis. The Apocalypse must, then, be interpreted in the light of Genesis. If, then, the serpent in both cases is the evil one,[64] if the seed of the Woman is Christ, for a Redeemer was promised immediately after the fall, and his combats and victory foretold, should not the Woman be she whose seed the man-child is? The first Woman is not an allegory, the second also should be real, for Mary is the second Eve. Whether Christ and His Mother or Eve and her seed are taken as the direct and immediate object of the divine oracle in the beginning, the conclusion is the same, for at the climax of the combat and the victory stand Mary and Jesus crushing the head of the serpent.

Newman assigns a third ground for his interpretation, no less effective than the other two: the Woman is not allegorical but has a real personage as type. Scripture does not have frequent recourse to allegories; figures are at times used in order to visualize still more something real, but there is no tendency to personify abstract qualities or generalizations; this is to be met with in classical, rather than in sacred authors. There may be some instances of this method in Scripture, but such poetical compositions are strikingly unlike its usual method. "Thus we at once feel the difference from Scripture when we betake ourselves to the Pastor of Hermas and find the Church a woman, to St. Methodius and find Virtue a woman, and to St. Gregory's poem and find Virginity again a woman. Scripture deals with types rather than personifications. Israel stands for the chosen people, David for Christ, Jerusalem for heaven."[65] The prophets dramatize their predictions, threats, and promises; the imagery of the Apocalpyse is founded on the

---

[63] Gen. 3:15.

[64] Cf. Dev. 116.

[65] Diff. II, 60.

Jewish ritual; the cures of our Lord symbolize the conferring of grace on the soul; His parables pertain to events which did or might occur. Even where such an abstraction as Wisdom presents itself, commentators could not accept it as a mere personification. They sought the type and at first claimed it to be our Lord, but as the Arians distorted the texts, they applied them to the Blessed Virgin. Since this is the conduct throughout Scripture, should not the Apocalyptic vision refer to the Woman as a real person, the great Mother to whom the chapters in the Book of Proverbs are referred in an accommodated sense.

A very significant and original remark is made by Newman in answer to the question that may at times be put, Why did not the other sacred writers make mention of our Lady's greatness? She was or may have been alive when the Apostles or Evangelists wrote; but the Apocalypse at least was written after her death, and "that book does (so to say) canonize and crown her."[66]

Newman indicates the conclusion to be drawn from these considerations on our Lady's dignity: "If all this be so, if it is really the Blessed Virgin whom Scripture represents as clothed with the sun, crowned with the stars of heaven, and with the moon as her footstool, what height of glory may we not attribute to her? and what are we to say of those who, through ignorance, run counter to the voice of Scripture, to the testimony of the Fathers, to the traditions of East and West, and speak and act contemptuously towards her whom her Lord delighteth to honor?"[67]

VIII. REASON FOR COMPARATIVE SILENCE OF SCRIPTURE ABOUT BLESSED VIRGIN

Why is there such a comparative silence of Scriptures and the early Fathers concerning the dignity of the Blessed Virgin, i.e., her present exaltation. Up to the Council of Ephesus in 431,

---

[66] Diff. II, 61.
[67] Ibid.

little is said of her. As an Anglican Newman explains why the Gospels do not tell us more about her. The reasons he assigns are twofold:

Scripture is not written to exalt any particular Saint, but rather to give glory to God. Our Savior did not wish to expose His more sacred feelings to the world as being unfit for the world to know, and more especially as *dangerous* lest the honor we should give Mary in consequence would eclipse the honor due to God. "Had the blessed Mary been more fully disclosed to us in the heavenly beauty and sweetness of the spirit within her, true, *she* would have been honored; *her* gifts would have been clearly seen; but, at the same time, the Giver would have been somewhat less contemplated, because no design or work of His would have been disclosed in her history. She would seemingly have been introduced for *her* sake, not for His sake. ... Thus, it is a dangerous thing, it is too high a privilege for sinners like ourselves to know the best and innermost thoughts of God's servants. ... The higher their gifts, the less fitted they are for being seen. ... In particular, it is in mercy to us that so little is revealed about the Blessed Virgin, in mercy to our weakness, though of her there are 'many things to say,' yet they are 'hard to be uttered, seeing we are dull of hearing'."[68]

The more she is considered in her person, the more dangerous is such knowledge for us, she is so close to God, too pure and holy a flower to be more than seen on earth. We hardly seem able to put her in her proper position. "We cannot combine in our thought of her, all we should ascribe, with all we should withhold. Consequently, we are to think of her only with her Divine Son."[69]

Though Newman's fears had vanished as to the danger of scrutinizing too closely the sublime dignity of Mary, he follows a somewhat similar line of thought when he reminds us that Mary's maternity, her sinless perfections, are for the sake of Jesus; so, too, her glory. She remained hidden during the public ministry of her Son; after His Ascension she held a subordinate

---

[68] P. S. II, 134–135; Heb. 5:11.

[69] Ibid. 135.

position in the Church. In the same manner, though elevated to the right hand of her Son, she did not ask Him to publish her name, or to hold her up to the world's gaze, but rather waited for the time when her glory would be necessary for His. She was to win her way to the world's homage by persuasion.[70]

Newman is convinced that the silence in the early Church about her person can be explained by the *disciplina arcani*. It was in force as regards her as well as in reference to the Blessed Trinity and the Eucharist. The Church was filled with such a deep sentiment of reverence in matters of sacred doctrine that it required a special effort and an indication of Providence for her to come forward and speak about the loveliest of creatures.[71]

The glory of Mary, her exaltation, seemed to be dependent upon the glory of her divine Son; only when it was necessary to secure a right faith in Jesus, was her manifestation to take place. "When His name was dishonored, then it was that she did Him service; when Emmanuel was denied, then the Mother of God (as it were) came forward; when heretics said that God was not incarnate, then was the time for her own honors. And then, when as much as this had been accomplished, she had done with strife; she fought not for herself. No fierce controversy, no persecuted confessors, no heresiarch, no anathema, were necessary for her gradual manifestation ... she has raised herself aloft silently, and has grown into her place in the Church by a tranquil influence and a natural process. ... Thus was she reared without hands, and gained a modest victory, and exerts a gentle sway, which she has not claimed. When a dispute arose about her among her children, she hushed it; when objections were urged against her, she waived her claims and waited."[72] She is not an earthly beauty dangerous to look upon, but rather tells us of heaven and peace. Like the morning star, the harbinger of day, she will lead us in

---

[70] Mix. 356, 357.

[71] Ath. II, 208. However, it would rather seem that the *disciplina arcani* had nothing to do with the Blessed Virgin.

[72] Mix. 358.

the dark night across the bleak wilderness of this world, on to Jesus, and will guide us safely to our heavenly home.

CHAPTER V
SANCTITY OF MARY

HE Eternal Word was not content with choosing a Mother who furnished Him with a body and, by her consent to the Incarnation, co-operated in the redemption of mankind. From a merely physical viewpoint she was privileged above other creatures in that she preserved intact her virginity and still was honored with the joys of motherhood. God desired her to take part in the restoration of the human race by a voluntary co-operation, for she was a free agent, as Newman repeats. Had she been solely a physical instrument in the Incarnation, we might conceive that Christ could have chosen any ordinary woman as His mother. But since she was to be associated intimately with Jesus in the Redemption, she has a role over and above that of the divine maternity.

I. HOLINESS PROPORTIONATE TO DIGNITY OF MOTHER OF GOD

Whenever God chooses creatures for some special office, He fits them out with a personal holiness that makes them worthy of their high spiritual dignity. Such is the ordinary rule of His dealings with us. The angels, who are His chosen messengers, were created in grace and were made perfect in holiness. Nothing defiled can enter into heaven and consequently it is to be expected that they who hold a higher position in heaven, should be proportionately superior in holiness. Thus, the

Seraphim, who immediately surround the throne of God, must be of a dazzling brilliancy because of the gifts of grace with which they are endowed. In like manner God communicates in various measures his holiness to rational creatures. Thus, the prophets, besides possessing gifts, also received graces. They were not merely inspired to make known God's will to others, but their souls were inwardly touched to make them docile to these inspirations of grace.

It is undeniable that there are exceptions to this rule. Caiaphas, who was one of the instigators to have Jesus put to death, prophesied on one occasion, for he was high-priest that year; Balaam desired to pronounce a malediction on God's chosen people and yet the Lord put words of blessing and prophecy in his mouth. Evil men are frequently used by God to effect a certain good. Even those who have been favored with gifts can fall away and lose their souls. Miraculous gifts may be found in one not in God's grace; the administration of the sacraments, though supernatural and miraculous, does not imply personal holiness; the worker of a miracle is an organ or instrument of divine power.

The case is different, however, for those to whom a particular mission is confided, i.e., prophets and preachers properly so called. This is manifest in the Old and New Covenants in the persons of Enoch, Noe, Moses, Samuel, David, Elias, Isaias, Jeremias, Daniel, John the Baptist, St. Peter, Paul, John, and a host of others—all of these are patterns of virtue. The same can be said of the remarkable figures in the history of the Church—a St. Athanasius, a St. Augustine, a St. Ambrose, a St. Thomas—each one speaks his own words in his own manner, while he speaks the words of God. Newman explains the reason for this: "The truth first goes into the minds of the speakers, and is apprehended and fashioned there, and then comes out from them as, in one sense, its source and parent. The Divine Word is begotten in them, and the offspring has their features and tells of them."[1]

And he continues in his discourse: "Now can you fancy, my

---

[1] Mix. 367.

brethren, such hearts, such feelings to be unholy? how could it be so, without defiling and thereby nullifying the word of God ... how can it be that the word of truth and holiness can proceed profitably from impure lips and an earthly heart? No, as the tree so is the fruit... . Which of you would go to ask counsel of another, however learned, however gifted, however aged, if you thought him unholy? nay though you feel and are sure, as far as absolution goes, that a bad priest could give it as really as a holy priest, yet for advice, for comfort, for instruction, you would not go to one whom you did not respect."[2] Those only can preach the truth duly, who feel it personally; those only transmit it fully from God to man, who have in the transmission made it their own.[3]

Places as well as individuals were made holy wherever God was pleased to come. So the burning bush and the ground about it were declared holy;[4] the ministers in the Temple were obliged to perform innumerable purifications; the Temple and Tabernacle were set aside with special ceremonies for the exclusive service of God. In the New Covenant confession is required before Communion whenever the soul is stained with grievous sin; without sanctity no one can enter heaven, for nothing defiled can be admitted to the presence of the All-holy.[5]

What shall be said of her who was chosen to hold God not merely in her arms, but to bear Him within her for nine months? Since holiness and divine favor go together, what must have been her transcendent purity, what must have been her gifts of holiness, since the Creator Spirit condescended to overshadow her with His miraculous presence, since she was chosen to be the only near earthly relative of the Son of God?[6] The Word of God dwelt within her and received from her the features in which He manifested Himself to men. The child is like the parent, and hence it may be supposed that He would

---

[2] Ibid. 367–368.

[3] These thoughts are developed in full in Mix. 364–368.

[4] Exod. 3:5.

[5] S. N. 106.

[6] P. S. II, 132.

show by His likeness to Mary the relationship existing between Him and her. Thus, the sanctity that we should naturally expect to find in her, comes not only from her being His Mother, but also from His being her Son.[7]

As far as a creature could, she reflected His sanctity and therefore became the Mirror of holiness, or, as is said in the Litany, the Mirror of Justice. Newman sees in the daily life of Jesus and Mary a ground for their mutual resemblance. Jesus resembled Mary because He was her Son; she had been prepared in advance with an incomparable measure of grace. She is in turn perfected to the resemblance of divine holiness by her continual intercourse with the Divine Word. Is it not a fact of everyday experience that people who love each other intensely, gradually become like each other in features as well as in tastes, habits, and dispositions? Now Mary loved her Divine Son with an unutterable love, she had Him all to herself for thirty years. Her sanctity must, then, have been vast, incomprehensible after such a lengthy and intimate intercourse with God; it must have been of an angelic order, reflecting back the attributes of God with a fulness and exactness to which no Saint upon earth can ever approach.[8]

II. Fulness of Grace in the Second Eve

A high degree of holiness must be attributed to the Blessed Virgin, since she is the second Eve. Newman advances here a strong apologetic argument. No objection can be raised against a comparison between Eve, who, though created to become the mother of the living, in reality became the mother of the dead, and the Blessed Mary, on the other hand, who blotted out Eve's fault and became, as Irenaeus says, "the cause or occasion of salvation" for the human race. We can hardly imagine Mary to have been less endowed than Eve.

God could have created man in a purely natural state, that is, possessing all natural gifts, but without any supernatural

---

[7] Cf. Mix. 369.

[8] M. D. I, 30, 31.

destiny, yet instead, He predestined Him to enjoy the beatific vision and so created him in grace. Adam and Eve were made partakers of the divine life and, over and above their supernatural condition, they received other gifts such as knowledge, immortality, and perfect subjection of the lower appetites to reason. Eve, created innocent and sinless, was to hold in her hands the destinies of her posterity; she could not gain admittance to heaven without meriting it. Consequently, she had to be put on trial; God does not, however, try anyone above his strength. He must, then, have conferred upon her an additional large grant of grace in order that she might resist the snares laid for her by the evil one. No one will dare to affirm that she did not possess sufficient grace to come out victorious from the trial. Thus, she was fully endowed with both sanctifying and actual grace; in accordance with God's usual proceedings she must have possessed both in a very high degree.

With this in mind Newman asks: "Is it any violent inference, that she who was to co-operate in the redemption of the world, at least was not less endowed with power from on high, than she who, given as a help-mate to her husband, did in the event but co-operate with him for its ruin? If Eve was raised above human nature by that indwelling moral gift which we call grace, is it rash to say that Mary had even a greater grace?"[9]

Protestants assume that grace is something merely external, an approbation or acceptance. It corresponds to the word "favor" and it is thus that Newman renders the words of the Angel in one of his Anglican sermons. He was but following the Revised Version, which translates the Catholic "Hail, full of grace" as "Hail, thou that art highly favored." The Protestant version is consequently fully in conformity with the Protestant notion of the whole supernatural system by which fallen man is purified or justified from sin and possesses the right to eternal beatitude. The sinner, according to Protestant principles, is not cleansed from his sins; these are not blotted

---

[9] Diff. II, 45.

out, but only covered over, as it were, by Christ's justice and merits. His sins are no longer imputed to him. Catholics, on the contrary, maintain that there is something positive taking place, there is a real interior sanctification, effected by grace, and thereby the soul once more becomes holy before God. It participates as before in the divine nature.

Such a doctrine is clearly affirmed not only in Scripture but also in the Fathers. The testimony of the earliest, St. Ignatius, will suffice: "You are all," says he, "companions in the way; God-bearers, temple-bearers, Christ-bearers."[10] The Epistle of Barnabas confirms the same doctrine: "Having obtained the remission of sins and with hope in the name of the Lord, we have been renewed and wholly re-created; therefore God truly dwells within us, in our dwelling-place."[11] The Fathers in countless passages give the lie to Protestant notions, for they assert repeatedly that a permanent supernatural gift is infused, sins are truly wiped out, man is renewed interiorly, becomes once more the temple of the Holy Ghost, the adopted child of God, and heir of heaven.[12]

This was the grace, the inherent gift bestowed upon Eve; should it not be supposed that Mary had even greater grace, nay, that she was "full of grace"? Were it supposed that the Angel wished simply to imply that Mary was the object of a special favor at that moment only, the text would have employed the present participle instead of the perfect in the original Greek form. Catholic belief in Mary's perfect sanctity or plenitude of grace does not repose solely on these words of the Angel, but on the fact of her divine maternity and her co-operation in the Redemption. It is rather these considerations, Newman points out, that give significance to the Angel's salutation,[13] and lead to a further deduction, namely, a perfect holiness and sinlessness, going to the first moment of Mary's existence. But this point merits a special development in the

---

[10] Ep. ad Eph. 9, 2; P. G. 5:652.

[11] Ep. Barnabae 16:8; P. G. 2:773.

[12] Cf. Rouët de Journal, *Enchiridion Patristicum* (1913), p. 773.

[13] Diff. II, 45.

succeeding chapter.

III. SINLESSNESS, A NEGATIVE CONDITION OF HOLINESS; PATRISTIC TESTIMONY TO THE CONTRARY EXPLAINED

Sanctity, while implying a real inward condition, a quality of the soul, necessarily presupposes a negative aspect as well, namely, the freedom from sin. Justification contains two simultaneous acts: the remission of sin and the infusion of grace.

From the earliest times Christians have instinctively been led not to associate the idea of sin with the Blessed Virgin, though some Fathers discussed whether she really possessed the privilege of sinlessness. Among these were Origen,[14] Basil,[15] Chrysostom,[16] Tertullian,[17] and Maximus of Turin.[18] On the other hand, Ephrem, Epiphanius,[19] Ambrose,[20] and others testify to her sinlessness.

Newman lays down the principle of the Catholic attitude on Mary's freedom from sin: "On the one hand, we will not allow that our Blessed Lady ever sinned; we cannot bear the notion, entering, as we do, into the full spirit of St. Augustine's words, 'Concerning the Holy Virgin Mary, I wish no question to be raised at all, when we are treating of sins.' On the other hand, we admit, rather we maintain, that, except for the grace of God, she might have sinned; and that she may have been exposed to temptation in the sense in which our Lord was exposed to it, though as His Divine Nature made it impossible for Him to yield to it, so His grace preserved her under its assaults also."[21]

Several of the Fathers, as was just mentioned, implied or

---

[14] In Luc. hom. 17; P. G. 13:1845.
[15] Ep. 260, 9; P. G. 32:965.
[16] Hom. 44 in Matt. P. G. 57:463.
[17] De Carne Christi 17; P. L. 2:766.
[18] Hom. in Epiph. Domini I; P. L. 57.
[19] Haer. 42; P. G. 41:696.
[20] De Virg. 2:15; P. L. 16:210.
[21] Diff. II, 136. Cf. Friedrich, op. cit. 234 sqq.

asserted that Mary on one or two occasions did sin venially or showed a certain infirmity. This might seem inconsistent with Newman's statement that, from the first, Christians regarded Mary as all-holy. For his purpose Newman selects three examples from Petavius.[22] The treatment of the two authors is, however, widely different. Petavius, after exposing the nature of the Fathers' arguments, notes that these Fathers, besides others, limit the possibilities of a sin of frailty to several occasions only in the life of the Blessed Virgin, as at the marriage feast of Cana, on Calvary, etc. The learned Jesuit poses as his thesis that the Fathers in question had no solid grounds whatever for their statements, which do little honor to Mary's purity. His method then is to give an exposition of the texts in Scripture which furnished them the occasion for their opinions. His counter-proof is consequently rather exegetical, basing his interpretations of the sacred texts on other Fathers.

Newman, as is to be expected, strikes out on a different line for his argumentation. He acknowledges his indebtedness to Petavius, whom he styles "a theologian too candid and fearless to put out of sight or explain away adverse facts, from fear of scandal, or from the expedience of controversy."[23]

The three Fathers who have pronounced themselves against the almost universal belief of Christians in Mary's sinlessness were Sts. Basil, Chrysostom, and Cyril of Alexandria. The two last mentioned are commenting on various passages of Scripture. A commentary on these passages of Scripture, though serving the purpose of Petavius, is of only partial use to Newman, who was looking to Antiquity for his foundations of devotion to Our Lady. He himself anticipates an objection that might have been made to him, that instead of looking to Justin, Irenaeus, or Tertullian for an evidence of early Christian belief, he might just as well have taken Basil, Chrysostom, and Cyril to prove the contrary. Why should the latter be the exception and not the rule? Why could not the contrary be just as true? Newman acknowledges that he is trying to make a case; even

---

[22] De Inc. XIV, cap. I.

[23] Diff. II, 129. For texts cf. Ibid. 129–133.

if he succeeds in doing only this, he would be justified because opponents of Catholic devotion to Mary presupposed *a priori* that it was not even possible to make any sort of case from the Fathers in behalf of Catholic doctrine concerning the Blessed Virgin.

Newman proposes to expose the statements of the Fathers and to give an explanation that is quite admissible—in fact, it is suggested by St. Cyril himself. The exposition is followed by an examination into the value of their testimony.

St. Basil considers the prophecy of Simeon, concerning the sword which would pierce the soul of Mary, as an announcement that she too would entertain some doubt concerning the divine mission of her Son. This sin, however, was only slight—a certain tossing or unsettlement of the soul.

St. Chrysostom has three passages. The first is concerned with the purpose of the Angel's visit to Mary, before the Incarnation. Had not the heavenly messenger come to her before the conception, she may have been exposed to violent temptation which could have even culminated in suicide. But God preserved her from this trial. In the second and third passages Chrysostom imputes the sin of vainglory to the Blessed Virgin at the marriage feast of Cana and when she sought to approach Jesus while He was addressing a vast crowd. Newman admits that these two passages are at variance with what is held and are exceptional in the writings of Antiquity.[24]

St. Cyril considers that Mary may have been tempted to doubt at the crucifixion of Jesus. To sum up: all three Fathers hold that she may have been exposed to the temptation of doubt; Basil and Chrysostom suppose that she actually did sin, though slightly, either by doubt or vainglory.

The explanation of these facts, according to Newman, lies in the views of the Fathers concerning womankind, views which were quite common in their times. These frailties of our Lady are to be attributed rather to her nature than to her person. In the earlier centuries of Christianity woman still held

---

[24] Diff. II, 134.

a very inferior position; her nature was held to be inferior to man's and intrinsically feeble. Consequently, the vainglory which Chrysostom attributes to Mary is no more than an infirmity. "He does not deny," says Newman, "that she had all the perfections which woman could have; but he seems to have thought the capabilities of nature were bounded, so that the utmost graces bestowed upon it could not raise it above that standard of perfection in which its elements resulted, and to attempt more, would have been to injure, not to benefit it."[25] Newman admits that his view is not substantiated in Chrysostom's writings, but St. Cyril confirms it in unequivocal terms in his commentary on St. John: "It is very natural that the woman in her, not knowing the mystery (of Christ's death and resurrection) should slide into some such trains of thought. For we must conclude, if we judge well, that the gravity of the circumstances was enough to overturn even a self-possessed mind; it is no wonder, then, if a woman begins to doubt. For if man himself was once scandalized ... what paradox is it if the soft mind of womankind was carried off to weak ideas?"[26] Elsewhere he says that "a woman's nature is the type of feebleness."[27]

Newman is quite right when he dismisses Cyril from consideration, for this Father does not impute any personal sin to the Blessed Virgin. He rather loves to praise in Mary her divine maternity and her virginity. In his estimation she is the Virgin *par excellence,* and with this term he almost invariably combines such expressions as holy, all-holy, all-pure, etc.[28] Furthermore, his panegyrics of the Blessed Virgin at the Council of Ephesus would rather incline us to the belief that he supposes her really to be sinless.[29]

The question to be resolved by Newman is, what value can be assigned to the teachings of these Fathers who seem so

---

[25] Ibid. 135–136.

[26] In Joann. P. G. 74:661.

[27] In Gen. P. G. 69:437.

[28] Cf. P. G. 76:17; 77:1065.

[29] Cf. Eberle op. cit. 124.

much at variance with the general belief of Christians on this point. His few preliminary remarks may be summed up in this manner:

1. The Fathers not only represent the people or countries for which they write, but they must witness to an uninterrupted tradition handed down from the Apostles; if they do not, their testimony is of no value. 2. In its *matter* the tradition must be a *positive* belief, whether the proposition itself be affirmative or negative. Thus "Christ is God" is an example of an affirmative tradition; "no one born of woman is born in God's favor" represents a negative tradition. 3. Before any tradition has weight, it needs interpretation. 4. Traditions are explicit or implicit. 5. A tradition may be determined as apostolical,

 a. When credible witnesses declare it such.
 b. When independent witnesses enunciate one and the same doctrine.

The application of these principles follows most naturally. Newman deduces the tradition of Mary's sinlessness as apostolical from the tradition of the "second Eve," which has, as he affirms, one of the two tests prescribed and which is an explicit tradition, whereas that of Mary's sinlessness is implicit, contained in the doctrine that she is the second Eve.

The remarks of Basil, Chrysostom, and Cyril by no means suppose a tradition in the Church as do the affirmations of other Fathers on Mary's role in the redemption.

1. They do not witness to any belief; they are interpreting passages of Holy Writ, and, further, do not interpret one and the same text; neither do they agree in the interpretation of the same text. It can hardly be inferred that a positive belief existed among the Christians that our Lady had committed actual sin; even if it be supposed that there was a tradition about her sinlessness, a contrary tradition could not be presumed in consequence.

2. The very form of the statements shows that the Fathers are not witnessing to an apostolical tradition. They do not claim their opinion to be such, nor do they testify to one and the same doctrine. Hence they do not fulfill the requirements

for an apostolical tradition. They are merely commentators of Scripture and so may be supposed to be giving a private and personal opinion, rather than to be making a dogmatic statement.

The notion, suggested by Basil, that our Lady admitted doubt at the passion of Jesus, traces its beginning to Origen[30] who says: "Thy soul also will be pierced by the sword of unbelief; thou wilt be struck by the point of doubt, thy thoughts will toss thee to and fro when thou seest how He, whom thou didst bear being called Son of God, is crucified, and dies." Newman judges Origen rightly when he says that this Father, "far from professing to rest it on Tradition, draws it as a theological conclusion from a received doctrine. His characteristic fault was to prefer scientific reasonings to authority."[31] The basis for the argument is this, that since Mary was one of the redeemed, she must have sinned at some time or other. Our Lord had foretold that all would be scandalized in Him at His passion; if she was not scandalized, then Jesus did not die for her sins. Such reasoning as that of Origen might have given rise to some sort of tradition as to the interpretation of Simeon's words, but this need not necessarily suppose that Mary really succumbed to temptation. From imputing a temptation the tradition may have been perverted to seeing sin in Mary. Basil derived this view from Origen. Chrysostom is the great Commentator of the Church ever "overflowing with thought, and he pours it forth with a natural engaging frankness and an unwearied freshness and vigor. ... He ever speaks from himself ... not speaking by rule. On the other hand, if it is not a paradox to say it, no one carries with him so little of the science, precision, consistency, gravity of a Doctor of the Church, as he who is one of the greatest. The difficulties are well known which he has occasioned to school theologians: his *obiter dicta* about our Lady are among them."[32]

When it is asked how one may account for the absence, at

---

[30] Hom. 17 in Luc. P. G. 13:1845.

[31] Diff. II, 143.

[32] Diff. II, 145.

Antioch or Caesarea, where Chrysostom and Basil lived, of a tradition of our Lady's sinlessness, Newman replies that "it was obliterated or confused for the time by the Arian troubles in the countries in which those Sees were situated. It is not surely wonderful if in Syria and Asia Minor, the seat in the fourth century of Arianism and Semi-Arianism, the prerogatives of the Mother were obscured together with the essential glory of the Son, or if they who denied the tradition of His divinity, forgot the tradition of her sinlessness. Christians in those countries and times, however religious themselves, however orthodox their teachers, were necessarily under peculiar disadvantages. ... Basil grew up in the very midst of Semi-Arianism. ... It is not wonderful, then, if he had no firm habitual hold upon a doctrine which (though Apostolical) in his day was as yet so much in the background all over Christendom as our Lady's sinlessness. As to Chrysostom, not only was he in close relations with the once Semi-Arian Cathedra of Antioch, ... but ... he came under the teaching of the celebrated Antiochene School, celebrated ... for the successive outbreaks of heresy among its members. ... The famous Theodore and Diodorus of the same school, who, though not heretics themselves, have a bad name in the Church, were, Diodorus the master, and Theodore the fellow-pupil, of St. Chrysostom. Here, then, is a natural explanation why St. Chrysostom, even more than St. Basil, might be wanting, great doctor as he was, in a clear perception of the place of the Blessed Virgin in the Evangelical Dispensation."[33]

It may be added, on the one hand, that Chrysostom made every effort to show that the words of our Lord at Cana imply no denial of His Mother,[34] for Jesus loved her, was subject to her, and worked the miracle at her prayer,[35] and still, on the

---

[33] Diff. II, 147.

[34] Cf. Hom. 44 in Matt. n. 1, 2: P. G. 57:463–466; Hom. 21 in Joan. n. 2, 3; P. G. 59:130–132.

[35] Hom. 22 in Joan. n. 1; P. G. 59:134.

other hand, he has such a low notion of her holiness.[36]

As to the interpretation of the "sword" spoken of by Simeon, there is no more reason to suppose that it means doubt than that it signifies anguish. And as for Mary's vainglory, which seems to provoke a rebuke from Jesus at the marriage of Cana, sufficient has been said in the preceding chapter.

IV. Virtues of the Blessed Virgin

Besides being free from all sin, Mary possesses all virtues in an eminent degree. She, the highest of all creatures, matured the graces conferred on her so abundantly, in solitude and silence. She advanced from day to day, from the initial plenitude of grace bestowed upon her at the moment of her conception to the sublimest heights of sanctity attained by her at the end of her mortal career, so that when she was transported to heaven she became the chief of all the undefiled followers of the Lamb.[37] She had the purity and innocence, the bright vision of faith, confiding trust in God which raised the feelings she had of her unworthiness to be Mother of God, to an intensity which ordinary mortals cannot understand.[38] The Fathers call attention to the faith, obedience, and virginity which merited for Mary the divine maternity and her position as Second Eve. Her virginity has already been considered in a special manner. Only a few words are required to see how Newman looks upon the virtues of which the Blessed Virgin gave such a shining example.

Mary is first of all a model of *faith*. She staggered not at the promise of the Lord; she believed when Zachary doubted, and was blessed for her belief.[39] Hers was not a faith that ended in a mere acquiescence in divine providences and revelations. She

---

[36] St. Thomas remarks about the passages of Chrysostom without any ambiguity: "In verbis illis Chrysostomus excessit." Summa, III, q. 27, a. 4 ad 3. Cf. also Bardenhewer, op. cit. III, 357–358.

[37] P. S. II, 137.

[38] Ibid. 128.

[39] Ibid. 137.

did not consider it sufficient to accept divine truth, but she dwelt upon it, she "pondered" it in her heart. She symbolizes the faith of the unlearned, and also that of the doctors of the Church, whose duty it is to investigate, weigh, and define, as well as to profess the Gospel, for she dwells upon divine truth, uses it, develops it, reasons upon it after believing.[40]

Newman does not touch upon the virtue of *hope* in our Lady, except to say that she must have had a trust in God in a very high degree.[41] What Newman says of the sanctity and *love* of John the Baptist and John the Evangelist, he applies *a fortiori* to the Blessed Virgin. They came so close to her in their all but sinlessness. "The rebellion of the reason, the waywardness of the feelings, the disorder of the thoughts, the fever of passion, the treachery of the senses, these evils did the all-powerful grace of God subdue in them. They lived in a world of their own, uniform, serene, abiding; in visions of peace, in communion with heaven, in anticipation of glory ... and therefore it is we speak of them rather as patterns of sanctity than of love, because love regards an external object, runs towards it and labors for it, whereas such Saints came so close to the object of their love ... that their hearts did not so much love heaven as were themselves a heaven. ... Thus these two were almost absorbed in the Godhead, living an angelical life, as far as men could lead one, so calm, so still, so raised above sorrow and fear, disappointment and regret, desire and aversion, as to be the most perfect images that earth has seen of the peace and immutability of God. Such too are the many virgin Saints ... and above all, the Virgin of Virgins, and Queen of Virgins, the Blessed Mary, who, though replete and overflowing with the grace of love, yet for the very reason that she was the Seat of Wisdom and the Ark of the Covenant is more commonly represented under the emblem of the lily than of the rose."[42]

Prudence is the queen of moral virtues, and the Blessed

---

[40] U. S. 312, 313; Dev. 337.

[41] P. S. II, 128.

[42] Mix. 66.

Mary has the right to be called "Virgin most prudent." According to Newman, Mary manifested this virtue in an exceptional degree in the midst of the trials and sorrows of her life. She is the great model of the practical life, which demands prudence as well as penance. All her duties, which varied in the different periods of her life, were performed with the greatest perfection whether she is viewed as a young maiden, a wife, a mother or a widow. She had her duties in the public and private life of Jesus, towards the Apostles, Martyrs, and Confessors. All her acts were perfect, all were the best that could be done. To be always mindful in the minutiæ of life demands a high degree of virtue guided constantly by prudence.[43]

Newman does not consider *justice* as a special virtue, but rather takes it as the ensemble of virtues in the Blessed Virgin, or, in other words, it becomes the synonym for holiness.[44] Thus, Mary is called the *Mirror of Justice* because she reflected in a most perfect manner the sanctity of her Divine Son. The particular virtue of justice itself shone forth in a splendid manner first of all by her intense *devotion to our Lord*. Her life was wholly absorbed in that of her Divine Son; for thirty long years she had been in closest intimacy with Him. This devotion was particularly apparent when Jesus suffered in His Passion, for then every indignity heaped upon Him found its counterpart in her own person.[45] Secondly, her *obedience* showed itself continually in her life. She obeyed the words of the angel and submitted to all the ordinances of God, particularly to the law of Purification. Though Jesus had been born without sin, and she required no purification in consequence, yet she submitted to the Law to do it reverence.[46]

Who shall speak of her *fortitude* and patience during the Passion of Jesus, when she stood upright to receive the blows which the sufferings of her Son inflicted upon her at every moment? Not only then but during her life, when she was in

---

[43] M. D. I, 57–58.
[44] Ibid. I, 30–31.
[45] M. D. I, 49, 50.
[46] P. S. II, 108.

exile with her Child among the heathen Egyptians and later on among the Greeks at Ephesus she had much to endure; what mother's sufferings could ever equal hers?[47] Jesus spared His sinless Mother the sufferings He bore in His own body, but she had to suffer in soul, in spirit. She had to agonize with Him in the garden and throughout His Passion. She was undergoing an interior martyrdom yet she stood on Calvary, still, collected, motionless, solitary but, for all that, heroically enduring the most acute anguish.[48]

The virtue of *temperance* shone out with particular splendor by reason of her inviolate virginity and also by her humility. Notwithstanding the awful dignity to which she was raised, she felt her own inexpressible unworthiness. Newman presupposes this virtue as a necessary condition for the divine maternity. Mary would without difficulty recognize "her humble lot, her ignorance and weakness in the eyes of the world," for the Lord had regarded the lowliness of His handmaid.[49]

V. Consequences of Her Sanctity

Mary's holiness produced its effects on her will, for she had no recognition of sin. Free from temptation and concupiscence by a special grace of God, she had not the experience of sin that innocent people ordinarily have. Temptation gives the latter some sort of knowledge of sin, but it was not so for Mary. She knew that she could disobey if she so desired it, but such a thought was like supposing her to be willing to jump off a precipice. She was certain that she would not consent to evil.[50]

A great trial to her holiness was the fact that other people sinned. She could not comprehend it, and if she was made to understand it, it would be through a supernatural indication which she would take on faith. Newman declares that the most unendurable penance for the Blessed Virgin was to be perfectly

---

[47] M. D. I, 55–56.
[48] Ibid. I, 51, 52.
[49] P. S. II, 128.
[50] S. N. 107.

holy and at the same time to live in a sinful world. He goes so far as to call this existence a sort of *poena damni* for her, living thus in the midst of sinners and separated from the possession of God.[51] How she must have thought of the blissful mysterious time between the creation of her soul and her birth, for Newman places knowledge and the use of reason in her from the first.

Another consequence of her holiness was in her person.[52] She became lovable by reason of her very sinlessness, for sin by its nature is something repulsive, while grace is beautiful and attractive. Not all holy people can attract others to them and make themselves loved; this is due to the remains of sin in them, or else they lack the degree of holiness powerful enough to overcome their defects of soul and body. As for Mary, her holiness must have reflected itself in her countenance, so that one could only describe it as angelic and heavenly. "Of course her face was most beautiful; but we should not be able to recollect whether it was beautiful or not; we should not recollect any of her features, because it was her beautiful sinless soul which looked through her eyes, and spoke through her mouth, and was heard in her voice and compassed her all about; when she was still or when she walked, whether she smiled or was sad, her sinless soul, this it was which would draw all those to her who had any grace in them, any remains of grace, any love of holy things. There was a divine music in all she said and did—in her mien, her air, her deportment, that charmed every heart that came near her. Her innocence, her humility and modesty, her simplicity, sincerity and truthfulness, her unselfishness, her unaffected interest in every one who came to her, her purity—it was these qualities which made her so lovable."[53]

Her holiness, her freedom from actual sin as we have considered thus far, reach a sublimity beyond comprehension when viewed in that ineffable privilege conferred on her, which

---

[51] Ibid. 108.

[52] M. D. I, 16–18.

[53] M. D. I, 18.

prevented her contracting even the stain of original sin. This bright jewel in the crown of our Lady, this unique prerogative bestowed upon her who is "our tainted nature's solitary boast" we call her Immaculate Conception.

CHAPTER VI
The Immaculate Conception

I. The Dogma Should Present No Difficulties

AMONG all the doctrines defined by the Church, hardly one caused such a stir in non-Catholic circles as did that of the Immaculate Conception. Immediately preceding the definition and subsequent to it, treatises appeared in great numbers outside the Church, protesting against or belittling the import of the dogma. The honor of the Blessed Virgin was in question, and hence they who had practically ceased to venerate the Incarnate Word, could not endure any additional glory for His Mother. In many cases, gross misconceptions were responsible for the attitude, where prejudice did not excite direct opposition to whatever emanated from the Roman Pontiff as head of the Church. This was the case, for example, in the Greek Church, which rejects the supremacy of the Pope and hence would repudiate any pronouncement *ex cathedra*.

After the proclamation of the dogma one of the most prominent opponents was Newman's friend Pusey. This opposition already signalized above, arose not so much from the doctrine as the mode of definition. Pusey saw in it just one more obstacle to reunion and, above all, "an insoluble difference between modern Rome and the ancient Church."[1] He hoped

---
[1] Eir. I, 121.

that he would even be able to induce the Fathers about to assemble for the Vatican Council (he was writing in 1869) to reconsider the Pontifical Bull of 1854 and modify the tenor of the definition. He was of the opinion that the Bull *Ineffabilis Deus* was only a one-sided explanation of the true doctrine and manifestly contradicted the universal tradition of the Church in all ages.[2]

Newman, even in his Anglican days, never had any doubt about the doctrine once he had been imbued with that strong tender devotion to our Lady which took root in him when he abandoned Liberalism. He was outspoken in affirming the doctrine of the Immaculate Conception, though not using the term for fear of giving offence to his co-religionists.[3] Since it held no difficulty for him, he was surprised that it should have caused difficulty to others.[4] As a Catholic, even before the definition of the dogma, the fact was so evident to him that it seemed practically axiomatic, so that he could not conceive how any Catholic, least of all any holy person, could have ever denied or opposed the doctrine as such.[5] Just a year before the proclamation of the dogma, he preached a sermon on the subject, and in his notes he writes: "Though the Church has never proposed it as a point of faith, it is not difficult to conceive it should be one, and there has been a growing wish that the Church could find it was part of the original dogma. Indeed, it is almost saying what has been said in other words, for if no venial sin, *must* there not be Immaculate Conception?"[6] On Christmas-day, 1854, he recalls to his hearers that this was not like other Christmases, for something special had been done, namely, the Pope had defined that Mary had nothing to do with sin. And he adds: "We were sure it was so. We could not believe it was not. We could not believe it had not been revealed. We thought it had, but the Church did not

---

[2] Pusey IV, p. 163.

[3] Cf. above pp. 6-7, P. S. II, 132.

[4] M. D. I, 78.

[5] S. N. 106.

[6] S. N. 106.

say it was, etc."⁷

For Newman the doctrine intimately harmonizes with the circle of recognized dogmatic truths into which it had been received.⁸ There should be no intellectual difficulties for Catholics on this score.⁹ The doctrine was defined precisely because Catholics believed and held it, and when it was promulgated it was acclaimed with universal enthusiasm.¹⁰

There were, however, some shining lights in the Church who in the past seemed to scruple on the point. The opposition of a St. Bernard or a St. Thomas, if it may be termed such, was rather due to a misunderstanding of the significance of the dogma as it is held today. In Newman's view, their difficulty was rather a matter of "words, ideas, and arguments."¹¹ He asserts also that they took the terms as referring to our Lady's mother, namely, that she virginally conceived the Blessed Virgin; nor could they reconcile this doctrine with others.¹² It was necessary, first, to precise the terms in which the doctrine was to be expressed, and then it would be found that those who seemingly opposed it would have become ardent proponents of the belief.

For both of these Doctors of the Church, the root of the difficulty lay in reconciling Mary's perfect sinlessness with the doctrine of the universality of original sin. "Whence would come the sanctity of this conception?" asks St. Bernard. "May it be said that Mary previously sanctified would have been holy already when she was conceived, and that in consequence her conception was also holy. Thus, she was said to have been sanctified in the womb of her mother so that her birth also might be holy. But Mary could not have been holy before she

---

⁷ Ibid. 116.

⁸ Apo. 254.

⁹ Apo. 255.

¹⁰ The sentiment of the faithful was not, however, the only ground for the definition; it had to be directed aright by theological reasoning. Cf. Marin-Sola, op. cit. I, 326–327.

¹¹ Apo. 255.

¹² M. D. 81.

existed, and she did not exist before she was conceived. Will it be said that in the act of generation, sanctity was associated with conception and thus there was simultaneously conception and sanctification? Reason opposes itself to such a hypothesis. How could there have been sanctity without the sanctifying Spirit? or how could the Holy Ghost have been associated with sin? or how could there not be sin when there was carnal pleasure? There is no way out of this unless we admit, what is unheard of, that Mary was conceived of the Holy Ghost and not of man."[13]

St. Thomas, on the other hand, distinguishes the time before the infusion of the rational soul and the very moment of this infusion. He rejects categorically a sanctification before the infusion of the soul; for if the soul is not present, there is no subject to receive grace. He held that the conferring of sanctifying grace at the very moment of union between body and soul cannot be admitted either, for this is the exclusive privilege of Jesus Christ, the Redeemer. It is not impossible that there should have been an exception to the universal law under which all men contract original sin, but it was not suitable to the dignity of the Redeemer, and hence even the Blessed Virgin had to contract the stain, for like every child of Adam she had to be truly and personally redeemed by the blood of Jesus Christ. Centuries had to elapse until the whole question had been elaborated by the Schools to show that the Immaculate Conception did not exclude personal redemption by Christ.[14]

Thus, as Newman taught, these Doctors could admit an Immaculate Conception that implied a miraculous conception. It is necessary for him also, to call the attention of non-Catholic opponents who stumble at the doctrine to the fact that it concerns only her own person and not her parents at all.[15]

---

[13] Ep. 174, P. L. 182,332.

[14] Cf. Del Prado, *Divus Thomas et Bulla Dogmatica "Ineffabilis Deus."* Marin-Sola, op. cit. p. 322 sqq.

[15] Diff. II, 47.

II. Protestant View of Original Sin, a Source of Difficulty

A great source of difficulties for Protestants in regard to the Immaculate Conception is their view of original sin, which is totally different from that of Catholics. For Catholics, original sin is not, strictly speaking, sin, but rather the sin of Adam as transferred to his posterity, or the state to which mankind has been reduced by reason of the first sin. Catholics conceive it as something negative, a deprivation of the supernatural, unmerited grace which Adam and Eve had at their creation; it includes, moreover, the consequences of this deprivation. The Protestant, on the other hand, holds it as something positive, somewhat like actual sin. For the latter it is a "disease, a radical change of nature, an active poison internally corrupting the soul, infecting its primary elements and disorganizing it."[16]

Such a view was no stranger to Newman in his Anglican days. All good principles that may be found in us, he held, are spotted and defiled, hopelessly and thoroughly steeped in evil, dissolved in evil. Whatever we do is pervaded with evil and odious to Almighty God, so that even our best services seem to be a sort of profanation.[17] Our very nature is sinful and so can produce no good whatever; and any good that is done, is to be ascribed to grace and not to nature.[18] The guilt may have been forgiven, but the infection remains; the evil principle is still within us, pride, deceit, unbelief, selfishness, etc., which have been transmitted to us by carnal descent.[19]

Adam had been created in grace, and endowed with privileges far above what his human nature was entitled to, the greatest gift conferred upon him being the divine indwelling in him.[20] But the presence of the Holy Ghost was lost by sin, and thus nature is absolutely evil prior to justification, so that

---

[16] Diff. II, 48. Cf. U. S. VII, 187.

[17] Jfc. 89, 90.

[18] P. S. V, 133. Cf. Ibid. 52, 53, 149.

[19] Ibid. 212.

[20] Jfc. 160. Cf. Mix. 352.

nothing good could come from it. The consequences of this infection remain to a great extent even after baptism.

Catholics, however, do not look upon human nature as essentially evil, as totally corrupt, as incapable of producing even natural good before justification. When man was created he was endowed with gifts above his nature, by which that nature was perfected. He was made according to the image and likeness of God. The soul itself was created a spirit, immortal, with knowledge and free-will; on the body was conferred beauty, perfection of form, etc., but certain defects remained inherent. As nature was constituted, the inferior passions would have warred against reason and the body against the soul. But God did not leave man thus; He gave him a supernatural gift—a likeness to Himself, with the participation of the divine nature. Besides, everything in him was duly subordinated: the soul was subjected to God, the passions to reason, and the body to the soul. Thus, all formed a harmonious whole, with nothing to disturb the perfect equilibrium in which human nature was placed.[21]

With the fall, man was stripped of the supernatural gifts of grace. The sin of Adam involved all his descendants. Had he remained faithful, he would have transmitted all the favors bestowed upon him to his posterity; but as a spendthrift who has squandered everything, so Adam had nothing to leave his children except bare human nature with the disorders consequent upon his sin. The passions and affections rebelled against reason, and the body against the soul. These disorders constitute the wounds of human nature, but human nature does not thereby become intrinsically corrupt, as the Protestants claim.

III. Nature of Immaculate Conception

In regard to the Immaculate Conception, Newman makes it clear that Catholics do not ascribe a different sort of nature to the Blessed Virgin; hers was like that of her parents; she also

---

[21] S. N. 174.

was a child of fallen Adam. Without the grace of God, she would have been frail as any other being. "We consider that in Adam she died, as others; that she was included, together with the whole race, in Adam's sentence; that she incurred his debt, as we do; but that, for the sake of Him who was to redeem her and us upon the Cross, to her the debt was remitted by anticipation, on her the sentence was not carried out, except indeed as regards her natural death, for she died when her time came, as others."[22]

Catholics simply state that Mary never had original sin; that is to say, she was never deprived of that supernatural grace which had been conferred on Adam from the first. A more abundant gift of grace made her what she was from the very beginning of her existence. She could not merit any more than we, the restoration of that grace lost by Adam; but God in His supreme bounty restored it to her from the outset, so that she never came under the original curse, which consisted in the loss of grace.[23] Her nature had nothing to do with this unique privilege, but an excess of grace hindered Nature from acting as it did in other cases.

Some of the so-called opponents of the doctrine could not reconcile it with the other dogmas of the universal transmission of original sin and universal redemption by Christ. They presupposed that without the contraction of the original stain Mary did not die in Adam, and hence would have to be excluded from the general sentence pronounced on mankind. How could the Psalm verse be true, which says: "In sin hath my mother conceived me"? But Mary would normally have come under the penalty of the fall, yet in her case the sentence was not carried out, for grace dwelt within her from the first moment. She was exempted by the eternal decree of God from original sin.

Simultaneously with the decree of man's creation by the Holy Trinity, existed the divine foreknowledge of the fall and

---

[22] Diff. II, 48. Cf. "Imm. Conc. and the 'Contracting of Sin'." *Eccl. Review*, Jan., 1925, Vol. 72, No. 1, pp. 76–82.

[23] Mix. 49.

the other decree to redeem the human race by the Second Person. He who was born from eternity, was born to save us in time and to redeem man. There was to be no exception for any creature. Mary was included in this need of salvation; she had to owe her salvation also to the death of her Son. However, her redemption was determined in the special manner which is called the Immaculate Conception. Not only was she dependent on her Son's Passion, but she is in a striking sense the true fruit and the purchase of His Redemption; to all others Christ gives grace and regeneration at a certain point in their earthly existence; she received it from the very beginning. Thus, we do not say of her that she was *cleansed* from original sin, but that she was *preserved* from it, from the first moment of her being, so that the evil one never triumphed in her. "Therefore she was a child of Adam and Eve as if they had never fallen; she did not share with them their sin; she inherited their gifts and graces (and more than those) which Adam and Eve possessed in Paradise. This is her prerogative and the foundation of all those salutary truths which are revealed to us concerning her."[24] In fact, Mary is the one in whose favor Christ performed His most wonderful act of redemption. By the merit of that Blood which was to be shed, He interposed to hinder her incurring the sin of Adam, before He had made atonement for it.[25]

IV. Inference from Doctrine on Second Eve

Most Protestants that hold to the fundamental teachings of Christianity admit that Adam and Eve were created in grace. Hence, there is nothing striking or shocking in the thought that Eve was created without original sin, for it did not exist as yet. Newman infers the Immaculate Conception from the doctrine, that Mary is the Second Eve. Mary was a typical woman like Eve; she was to co-operate in the redemption of the world, where Eve had co-operated for its ruin. Eve had been deceived, Mary was to conquer. But since she had a great part to play in

---

[24] M. D. I, 7.
[25] Ibid. 9.

the restoration of mankind, should she not have at least been as fully endued with grace as Eve was, who, though chosen to be the mother of all the living, contributed to the downfall of the human race? Mary had succeeded where Eve had failed. To fulfill the function confided to her, she too had to receive a certain degree of grace, for, as Newman insists, "holiness and divine favor go together."[26]

Mary *undoes* what Eve had done; mankind is *saved* through a Virgin; the obedience of Mary becomes the *cause of salvation* to all mankind. She does this in a special way, as is shown by the title of Advocate given her by the Fathers. This word is ordinarily used of our Lord, who intercedes for us in His own Person, and of the Holy Ghost, who intercedes in the Saints.[27] If Mary had such an important position, it is impossible to deny that she should have at least the gifts which Eve had. As Eve was raised above human nature by grace, it may be said that Mary had a greater grace. If Eve had this supernatural gift from the first moment of her personal existence, may it be denied that Mary had it also from the first instant of her being?[28]

It may perhaps seem that Newman is driving the parallel a little too far, for Mary did not resemble Eve insofar as her natural gifts were concerned. She was mortal and subject to suffering. The same may be said of our Lord, who, by reason of the hypostatic union, was not subjected to suffering and death, but He submitted to them. These natural gifts such as knowledge, freedom from suffering, immortality, etc., were superadded and do not pertain to the essence of the state of original justice. They are merely accidental, and with the deprivation of grace were likewise lost; just as in Baptism, though sanctifying grace is restored, certain consequences of original sin nevertheless remain. Mary was not a complete exception in this regard. Newman's argument implies simply that according to the ordinary designs of Providence, grace is proportionate to the office, and since the Blessed Virgin had a

---

[26] P. S. II, 131.

[27] M. D. I, 82.

[28] Diff. II, 45, 46.

greater work to perform than Eve, she should also have greater grace. If Eve had grace from the first moment, Mary should also have it. Newman admits that in certain things the curse was not reversed in Mary's favor: "She came into a fallen world," he says, "and resigned herself to its laws; she, as also the Son she bore, was exposed to pain of soul and body, she was subjected to death; but she was not put under the power of sin. As grace was infused into Adam from the first moment of his creation, so that he never had experience of his natural poverty till sin reduced him to it; so was grace given from the first in still ampler measure to Mary and she never incurred, in fact, Adam's deprivation. She began where others end.... She was from the first clothed in sanctity, destined for perseverance, luminous and glorious in God's sight, and incessantly employed in meritorious acts which continued till her last breath."[29]

Had Eve not fallen, the grace given to her would have been transmitted to her children, and that, from the first moment of their existence, for they would have been entitled to the same privilege as she. "They would have then been conceived in grace, as in fact they are conceived in sin. What is there difficult in this doctrine?

What is there unnatural? Mary may be called, as it were, a daughter of Eve unfallen. ... St. John Baptist had grace given to him three months before his birth.... He accordingly was *not* immaculately conceived, because he was alive before grace came to him; but our Lady's case differs only from his in this respect, that to her the grace of God came, not three months merely before her birth, but from the first moment of her being, as it had been given to Eve."[30]

It is not a little strange to find mention of exemptions from sin both in Scripture and in the early writers but not the slightest reference to the sanctification of the Blessed Virgin. Scripture expressly refers to the purification of Jeremias and John the Baptist in the womb, and some Fathers include Moses and Jacob as being similarly favored. St. Jerome implies a like

---

[29] Mix. 354.
[30] Diff. II, 47.

gift in the case of Asella.[31]

The Immaculate Conception remains a mystery, and consequently no argument that may be adduced for it is apodictic. The Bull of proclamation brings out in strong relief the parallel of Eve and the Blessed Virgin. The final proof of the doctrine, however, rests with the authority of the Church, which defines that the truth has been revealed by God. The definition does not rest upon any single text alone of Holy Scripture, but rather on an ensemble of texts, which, taken together, have a cumulative value and give authority. The text from Genesis, *"Ponam inimicitias"* has great weight, but requires the support of others besides the common sentiment of the faithful. Newman substantiates and explains its force from the Apocalypse, which he uses also to prove the present exaltation of the Blessed Virgin. Pusey had accused Catholics of supporting the doctrine of the Immaculate Conception on an erroneous reading of the Hebrew version, which has "and he shall crush thy head," whereas the Vulgate gives "she."[32]

Newman holds to the Catholic reading, for he declares: "Now this fact alone of our reading, 'She shall bruise' has some weight, for *why* should not, perhaps, our reading be the right one?"[33] The fact that this reading is in use from early times and is to be found in the official version of the Church is sufficient guarantee for him.[34]

He combines Genesis with the Apocalypse to develop a complete argument. On comparing Scripture with Scripture, it is seen how the whole hangs together as we interpret it. The Apocalypse furnishes the complement to Genesis. A war is announced between the serpent and the woman. In the

---

[31] Cf. Ath. II, 207; Hieron. Ep. ad Marcell. 24, 2. Mix. 370.

[32] The direct sense of the Hebrew is that the posterity of the woman will crush the head of the serpent; the Greek has the same. The *ipsa* is already to be found in the Old Latin version though less frequently than *ipse,* and is used almost exclusively in the MSS. of the Vulgate. The Fathers of the fourth century use it. Cf. Dom Henri Quentin, *Essais de Critique Textuelle* (Paris, 1926), p. 113 sqq. Cf. I Eir. 168.

[33] M. D. 83.

[34] Cf. V. M. I, 112.

Apocalypse the serpent is introduced as Satan; here he again appears with a woman as his enemy. In Genesis the woman has a "seed"; here, a Child. If the woman in the Apocalypse is Mary,[35] then it is Mary also who is foretold in Genesis; so that the very first prophecy contrasts Mary with Eve as do the Fathers. In these texts Newman witnesses a direct bearing upon the Immaculate Conception. "There was *war* between the woman and the serpent. This is most emphatically fulfilled if she had nothing to do with sin—for, so far as any one sins, he has an alliance with the Evil One."[36]

V. A NECESSARY PREPARATION FOR THE DIVINE MATERNITY; CONSEQUENCE OF FREEDOM FROM VENIAL SIN

Lost in contemplation of Mary's dignity, Newman was perforce led to admit the Immaculate Conception as a necessary predisposition for the divine maternity. What must have been the purity and holiness of her whom the Divine Spirit deigned to overshadow? Such is the question he puts, but hesitates then to enunciate the conclusion which he already accepts and which lies evidently before him.[37]

Because of the high office to which the Blessed Virgin was to be raised, Newman teaches that she had to have other prerogatives; she had to be personally endowed in order to be worthy of her function.[38] She was more glorious in her person than in her office, for her purity is a higher gift than her relationship to God. Christ implied this Himself when he answered the woman who glorified His Mother: "Yea, rather, blessed are they who hear the word of God and keep it."[39]

Commenting on this passage, Newman says: "Protestants take these words in disparagement of our Lady's greatness, but they really tell the other way. ... He lays down a principle, that

---

[35] Cf. above, Chap. V.

[36] M. D. I, 83.

[37] P. S. II, 132.

[38] Mix. 350.

[39] Luke 11:28.

it is more blessed to keep His commandments than to be His Mother; but who, even of Protestants, will say that she did *not* keep His commandments? She kept them surely, and our Lord does but say that such obedience was in a higher line of privilege than her being His Mother."[40] The Fathers also teach that she was more blessed in her virtues than in her maternity. She had been made holy precisely that she might become the Mother of God, and these two prerogatives cannot be separated.

The coming of Christ was to herald a season of grace, and thus it was most fitting that His own Mother should be the first beneficiary of this great event. She who was to be the instrument of His bodily presence, should first be a miracle of grace; she should triumph by the spotlessness of her sanctity. She was to be a specimen in the purity of her soul and body of what man was before his fall, and what he would have been had he risen to his full perfection. "It had been hard, it had been a victory for the Evil One, had the whole race passed away, nor any one instance in it occurred to show what the Creator had intended it to be in its original state."[41] In order to show what human nature, His handiwork, was capable of becoming; to show how utterly He could bring to naught the utmost efforts of the foe and reverse the consequences of the fall, our Lord began, even before His coming, to do His most wonderful act of Redemption, in the person of her who was to be His Mother.[42]

An *a posteriori* argument that has weight with Newman in reference to the Immaculate Conception lies in Mary's freedom from venial sin. St. Augustine and, in his turn, Pius IX could claim that Christians instinctively dissociated from the thought of the Blessed Virgin the idea of sin.

From the first, Mary had the gift of indefectibility. She never committed any sin, even the least; sin had no part in her; not a thought, word, or action but was most pleasing to

---

[40] Mix. 351.

[41] Ibid. 352, 354.

[42] M. D. I, 9.

Almighty God.[43] Hence, there is no venial sin, notwithstanding the expression of a few Fathers, which might seem to imply the contrary.[44] Newman can see the Immaculate Conception as a presupposition of the freedom from venial sin. "If no venial sin, *must* there not be Immaculate Conception?"[45] There is such a vast difference between the souls of holy men and that of the Blessed Mary. However holy they may be, they cannot be wholly free from lesser transgressions, for they suffer necessarily from the spiritual wounds inflicted upon them by original sin, the remains of which are not and cannot be wholly eradicated from their beings. Mary alone was without venial sin, as is taught by faith. Hence, the source must have been wholly pure, so that perfect harmony reigned in her being, for venial sins arise from ignorance, frailty, and inadvertence, which are the unfortunate consequences of original sin. Since these were not to be found in Mary, neither could there be original sin in her.

VI. Unreasonableness of Objecting to Dogma if Doctrine is Admitted

For the benefit of a friend, Newman prepared a Memorandum on the Immaculate Conception to meet the objections of Protestants to the doctrine. He adduces Scripture and the Fathers not so much to prove the doctrine, as to rid it of the improbability that would make a person scruple to accept it when the Church defines it. Newman gives the possible declaration of a Protestant, who can never accept the truth of so "terrible a doctrine", and goes on: "Is it, after all, *certainly* irrational? is it *certainly* against Scripture? is it *certainly* against the primitive Fathers? is it *certainly* idolatrous? ... Rather may not *something* be said for it from reason, from piety, from antiquity, from the inspired text? ... Many, many doctrines are far harder than the Immaculate Conception. The doctrine of

---

[43] S. N. 79.

[44] S. N. 106.

[45] Cf. above, p. 232 sqq.

Original Sin is indefinitely harder. Mary just had not this difficulty. It is *no* difficulty to believe that a soul is united to the flesh *without* original sin; the great mystery is that any, that millions on millions are born with it. Our teaching about Mary has just one difficulty less than our teaching about the state of mankind generally."[46] The doctrine of the Immaculate Conception cannot be derogatory to God's grace, inconsistent with the Passion of Christ, nor at variance with Holy Scripture, nor unlike the teachings of the primitive Fathers, and so it gives no one the right to reject it and the Church which teaches it.

---

[46] M. D. 84–85.

CHAPTER VII
THE ASSUMPTION

I. NATURE OF THE DOCTRINE

THE Fathers of the Vatican Council were the first to give a solemn expression to their desire of seeing the Assumption of the Blessed Virgin proclaimed a dogma of faith. For the faithful Catholic there can be no doubt about this belief, and to deny it were culpable temerity. The privilege itself seems to be the most logical conclusion to all the prerogatives with which the Blessed Virgin was favored. The universal belief of the faithful, the tradition of the Church, its teaching through the Liturgy, gives this doctrine such a character of certainty that the only thing wanting is the express, formal definition of the Infallible Teacher of Christendom.

When compared with the belief in the Immaculate Conception previous to 1854, the Assumption seems to have had a more certain hold on the minds of the faithful. In order that it, too, may become a point of faith, it must have a solid dogmatic basis.

Taken in itself, what is meant by the Assumption? It is an exception to the general law by which God has decreed that all men shall rise on the last day. It is an anticipated application of the law in favor of the Blessed Virgin. Consequently, the divine Mother similarly escapes the corruption of the tomb, to which all men are condemned in virtue of the sentence "Dust thou art and into dust thou shalt return."[1] The Assumption, then, is the fact of the union of the body and soul of Mary and her glorious entry into heaven, operated by the power of God.

The question of the Assumption is not treated by Newman in his *Letter to Pusey*, for the simple reason that he could not have given an absolutely convincing argument for it. The Assumption is not implicitly contained in some other dogma of faith; e.g., Mary's title *Theotokos* is intimately bound up with the mystery of the Incarnation. On the other hand, the virginity of Mary is not essentially associated with the divine maternity, so that a formal explicit revelation was required for it. In order that the Assumption may be proclaimed a dogma of faith, it must be clearly shown that, in view of the constant tradition of the Church, there must have been at least an implicit revelation to one or more of the Apostles, which was handed down through succeeding generations of the faithful until at length the oral tradition was consigned to writing. The first express mention of the belief in authentic, orthodox writings occurs before the fifth century, and certainly not before the fourth.[2] This fact, however, does not destroy the probability of an oral tradition.

It becomes evident at once why Newman did not attempt an *ex professo* doctrinal treatment of this question in his *Letter*, for, since he was appealing to the Fathers, he had confined himself strictly to the Patristic Period. Elsewhere, however, he shows the propriety of such a conclusion to the life of her who had been called to be Mother of God and, to this end also, was conceived immaculate. In other words, Newman does not investigate the profound doctrinal reasons that could serve as a basis for a definition of the Assumption as an article of faith. But he does not ignore the subject. He seems to have entertained a particular attraction for this mystery, since he considers it as a sort of necessary consequence of the divine maternity and the Immaculate Conception. He dedicates three sermons in his *Sermon Notes* directly to the mystery itself, and

---

[1] Gen. 3:19.

[2] Renaudin, *La Doctrine de l'Assomption de la T. S. Vierge*, p. 123 sqq.

two others to its consequence, namely, the intercessory power of Mary. One of the most beautiful sermons on the Blessed Virgin is devoted to the Assumption; the fourth section of his *Meditations,* in the Litany, center about it also. In all of these sources Newman takes it for granted that Christian sense necessarily accepts the Assumption as a fitting conclusion to the life of the Divine Mother, and thus concerns himself only with exposing the fact itself, its suitableness, and its connection with other prerogatives of Mary.

II. THE FACT OF MARY'S DEATH AND ASSUMPTION

There is an infinitesimally small group of modern theologians who have attempted to teach that our Lady was not at all subject to death.[3] Among the Fathers, only one, St. Epiphanius, seems to doubt whether the Virgin of Virgins, so pure and holy, could have been obliged to die. The Saint is merely putting the case as hypothetical or very doubtful, in contrast with the doctrine of Mary's virginity which he is affirming categorically.

Newman has no hesitation on this score; the testimony to the contrary is too strong to admit of any doubt. The universal persuasion of the Church, attested to by the Liturgy, the statements of the Fathers from the fifth century onwards, are there to guide Catholics in a safe course.

The ordinary lot of mortals is to die and be subject to the corruption of the tomb. The curse pronounced upon Adam "Dust thou art and into dust shalt thou return" is the punishment inflicted for sin. This same curse falls upon each one of his posterity. The Blessed Virgin, however, did not know sin, and consequently ought not to see corruption;[4] but she had

---

[3] Dr. Arnaldi, professor at Genoa, during the second half of the nineteenth century, was the principal defender of the theory that the Immaculate Conception necessarily brought with it the impossibility of death for the Blessed Virgin. Concerning this and St. Epiphanius' view, cf. Renaudin, op. cit. p. 58. Cf. S. Epiph. Haer. 78 n. 11. P. G. 40:716; Terrien, op. cit. II, p. 317 sqq.

[4] Mix. 372.

to die, for she was mortal, and so she died in all reality.[5] The principal reason assigned by Newman for Mary's death lies in the fact that our Lord Himself submitted to die.

It may at first sight seem inconsistent that she who had been conceived without sin, should be obliged to yield to death, since death is the punishment of sin. As the Apostle declares, "The wages of sin is death." Mary never inherited Adam's sin, consequently it would seem natural that she should have been spared the humiliation of death. Though she knew no sin, she was not exempted from the laws of fallen nature, but inherited its evils.[6] The Son of God Himself took upon Himself all the infirmities of our nature; He became like to us in all things, sin excepted. He suffered fatigue, pain, mental anguish, and became veritably the Man of Sorrows. His death on the Cross was a fitting close to a life of suffering. In like manner Mary died, as she suffered, because she was in a state in which sufferings and death are the rule. When God willed it, she yielded to the tyranny of death and was dissolved into soul and body, as well as other men.[7]

However, her exemption from sin, conferred upon her special privileges insofar as her body was concerned. The reasoning cannot be absolutely convincing, but suggests itself very forcibly, for the whole argument is based on analogy, namely, resemblance to her divine Son and to our first parents in the state of original justice. Jesus, in coming to earth, submitted to certain defects of nature which were not inconsistent with His sanctity and dignity of Redeemer.[8] Adam and Eve were endowed with supernatural gifts of grace, together with certain natural and preternatural favors. Mary surpassed them in the wonderful effusions of grace poured out upon her; though she did not inherit all their natural and preternatural gifts, nevertheless, Christian sentiment would seem to demand that she, who did not contract original sin,

---

[5] M. D. I, 61.
[6] S. N. 104.
[7] Mix. 372.
[8] Summa III, q. 14 a. 4.

should not contract all the defects coincident with it. Like her Son, however, she would submit to those not inconsistent with her dignity of Mother of God.[9]

Thus Newman, conformably to Christian ideas about the Blessed Virgin, holds that our Lord observed a special dispensation in her regard even concerning her body. Like Jesus, she was preserved from disease and anything that could cause her bodily frame to weaken and decay. Jesus submitted to physical torture and to a violent death; He spared His Mother this physical suffering, yet she was not exempted from the most excruciating anguish in her soul.[10]

She was to live to the full age of human kind, but though she had reached the age of sixty and more, as is usually believed, she looked as beautiful and young as ever and more heavenly than before. "Original sin had not been found in her, by the wear of her senses and the waste of her frame, and the decrepitude of years, propagating death."[11]

How contrary to our sense of propriety would be the supposition that Mary should have been subjected to the ravages of disease or old age. Jesus did not subject Himself to them, and we may well suppose that He wished His Mother to be exempt from them. Could we picture the Blessed Mother of God bowed down by the weight of years and infirmities; could we recognize in her the one whose beauty ravished the heavens themselves? Why should our Savior have permitted sin to imprint its marks on her who never knew sin?[12] "By the grace of Christ ... she was also saved from disease and malady, and all that weakens and decays the bodily frame."[13]

For long years she had to wait for the hour of her delivery, which would once more unite her to her Divine Son. Her martyrdom had been in living; she had to suffer from the prolonged separation from Jesus. Newman calls her waiting for

---

[9] Renaudin, op. cit. 59, 60.

[10] S. N. 104.

[11] Mix. 372.

[12] Terrien, op. cit. II, 325.

[13] Mix. 372.

Christ's face "like a purgatory,"[14] with this difference, that it was not for sin, but rather combined with merit.

Since she was free from malady and the infirmities of old age, these could not kill the body. Hence, Newman speaks of her death not as an *effect*, for it was not the result of natural decay, but it was merely a *fact*. "She died that she might live, she died as a matter of form or an observance, in order to fulfill the debt of nature, not because of sin, but to submit to her condition, to glorify God, to do as her Son did, in order to finish her course and receive her crown."[15]

What could have caused her death? It is a pious belief that she died of love, for it was most fitting that love should strike the blow that would break the bonds uniting soul and body. Soul and body were engaged in a contest; the body was strong and the soul, inundated by love, longed to be with Christ. It languished for love and strove to part from the body which was still holding it captive. The ardor of her love increased from day to day until at length the soul gained the victory and took its flight to heaven. Her death was a sort of miracle, or, rather, it was the cessation of a miracle, for the greatest miracle of all was that she could have lived such a length of time separated from her beloved Son.

The death of Mary was unlike that of her Son, for she died in silence, in private, unknown to the world, whereas "it became Him, who died for the world, to die in the world's sight; it became the Great Sacrifice to be lifted up on high as a light that could not be hid. But she, the lily of Eden, who had always dwelt out of the sight of men, fittingly did she die in the garden's shade, and amid the sweet flowers in which she had lived. Her departure made no noise in the world. The Church went about her common duties, preaching, converting, suffering; there were persecutions, there was fleeing from place to place, there were martyrs, there were triumphs; at length the rumor spread abroad that the Mother of God was no longer

---

[14] S.N.105.
[15] Mix. 372, 373.

upon earth."[16] The place of her death remains ever a matter of dispute; did she die at Ephesus or Jerusalem? It is impossible to say.

As for the details connected with Mary's death and Assumption, Newman does not hesitate to recount them, even though it is not necessary to accept them as so much history. Whatever stand may be taken, there is nothing in these narrations, apocryphal to a certain extent, which need be unwelcome or difficult to piety. He portrays in a vivid fashion what may have taken place among the early Christians when the news reached them of Mary's death, which was not really something painful or sad, but rather a triumph, a gentle falling to sleep. "Pilgrims went to and fro; they sought for her relics, but they found them not; did she die at Ephesus? or did she die at Jerusalem? reports varied; but her tomb could not be pointed out or, if it was found, it was open; and instead of her pure and fragrant body, there was a growth of lilies from the earth which she had touched. So inquirers went home marvelling and waiting for further light. And then it was said, how that when her dissolution was at hand, and her soul was to pass in triumph before the judgment-seat of her Son, the Apostles were suddenly gathered together in the place, even in the Holy City, to bear part in the joyful ceremonial; how that they buried her with fitting rites; how that the third day, when they came to the tomb, they found it empty, and angelic choirs with their glad voices were heard singing day and night the glories of their risen Queen."[17]

Perhaps such a description may excite surprise in all who see in Newman a true devotee of the Blessed Virgin indeed, but one who does not let imagination run away with reason. In citing these details, which are given by St. John Damascene,[18] as a very "ancient and true tradition," Newman states expressly

---

[16] Mix. 373.

[17] Mix. 373, 374.

[18] *Hom. 2 in Dormit. B. V. M.* n. 18. P. G. 96:748 sqq. This narration forms the Lessons of the second Nocturn, on the fourth day within the Octave of the Assumption.

that there is a difference between accepting these merely historical details and the fact of the Assumption itself which followed upon her death. The whole Catholic world is in accord that she is now, soul and body, with her Son and God in heaven; before her body could undergo corruption, Jesus raised it up from the tomb and united it once more with her spotless soul, so that for her the resurrection was anticipated.

III. THE DOCTRINE IS CONSISTENT WITH THE REST OF REVEALED TEACHING

The account of Mary's death just narrated has nothing to do with the doctrinal value of the Assumption, though what is related may well be accepted. The historical circumstances under which the Assumption took place are not so important as the fact of the glorification of Mary's soul and body. The apocryphal writings which narrate these events may be invoked as testimonies of the Church's tradition, from which they took birth. Even if there is a certain amount of imposture and heresy in these accounts, they give testimony to the truth, for insofar as they speak of the *fact* of the Assumption, they testify to a universal belief. Accidental circumstances may be left aside.[19]

Newman, as has been said, does not consider the Assumption from an absolutely dogmatic viewpoint, that is to say, from his argumentation one could not deduce the possibility of making the Assumption an article of faith. He is satisfied with showing how intimately this mystery is connected with the prerogatives of Mary and with the tradition of the faithful. He who learned well how to weigh his words never purposes to draw an undeniable conclusion, but insists continually that the Assumption is a *fitting* termination of Mary's career; that this belief is simply in harmony with the substance and main outlines of the Incarnation, and that without it Catholic teaching would seem to be incomplete, and

---

[19] Cf. Renaudin, op. cit. 126 sqq.

our pious expectations disappointed.[20] It became our Lord to do this for His Mother—such is the summary of Newman's argument. He prefers to view the question in the light of reason, so that its very fitness recommends the Assumption to our minds even though we receive the doctrine on the belief of ages.

The principle here laid down by Newman is the consistency manifest in all revealed teaching. One doctrine must fit into what is already received. Christ, as well as St. Paul, calls attention to the "analogy of faith." Both appeal to the fitness and congruity which exist between the Passion and the other truths revealed concerning the salvation of mankind. It is a great evidence of truth in the case of revealed teaching that one thing springs out of another, and each part requires and is required by the rest.[21]

Applying this principle to the mystery of the Assumption, we say with Newman: It is fitting; we feel that it *ought* to be so, it *becomes* the Son of Mary to act thus in her regard. The Assumption is in harmony with the Incarnation and completes Catholic teaching.[22]

IV. THE ASSUMPTION AND THE DIVINE MATERNITY

"What ought to be done to the man whom the king is desirous to honor?" asked King Assuerus of Aman.[23] In like manner it may be asked: What shall be done to Mary, who gave birth to the Creator, who had the most intimate relationship with the Most High? And Newman answers the query: "Nothing is too high for her to whom God owes His human life; no exuberance of grace, no excess of glory but is becoming, but is to be expected there, where God has lodged Himself, whence God has issued."[24] She had, then, to be endowed with grace and

---

[20] Mix. 361.

[21] Mix. 360.

[22] Ibid. 361.

[23] Esther 6:6.

[24] Mix. 363.

glory. Her life was one of the utmost purity and sanctity; she participated in such great mysteries and miracles that we should be disappointed were her death, and what followed, similar to that of other men. "It would be a greater miracle if her life, being what it was, her death was like that of other men, than if it were such as to correspond to her life. Who can conceive that God should so repay the debt which He condescended to owe to His Mother, for the elements of His human body, as to allow the flesh and blood from which it was taken to moulder in the grave? Do the sons of men thus deal with their mothers? Do they not nourish and sustain them in their feebleness and keep them in life while they are able?"[25]

Furthermore, we read in Scriptures that by the power of God other Saints had been raised from the grave. At our Lord's death "many of bodies of the Saints that had slept, came out of their tombs and appeared to many in Jerusalem."[26] These Saints, according to Newman, were the Prophets, Priests, and Kings of former times, who rose again in anticipation of the last day.[27] The law of the grave had admitted a relaxation in their case. Did body and soul reunite in these Saints, who had long been dead? Newman would seem to say so, for if they rose in anticipation of the last day, they must have risen in the same manner as all men will on the dread judgment-day. We are not told what became of these Saints after the apparitions in the Holy City.

From the fact that some Saints of the Old Covenant were thus favored, Newman demands to know whether we could exclude God's own Mother from such a privilege; for had she not a greater claim on the love of her Son than the others? Was she not nearer to Him than the greatest Saints before her?

V. THE ASSUMPTION AND THE IMMACULATE CONCEPTION

The doctrine of the Immaculate Conception suggests

---

[25] Ibid. 371.

[26] Matt. 27:52–53.

[27] M. D. 62.

another reason for the fitness of Mary's Assumption. She was so transcendently holy, full of grace, that it was not fitting that her virginal frame should remain in the grave. Though she died as her Son did, yet she was not to die the death of a sinner, for she had no knowledge of sin; hence she ought not to see corruption.

The comparison between Mary and Eve once more recurs to Newman in this connection. Adam and Eve had both been created upright and sinless; had they been faithful to God's command, they would have been immortal in spite of the corruptibility of their bodies. Only when they had sinned, did their bodies follow the ordinary law of their corruptible nature. From thenceforth all who share in their curse must share in the punishment. "If Eve, the beautiful daughter of God, never would have become dust and ashes unless she had sinned, shall we not say that Mary, having never sinned, retained the gift which Eve, by sinning, lost? What had Mary done to forfeit the privilege given to our first parents in the beginning? Was her comeliness to be turned into corruption and her fine gold to become dim, without reason assigned? Impossible. Therefore, we believe that, though she died for a short hour, as did our Lord Himself, yet like Him and by His Almighty power she was raised again from the grave."[28]

VI. AN EXTRINSIC, HISTORICAL PROOF

Another reason presents itself to the mind of Newman; he draws it not from any doctrine, but from a mere extrinsic historical fact, which would serve as an adequate reply to any one who might be so rash as to deny the doctrine of our Blessed Lady's Assumption. It is inconceivable that Christians, impressed by the awful dignity of the Mother of their Lord, should have lost sight of her burial place and of her remains.

"If her body was not taken into heaven, where is it? how comes it that it is hidden from us? why do we not hear of her tomb as being here or there? why are not pilgrimages made to

---

[28] M. D. I, 64

it? why are not relics producible of her, as of the Saints in general? Is it not even a natural instinct which makes us reverent towards the places where our dead are buried?" Our Lord's tomb was honored; in like manner the tombs and relics of John the Baptist, the Apostles and Martyrs. "Now if there was any one who more than all would be preciously taken care of, it would be our Lady. Why, then, do we hear nothing of the Blessed Virgin's body, and its separate relics? Is it conceivable that they who had been so reverent and careful of the bodies of the Saints and the Martyrs should neglect her—her who was the Queen of the Martyrs and Queen of the Saints, who was the very Mother of Our Lord? It is impossible. Why, then, is she thus the *hidden* Rose? Plainly because that sacred body is in heaven, not on earth."[29]

---

[29] M. D. I, 66–67.

CHAPTER VIII
INTERCESSORY POWER OF THE BLESSED VIRGIN

ITH her Assumption into heaven the Blessed Virgin does not cease to continue her relations with humanity. Her death ushered in a new function, or, rather, the continuation of the one she had exercised upon earth, namely, that of Advocate, to which St. Irenaeus refers when he declares: "And though the one had disobeyed God, yet the other was drawn to obey God; that, of the virgin Eve, the Virgin Mary might become the Advocate."[1] Seated at the right hand of her Son in glory, raised to the dignity of Queen of Angels and Saints, Mary cannot forget the Church militant, for the salvation of which she had consented to become Mother of the Redeemer, had co-operated in the Redemption, and had suffered courageously the greatest spiritual anguish that could ever have been endured by a mere creature.

As has been remarked hitherto, Newman is always preoccupied with finding a solid doctrinal basis for any prerogative or dignity possessed by the Blessed Virgin. The intercessory power of Mary is no exception to the rule. It is founded on the Christian doctrine of prayer, which in its turn rests solidly on the fundamental tenet of the Communion of Saints. This same belief in her intercession is an inference drawn from the practical utility and benefits accruing from the invocation of Mary, who is so singularly dear to her divine Son.

---

[1] Diff. II, 68.

I. BASED ON THE DOCTRINE OF PRAYER

The teaching of Catholics about the Blessed Virgin's prayerful omnipotence is not a mere pious invention of the imagination, but is grounded on the solid doctrine of prayer, which is accepted by Protestants and Catholics alike.[2] The immutability of natural laws furnishes some unbelievers with the pretext of rejecting all religion, since fate seems to determine everything. The Creator has imposed these fixed laws upon the universe so that it may be protected against substantial injury and loss. Everything proceeds in order; there seems to be an illimitable system of cause and effect, that unaided reason, confused by the regularity, is led to believe in mere fate, so that if it admits a God, it does not accept a religion as necessary, since God seems able to enter into direct communication with the world only through a system.[3] Such sceptics are wont to demand: Of what use is prayer, since the natural laws will continue to function whether man prays or not?

Conscience and the innate religious sense, both of which hold such an important place in Newman's religious views, speak to us of a particular Providence; these, confirmed by revelation, tell us of a still more wonderful world in which there is a power of avail to alter and subdue the visible world, to suspend and counteract its laws. This is the world of the Angels and Saints, of the Church and her children, all of whom possess a weapon by which they render themselves masters of these laws of the visible universe. This weapon is the power of prayer, which renders possible what seems impossible of achievement.[4]

Mere natural religion even, has as one of its doctrines that of meritorious intercession by certain ones whose lives of austerity and prayer seem to mark them as particularly

---

[2] S. N. 42.

[3] M. D. I, 70.

[4] P. S. III, 116; S. N. 42.

agreeable to the divinity or divinities worshipped. This idea is expressed by the young man cured of his blindness by our Lord: "We know that God doth not hear sinners ... unless this man were of God, he could not do anything."[5] Apart from the superstitions to which some of these views gave rise among the pagans, the fundamental notion of intercessory prayer was there.[6]

Pagans must have been astonished to see what a vital part prayer took in the organization of the Christian Church; no matter how scattered the members were, mutual intercession served as the bond of union and the solace of a spiritual intercourse. Newman insists again and again that intercessory prayer is "the special function of the justified,"[7] "the Christian's especial prerogative."[8] God will hear the prayer of the righteous, not that of the unregenerate and the carnal, for there is an incongruity that exists in a habitual, deliberate sinner presuming to intercede for others.[9] The friends of Christ on earth give power to their prayer by the practice of virtue.[10] Even in the natural order, mediation is sought for when one has been offended;[11] how much more in the supernatural order must not Saints possess the privilege of being intercessors on earth between God and man?[12]

Nay, even the ordinary Christian unites with others in praying for the needs of the Church, of his country, and of those that are near and dear to him.[13] Though the Anglican Newman hesitated about admitting the intercession of the

---

[5] John 9:31, 33.
[6] G. A. 407, 408.
[7] P. S. III, 354.
[8] Ibid. 362.
[9] P. S. III, 355.
[10] Ibid. 356.
[11] Ibid. 94.
[12] Ibid. 358.
[13] Ibid. 116.

Saints in heaven,[14] he never had the slightest doubt about the power of the faithful on earth to intercede for one another. He was fully aware that great services were rendered the Church by those who had leisure for prayer. In begging the prayers of one of his aunts in order that he might be useful in the service of God, he adds: "I am quite sure it is by prayers such as yours, of those whom the world knows nothing of, that the Church is saved, and I know I have them in particular, as you have also mine, ... every morning and evening."[15]

In fact, in his Anglican days, Newman advocated a life of which "prayer, praise, intercession, and other devotional services are made the object and business of life, one in which devotion is the end to which everything else subserves."[16] In his view, the privilege of intercession is a trust committed to all Christians, whose prayers may benefit the world and every individual of it; this charge is so august, so sacred, and so awful that their neglect of prayer may be even the occasion of the difficulties in which a country and its rulers find themselves.[17]

Intercession is particularly characteristic of the priestly order, and a prerogative of the Gospel Ministry. This thought is repeatedly brought out by Scripture, and particularly by Isaias when he wrote: "Upon thy walls, O Jerusalem, I have appointed watchmen all the day and all the night, they shall never hold their peace. You that are mindful of the Lord, hold not your peace and give him no silence till he establish, and till he make Jerusalem a praise in the earth."[18]

II. And also on the Communion of Saints

Prayer is the very essence of all religion; among pagans it was public or personal for the attainment of temporal goods,

---

[14] "We do not know, we may not boldly speculate—yet, it may be that Saints departed intercede, unknown to us." P. S. II, 214.

[15] Moz. II, 117.

[16] P. S. III, 334.

[17] P. S. III, 364–365.

[18] Is. 62:6, 7; P. S. II, 312 sqq.

among Christians it was the link that united them, it knit them together into one body. No matter how they were hindered in their social intercourse by iniquitous laws, yet they could pray for one another. In fact, this was but the continuation of the tradition established at the very inception of the Church, for it was founded in prayer. The Apostles and other holy souls persevered with Mary the Mother of Jesus, in prayer. The whole Christian community offered up unceasing prayer for the Prince of the Apostles while he was in prison.

St. Paul exhorted his brethren to "pray in every place," "to make supplications, prayers, intercessions, thanksgiving for all men."[19]

The bond of union between Christians was maintained after the death of the brethren. The early ages testify to the use of the prayers for the dead. Such a practice, though perhaps offensive in the eyes of Protestants in general,[20] because it implies the existence of Purgatory, seemed perfectly intelligible to a man like Pusey, who writes to Newman in 1826 on the death of his own brother: "They are not separated who are not visibly with us. Dare one pray for them? Will you answer me when I see you? Nothing, I am sure, can be found in Scripture against praying for the dead."[21] Pusey certainly would not have posed such a question did he not consider that the departed may stand in need of the prayerful assistance of their brethren on earth. Thus prayer and intercession unite the militant with the suffering Church.[22]

The same must be said with regard to the Church triumphant. A sacred communion extends even to the inhabitants of heaven. This fact was accepted by Pusey and also by Newman in his Tract 90. They both admitted that it was good and useful to invoke the Saints, to obtain favors from God through their intercession.[23] There can be no question of

---

[19] 1 Tim. 2:1, 8; Diff. II, 69.

[20] Cf. P. S. III, 372.

[21] Pusey I, 112.

[22] V. M. II, 296 sqq.

[23] Ibid. 305 sqq.

praying for those already in glory, but these can pray for us and we can address our prayers to them. Should it not be expected that they may do for us in heaven what they could do on earth and what Christians are bound to do for one another?[24]

In the Apocalypse, Angels are introduced as sending us their blessings and offering up our prayers before the Divine Presence. The Angel "came and stood before the altar, having a golden censer" and "there was given to him much incense, that he should offer of the prayers of all Saints upon the golden altar which is before the Throne of God."[25] From this fact, Newman is led to conclude that the Angel surely performed the office of Mediator or Intercessor above, for the children of the Church Militant below.[26] In like manner the Eternal seems to associate Himself with the ministers of His mercies, in conferring on us grace and peace.[27] St. Justin, in a remarkable passage, speaks of Angels as receiving from men a reasonable and true honor, and as therefore being objects of worship.[28]

The spirits of the just, as well as the Angels, enter into this communion with us, as is declared by St. Paul: "You are come to mount Sion ... the heavenly Jerusalem ... to the company of many thousands of Angels ... to God the judge of all, and to the spirits of the just made perfect, and to Jesus the Mediator of the new testament."[29] Commenting on this, Newman asks: "What can be meant by having 'come to the spirits of the just,' unless in some way or other, they do us good whether by blessing or by aiding us? that is, in a word, to speak correctly, by praying for us, for it is surely by prayer that the creature above is able

---

[24] I Eir. 100.

[25] Apoc. 8:3.

[26] Diff. II, 70.

[27] Cf. for example, John 5:4; Apoc. passim.

[28] The passage in question has been much disputed; some would wish to remove mention of the angels and thus find a clear expression on the Blessed Trinity, while others find difficulty in accepting the words "worship and adore" used in reference to God and the angels. Cf. Dev. 411 sqq.

[29] Heb. 12:22, 24.

to bless and aid the creature below."[30]

We are told that the "prayer of a just man availeth much" and religious men are certain of being answered.[31] What makes intercession really so powerful, is sanctity. St. John reminds us that "Whatsoever we ask, we receive of Him, because we keep His commandments and do those things that are pleasing in his sight."[32] Thus it is that consistent obedience, mature, habitual, lifelong holiness is made the condition of Christ's intimate favor and of power in intercession. "If you abide in Me," says Christ Himself, "and My words abide in you, you shall ask whatever you will and it shall be done unto you."[33] God revealed to Abraham and Moses His purposes of wrath that by their prayers they might avert its execution. Job was made the intercessor of his erring friends. Moses and Samuel are spoken of as mediators so powerful that only the sins of the Jews hindered the success of their prayers. Noe, Daniel, and Job could have saved guilty nations from judgment.[34] This same high office is continued even after this life as is shown by the mention of Abraham, who is spoken of in Scripture as having charge of Lazarus. Newman admits, in this latter respect, the contention of some, that though the expression "Abraham's bosom" is a Jewish mode of speech, nevertheless it has its very particular significance since our Lord Himself sanctioned and recognized this belief.[35]

Since the prayers of the just upon earth are of such avail, it must follow that as the Saints in heaven are free from every stain of sin and are confirmed in grace and glory, so their

---

[30] Diff. II, 71.

[31] James 5:6; S. D. 352.

[32] I John 3:22.

[33] John 15:7.

[34] Cf. P. S. III, 356–357. The preliminary matter on Mary's intercessory power, as exposed in the *Letter to Pusey* lies at the basis of an entire sermon on Intercession preached in 1835. The basic principles developed in both are identical, though a span of thirty years separates the two writings. Cf. P. S. III, Sermon XXIV.

[35] Diff. II, 72.

prayers must be proportionately more efficacious.[36] What shall be said of the intercession of her who is not merely the "friend" but the very "Mother of God", whose sanctity surpasses that of every other creature.

III. Mary's Special Intercession Because of Her Sanctity and Dignity

Now, combining the three beliefs in the Communion of Saints, the power of prayer, and the sanctity and dignity of the Blessed Virgin, the conclusion is obvious. Newman sums it up concisely: "I consider it impossible, then, for those who believe the Church to be one vast body in heaven and on earth, in which every holy creature of God has his place, and of which prayer is the life, when once they recognize the sanctity and dignity of the Blessed Virgin, not to perceive immediately, that her office above is one of perpetual intercession for the faithful militant and that our very relation to her must be that of clients to a patron, and that, in the eternal enmity which exists between the Woman and the serpent, while the serpent's strength lies in being the tempter, the weapon of the Second Eve and Mother of God is prayer."[37]

Thus it is seen that Newman, on the question of intercession, has not failed to look also to Mary's position as Second Eve for confirmation of his arguments. As she had foiled the tempter on earth, she must continue to do so in her glorified state by means of prayer. Here Newman is applying the suggestion given by Irenaeus and other Fathers, to whom Mary appeared in the character of Patroness or Paraclete, a "loving Mother with clients."[38] Thus, as soon as the idea of her

---

[36] I Eir. 100.

[37] Diff. II, 73.

[38] Dev. 418. Newman considered that the term *Advocata* could be applied as well to Mary's intercession as to her reparation of the evil done by Eve. Robinson translates the word by "Intercessor." Cf. Irenaeus, "The Apostolic Preaching," No. 33. Neubert does not accept this meaning: Advocate connotes the idea of consoling, or of coming to the aid of someone. This is the meaning to be understood here. Cf. Neubert, op. cit. 263–264.

dignity penetrated the minds of the first Christians, that of her intercessory power followed close. The first representations of her in the Catacombs portray her as Mother of Jesus, but soon she is pictured with arms outstretched in prayer, either with Jesus before her or standing between the Apostles Peter and Paul.[39]

Newman looks to Antiquity for further confirmation of his statements and cites two of the earliest known documents that manifest a belief in Mary's intercession. St. Gregory Thaumaturgus was perplexed on some religious questions, when during the night the Blessed Virgin appeared to him with St. John. She bade the Evangelist disclose to him the mysteries over which he had been pondering so deeply. St. John enunciated a concise but complete formulary and both of the visitors disappeared.[40] As for the second account, Newman omits it in the *Letter to Pusey* though he had given it in the *Essay on Development,* because, as he says: "It is attended with some mistake in the narrative which weakens its cogency as an evidence of the belief, not of the fourth century, in which St. Gregory (Nazianzen) lived, but of the third."[41] St. Justina had recourse to the protection of the Blessed Virgin, was preserved from impurity, and obtained the conversion of a magician who had attempted to practice his arts on her. Both died as martyrs.[42]

Apart from these historical documents, which show the mind of the early Christians, a more potent demonstration lies in the mere application of the doctrine of prayer to the intercession of Mary. With an argument to the point, Newman answers Pusey's condemnation of the expression "All heresies

---

[39] Cf. above, p. 218.

[40] Even the Protestant divine, Bull, accepts this account. Cf. Dev. 417–418; Diff. II, 74–75.

[41] Dev. 418.

[42] S. N. 93; Cf. I Eir. 110 note.

thou hast destroyed alone."[43] In spite of Pusey's objection, Newman claims that its truth "is surely verified in this age, as in former times. ... She is the great exemplar of prayer in a generation which emphatically denies the power of prayer *in toto,* which determined that fatal laws govern the universe, that there cannot be any direct communication between earth and heaven, that God cannot visit His own earth and that man cannot influence His providence."[44] Protestants frequently object that Catholics exaggerate the power of our Lady. We call her the powerful Virgin, nay, we sometimes speak of her as all-powerful.[45] Yet, as Newman shows, her power is nothing else than the greatest exemplification of the power of prayer, for she has, more than any one else, the prevailing gift of prayer. She is the great advocate of the Church. She has nothing to do with Atonement properly so called, it is true; Jesus remains as ever the sole absolute Mediator between God and man; He it is who redeems and saves mankind. "He alone has an entrance into our soul, reads our secret thoughts, speaks to our heart, applies to us spiritual power and strength. On Him we solely depend. He alone is our inward life; He not only regenerates us, but (to use the words appropriated to a higher mystery) *semper gignit;* He is ever renewing our new birth and our heavenly sonship. In this sense He may be called, as in nature, so in grace, our real Father. Mary is only our mother by divine appointment given us from the Cross; her presence is above, not on earth; her office is external, not within us. Her name is not heard in the administration of the Sacraments. Her work is not one of ministration towards us; her power is indirect. It is her prayers that avail, and her prayers are effectual by the *fiat* of Him who is our all in all. Nor need she hear us by an innate power or any personal gift; but by His manifestation to her of

---

[43] I Eir. 124, note. Pusey maintained that this phrase applied to Mary's present personal power by Catholics, was originally said of the Incarnation, which, if rightly believed, is the destruction of all heresies.

[44] Diff. II, 75–76.

[45] M. D. 71.

the prayers which we make to her."⁴⁶ Thus Newman sketches the essential difference which lies between our Lord as Mediator and the Blessed Virgin as our advocate. Her intercession cannot interfere with the Mediatorship of Jesus. To her we ascribe prayer as we do to ourselves and all Christians. The power of our intercession is, however, very limited, depending upon the degree of holiness attained; whereas Mary, the sinless and immaculate Virgin, possesses this power in its fulness. It was unintelligible to Newman that Non-Catholics should be taken aback at the assertions of Catholics on Mary's power. Persons may reject the power of prayer altogether, but why should they scruple at admitting a great exemplification of it? "We do not introduce a mystery but realize it. The great mystery is that prayer should have influence."⁴⁷ Once the power of prayer is admitted, an almost unlimited number of possibilities present themselves to the mind.

Do not Protestants say strong things about prayer? Such is Newman's retort. Scripture itself speaks of the prayer of faith which removes mountains and can do all things. Prayer constrains God, as it were. Thus, too, we say that Mary's prayer is omnipotent and that it constrains God. For an assurance that a prayer will be heard, sanctity and perseverance must go hand in hand. Who can persevere as Mary? who is as holy as she?⁴⁸

Should it cause any wonderment to any one that her prayer should be so effectual when her dignity, sanctity, and prerogatives are borne in mind?⁴⁹ The omnipotence assigned to

---

⁴⁶ Diff. II, 84. "The Catholic Church allows no image of any sort, material or immaterial, no dogmatic symbol, no rite, no sacrament, no Saint, not even the Blessed Virgin herself, to come between the soul and its Creator. It is face to face, 'solus cum solo', in all matters between man and his God. He alone creates; He alone has redeemed; before His awful eyes we go in death; in the vision of Him is our eternal beatitude." Apo. 195.

⁴⁷ S. N. 43.

⁴⁸ "Thus, to say that prayer (and the Blessed Virgin's prayer) is omnipotent is a harsh expression in every-day prose; but if it is explained to mean that there is nothing which prayer may not obtain from God, it is nothing else than the very promise made us in Scripture." Diff. II, 104.

⁴⁹ S. N. 44.

her is participated in a manner likewise possessed by the Saints, but she in a higher degree and greater perfection. Because of her position in the Incarnation, she stands alone between God and the rest of creation; she may thus be called the center of all things. Consequently, a special office is assigned to her distinct from that of other Saints, yet also distinct from that assigned to our Lord. In the words of Segneri, she has been made "the arbitress of every effect coming from God's mercy." Because she is Mother of God, the salvation of mankind is said to be given to her prayers *"de congruo,* but *de condigno* it is due only to the blood of the Redeemer."[50] Her prayer is especially powerful because no one has access to God as she has, for she is the Mother of God; none could have merit such as hers. Could Jesus deny her anything in heaven, who had been so near to Him on earth?[51]

If holy men of the Old Testament had such power over the heart of God, if the Apostles served as mediators to bring others to Jesus, "is it strange that the Mother should have power with the Son, distinct in kind from that of the purest Angel and the most triumphant Saint? If we have faith to admit the Incarnation itself, we must admit it in its fulness; why, then, should we start at the gracious appointments which arise out of it, or are necessary to it, or are included in it?"[52]

IV. Exercise of Mary's Intercession

As Advocate, as Queen of Heaven, Mary exercises her benignant offices on behalf of the Church militant at large and of individual members in particular. In the words of the Litany she is the true *Auxilium Christianorum,* the minister of numberless services to the elect people of God and to His holy Church.

Newman recounts five events in the history of the Church in which, according to the Divine Office, Mary is displayed as

---

[50] Cf. Dev. 435.

[51] M. D. I, 71.

[52] Mix. 355.

the Help of Christians. All of them are connected more or less with the Rosary. The first refers to the institution of the Rosary by St. Dominic, who used it in combating the Albigensians.[53] Then there were three victories gained over the Turks, in the Gulf of Lepanto, at Vienna, and in Hungary. Lastly, Pius VII ascribed to our Blessed Lady the restoration of the temporal power taken from him by Napoleon I. The feasts of the Holy Rosary, of the Holy Name of Mary, and of Our Lady Help of Christians are associated with these events.[54]

By her intercession Mary is of aid to the Christian upon earth. He has his struggle to wage, but he must recall that he is the child of the sweetest of mothers. Hence, he must endeavor in the measure of his abilities to imitate her virtues, her meekness, her simplicity, her faith and obedience and, above all, her purity. Newman develops in a most forceful and beautiful manner the thought that Mary's help and intercession are particularly necessary for the young in order to maintain them in their purity. Addressing young men and women, he says: "What shall bring you forward in the narrow way, if you live in the world, but the thought and patronage of Mary? What shall seal your senses, what shall tranquillise your heart, when sights and sounds of danger are around you, but Mary? What shall give you patience and endurance, when you are wearied with the length of the conflict with evil, with the unceasing necessity of precautions, with the irksomeness of observing them, with the tediousness of their repetition, with the strain upon your mind, with your forlorn and cheerless condition, but a loving communion with her? She will comfort you in your discouragements, solace you in your fatigues, raise you after your falls, reward you for your successes. She will show you her Son, your God, and your All. When your spirit within you is excited, or relaxed, or depressed, when it loses its balance,

---

[53] Newman does not investigate from a critical historical viewpoint the beginnings of this popular devotion, but accepts the fact on the authority of the Breviary. The form of prayers comprising what is now called the Rosary, seems to have begun at a date even earlier than the thirteenth century. Cf. *Katholik,* 1913, I, p. 320.

[54] M. D. I, 72–73.

when it is restless and wayward, when it is sick of what it has, and hankers after what it has not, when your eye is solicited with evil and your mortal frame trembles under the shadow of the tempter, what will bring you to yourselves, to peace and to health, but the cool breath of the Immaculate and the fragrance of the Rose of Sharon? It is the boast of the Catholic Religion, that it has the gift of making the young heart chaste; and why is this, but that it gives us Jesus Christ for our food, and Mary for our nursing Mother? Fulfil this boast in yourselves; prove to the world that you are following no false teaching, vindicate the glory of your Mother Mary, whom the world blasphemes, in the very face of the world, by the simplicity of your own deportment, and the sanctity of your words and deeds. Go to her for the royal heart of innocence. She is the beautiful gift of God, which outshines the fascinations of a bad world, and which no one ever sought in sincerity and was disappointed."[55]

This lengthy citation is pregnant from first to last with a deep psychological insight into the trials and temptations with which the young especially are beset, and at the same time brings out in relief the fruit of Mary's intercession in behalf of those who call upon her in the hour of peril. She, the purest of creatures, can obtain the gift of purity for those who invoke her with confidence.

Mary concerns herself in all that pertains to our spiritual life. She aids us by her prayers to live in the grace of God and she is of special assistance to persevere and die in that blessed grace which assures us of our future predestination. Newman can find no more effective means for guaranteeing perseverance than Mary's intercession. "Interest your dear Mother, the Mother of God, in your success; pray to her earnestly for it; she can do more for you than any one else. Pray her by the pain she suffered, when the sharp sword went through her, pray her, by her own perseverance, which was in her the gift of the same God of whom you ask it for yourselves. God will not refuse you, He will not refuse her, if you have recourse to her succor. It will be a blessed thing in your last

---

[55] Mix. 375, 376.

hour ... to have her at your side more tender than an earthly mother, to nurse you and to whisper peace.... . That dread day may be sooner or later ... but if Mary intercedes for you, that day will find you watching and ready."[56]

---

[56] Mix. 143–144.

CHAPTER IX
Devotion to the Blessed Virgin

I. Newman's Peculiar Fitness to Treat This Question

THE Newman, who at the age of fifteen was I overpowered by the thought of two luminously self-evident beings, *his Creator and himself,* and lived under its constant influence, did not cast aside what might be called the center of his Anglican spirituality, when he joined the Catholic Church. Henceforth, he is no longer alone with his Creator; the Blessed Virgin, the Angels and Saints are with him. The same center remains as ever; God is ever his *All in all.* His Anglican notions had once told him that these creatures, holy though they be, intervened in the soul's onward march towards the Creator and became snares in the path. He discovered, at length, that the contrary was really the case; that they are the surest guides towards the Sovereign Good, in whom they repose as their supreme happiness, to whom they wish to direct the pilgrims still wandering upon the earth.

Newman's intense personal devotion to Christ, which transforms and marks his whole Anglican career, bears along with it in due time a correspondingly ardent devotion to His Blessed Mother. The devotion to Christ was fixed in him from an early hour; not so for devotion to Mary. At first he seems to be defending himself against an attraction which draws him instinctively towards her; in later years he wishes to make up for time lost when he failed to tender towards the Blessed Mother of God a worship befitting her who is "blessed among women." He discovered as time went on and his difficulties melted before him, that devotion to Mary, instead of being an obstacle in the way of devotion to Jesus, was rather the necessary consequence of it. As the river is traced back to its source, so the cultus of Mary springs from a true knowledge of the person and dignity of the Word Incarnate.

No one was, then, better fitted than Newman to give a psychological analysis of devotion to Mary and to defend it against the aspersions of those who were unable to comprehend it. No one was more capable of entering into the difficulties of others, for he was possessed by nature with the gift of throwing himself into the minds of others. Besides, he himself had had experience of these presumedly insurmountable obstacles that long hindered him from giving his adhesion to the Church of Rome. The difficulties propounded by Pusey in his *Eirenicon* were not at all unfamiliar to Newman. They had been his, and perhaps even more so, in his pre-Roman days. Having recognized that these objections were, if not puerile, at least unfounded, he could serve as a most apt guide to others who were stumbling over these self same obstacles and could not submit to Rome because of her alleged "corruptions." His study of the bases and practice of Marian devotion is one of the most serious and at the same time most original ever presented from a psychological point of view. This is sufficiently evidenced by a casual glance at all the modern works on devotion to Mary which claim to treat the question apologetically. Newman stands as the guide and master of many in this field of Catholic devotion.

It will be recalled that Newman made a distinction as an Anglican which he abandoned as he approached the Roman Church. Doctrine was one thing; devotion and devotional manifestation were as distinct from each other as doctrine and devotion. His Marian doctrine underwent no transformation save on the question of intercession, which he had considered an open question in the Anglican Church. He professed true devotion to Mary as an Anglican, but rejected devotional manifestations, which were his particular *crux* as regards Catholicism. The system of Romanism, altogether too thorough, too complete, had baffled him; it seemed to profess a knowledge that went far beyond actual revelation. This same systematic development of Marian doctrine was likewise too much for Pusey.[1] The practical system of Rome, had, according to the Anglicans, put the Blessed Virgin on a par with our Lord, making her office of intercession co-extensive with that of her Divine Son.

II. DEVOTION IS THE CONSEQUENCE OF DOCTRINE

Bearing in mind the difficulties of Anglicans, Newman begins the doctrinal portion of his *Letter to Pusey* with a definition of terms. He no longer distinguishes between devotion and devotional manifestations; for him, as for all Catholics, they are integral parts of the cultus due to Mary. Faith or doctrine is the Creed and assent to it; devotion is the religious honors due to the objects of faith, and the payment of these honors. The doctrine concerning the Blessed Virgin has been fixed once and for all from the beginning; it is substantially the same now as in Apostolic times; development may take place but not transformation. Devotion, on the other hand, is something accidental that follows upon faith and consequently may be subject to increase among Catholics with the progress of centuries.[2]

The Council of Trent, in defining the invocation of the Blessed Virgin and Saints, admits the accidental character of devotion by declaring the practice "good and useful," but does not go beyond to impose anything in this regard. Practices of devotion are almost infinite in their variety, differing from place to place, from individual to individual, and also according to time. But doctrine is something fixed, firmly established, and immutable. No Pope or Council can undo what was once declared of faith and imposed as such upon all the faithful.

---

[1] I Eir. 101.

[2] The first light that came to dispel Newman's own doubts in the matter, showed him that the idea of the Blessed Virgin was gradually *magnified* in the Church. Apo. 196.

In proportion as Christians penetrated more and more deeply into an understanding of the natures and personality of Christ, they were led to look upon Christ's Mother and to appreciate her lofty position in the economy of grace. But it does not suffice to entertain a high notion of the Blessed Virgin in consequence of her dignity as Mother of God and Second Eve. Honors may be paid to her as also to the Saints. This cultus in general is independent even of our Lady's personal office, since it is due to all the elect who have died in the grace of God.

Newman again lays down a solid dogmatic basis for the worship of the Saints in general and a superior cult for the Blessed Virgin in consequence of her dignity and prerogatives. This brilliant thinker is never content unless he can trace a doctrine back to some primary one in which it is either implicitly contained or with which it is intimately connected. He maintains that cultus forms part of the theological system which revolves about the Incarnation as the antecedent doctrine. "The Incarnation is the antecedent of the doctrine of Mediation and the archetype both of the Sacramental principle and of the merits of Saints."[3] Where does the devotion to the Saints find its natural place. Devotion is a very general term with Newman and includes invocation and cultus, which in turn embrace the veneration of the persons themselves with their images and relics.

The merits of Angels and Saints, together with invocation and cultus, follow from the doctrine of Mediation as do the Atonement and the Mass. The veneration of images follows from the sacramental principle; the virtue of relics is associated with the Eucharist.[4] And yet all these combine and form parts of one.

Newman considered the Catholic polemic waged against

---

[3] Dev. 93.

[4] Dev. 94. Newman repeatedly points out the wonderful harmony existing in the system of revealed truth. Every article of faith is consistent with every other. The rejection of one doctrine entails that of others. He realized in himself what he says in this connection: "It is a solemn thing to accept any part, for before you know where you are, you may be carried on by a stern logical necessity to accept the whole." Ibid.

the Arian and Monophysite heresies the natural introduction to the *cultus Sanctorum,* which developed in proportion as the doctrine of the Mediation became clear.[5] Texts descriptive of created mediation were no longer applied by the Fathers to our Lord because of Arian distortion of them, and so room was opened for created mediators. Another fact that tended in the same direction was the insistence of the Fathers on the spiritual benefits accruing to man from the Incarnation, by which human nature is exalted, deified. "Intimate must be the connection between Christ and His brethren and high their glory, if the language which seemed to belong to the Incarnate Word really belonged to them. Those who are formally recognized as God's sons in Christ, are fit objects of worship on account of Him who is in them."[6] This doctrine accounts for the invocation of Saints, the cult of relics, and the veneration of even living personages distinguished by their holy lives. "Worship, then, is the necessary correlative of glory; and in the same sense in which created natures can share in the Creator's incommunicable glory, are they also allowed a share of that worship which is His property alone."[7] Such were the broad deep premises laid by the controversies of the fourth and fifth centuries, and which ultimately led to a formal, public payment of honors to the Saints and, above all, to the Blessed Virgin, who was found to be the immediate object of certain Scriptural passages previously applied to the Eternal Son.

So intimately is the honor paid to the Saints associated with the Incarnation, that the Nestorian heresy and the others which had their rise in the Antiochene School, tended to separate Christ from His Saints and, by that fact, the Saints were separated from Christ. Thus, an opening was made for a denial of their cultus.[8]

The mystery of the Incarnation together with that of Christ's Resurrection gave the lie to the erroneous belief that

---

[5] Dev. 138.

[6] Dev. 138.

[7] Cf. Ath. II, 195. Dev. 142.

[8] Dev. 290.

matter was intrinsically evil. In consequence of these mysteries comes the doctrine of the resurrection of the Saints' bodies and of their future glorification with Christ; next follows the sanctity of their relics. From the earliest ages of the Church, the martyrs and their relics and all which came into contact with their blessed remains became objects of special veneration. Evidences are extant that Angels and Saints were worshipped in Antiquity, though their images did not receive a recognized honor until considerably later.[9]

The doctrine of the Incarnation involves, moreover, the special prerogatives of the Blessed Virgin, although these were not recognized in the ritual of the Church until a late date. Yet, they were known to the early Fathers, as has already been pointed out.[10] It is impossible not to conceive a deep-seated feeling of reverence and devotion towards her when once she is regarded in her true light. "When once we have mastered the idea that Mary bore, suckled, and handled the Eternal in the form of a child, what limit is conceivable to the rush and flood of thoughts which such a doctrine involves? What awe and surprise must attend upon the knowledge that a creature has been brought so close to the Divine Essence? It was the creation of a new idea and of a new sympathy, of a new faith and worship, when the holy Apostles announced that God had become incarnate; then a supreme love and devotion to Him became possible, which seemed hopeless before that revelation. This was the first consequence of their preaching. But besides this, a second range of thoughts was opened on mankind, unknown before, and unlike any others, as soon as it was understood that that Incarnate God had a mother. The second idea is distinct from the former and does not interfere with it. He is God made low, she is a woman made high. ... When He became man, He brought home to us His incommunicable attributes with a distinctiveness which precludes the possibility of our lowering Him merely by our exalting a creature."[11]

---

[9] Ibid. 410.

[10] Cf. Dev. 415.

[11] Diff. II, 82–84.

III. Foundation of Present Devotion of Catholics Laid in Antiquity

Thus, the Incarnation exerted a broader and stronger influence on Christians as they began to apprehend the notion that the Word had been made flesh and had a Mother. Time was required to impress the full import of so sublime an idea upon their faith as well as upon their worship. Newman ascribes the laying of the solid foundations of devotion to our Lady, to his favorite Father, St. Athanasius, though there is no proof that he himself had any special devotion to the Blessed Virgin. He was the first and great teacher of the Incarnation. "He collected together the inspired notices scattered through David, Isaias, St. Paul, and St. John, and he engraved indelibly upon the imaginations of the faithful, as had never been before, that man is God and God is man, that in Mary they meet, and that in this sense, Mary is the center of all things. He added nothing to what was known before, nothing to the popular and zealous faith that her Son was God; he has left behind him in his works no such definite passages about her as those of St. Irenaeus or St. Epiphanius; but he brought the circumstances of the Incarnation home to men's minds, by the multiform evolutions of his analysis, and thereby secured it to us for ever from perversion."[12] Athanasius set down the solid foundations, but other Fathers before him and countless others after, are high in their praises of her person and office. Newman, who at one time thought that Rome had added to the primitive teaching by her practical system, had been convinced of the contrary. Her Marian teaching, besides being a natural consequence of the Incarnation, is attested to by Antiquity and is but a legitimate development of the primitive teaching. Any one acquainted with the teaching of the Fathers concerning the Blessed Virgin could not maintain an attitude of opposition to the present beliefs of Catholics on the subject. Thus, Newman could tell Pusey that the latter's beliefs and statements about

---

[12] Diff. II, 87.

the high dignity of Mary were little different from those of the Fathers. "Though you appealed ever so much in your defence," he says to him, "to the authority of the 'undivided Church,' they (Protestants in general) would have said that you, who had such high notions of the Blessed Mary, were one of the last men who had a right to accuse us of quasi-idolatry."[13] One need but consult the works of an Irenaeus, an Epiphanius, Ephrem, and Cyril of Alexandria, a Jerome and an Augustine and a galaxy of other Fathers to see what their views were concerning the Mother of God. Were their expressions extravagant?

In general, the Anglicans of Pusey's type seemed to overlook the strength of the argument adducible from the Fathers in favor of the Catholic doctrine. While attacking medieval and modern writers, they forgot that by that fact they were opposing what the primitive Church held; and yet they maintained that Antiquity was their stronghold.[14] It may be that some individual writers do really go beyond what the Fathers taught but, still, the line cannot be logically drawn between their teaching on the Blessed Virgin and that of the present time.

The consequence of this doctrine is summed up by Newman thus: "This being the faith of the Fathers about the Blessed Virgin, we need not wonder that it should in no long time be transmuted into devotion. No wonder that their language should become unmeasured, when so great a term as 'Mother of God' had been formally set down as the safe limit of it! No wonder if it should be stronger and stronger as time went on, since only in a long period could the fulness of its import be exhausted! And in matter of fact, and as might be anticipated ... the current of thought in those early ages did uniformly tend to make much of the Blessed Virgin and to increase her honors, not to circumscribe them."[15]

---

[13] Diff. II, 78. Newman, however, admits that there is a real difference between what Pusey holds with the Fathers and what he protests against.

[14] Ibid. 77.

[15] Diff. II, 65, 66.

IV. The Greek Church Witnesses to It

By a very curious procedure, Anglicans as well as Protestants of other denominations have held aloof from Rome but inconsistently turn to the Greek Church, which holds practically all the doctrines of the Roman communion and admits precisely those that are declared stumbling-blocks for Protestants in their attitude to Rome. Antiquity, as just considered, not only stands as a witness of devotion to the Blessed Virgin, but the Greek Church, though separated from Rome for nearly a thousand years, strengthens the argument in favor of this devotion. No Protestant need be shocked or surprised at the sight of Roman Catholic devotion to our Lady if he becomes a little acquainted with the Greek ritual. "Is it not a very pregnant fact," asks Newman, "that the Eastern Churches so independent of us, so long separated from the West, so jealous for Antiquity, should even surpass us in their exaltation of the Blessed Virgin?"[16] Some may deny that the Greeks go further than the Roman Catholics, because the Western devotion is brought out into a system, whereas the Eastern is not. This implies only that there is more strength of intellect, less of mechanical worship among the Latins than among the Greeks; the former can give a better account of their devotion than the latter.

Yet, for all that, the Latins have been much more reserved than the Greeks; these have substituted the name of Mary for that of Jesus at the end of the Collects in the Breviary, as well as in the Ritual and Liturgy. Even in the formal prayers of the Eucharistic service, petitions are offered in the name of the *Theotokos* instead of that of Jesus Christ.[17]

In the authoritative books of the Latin Rite, namely, Missal, Ritual, and Breviary, Saints are not directly addressed, and all prayers end with the name of Jesus. The intercession of the Blessed Virgin and of the Saints is sought for, but the petition

---

[16] Diff. II, 90.

[17] Diff. II, 91.

is addressed to the Blessed Trinity, or to one of the Divine Persons. But the formal Greek devotion is "far less observant of dogmatic exactness ... (it is more) free and fearless in its exaltation of the Blessed Virgin."[18]

Newman has taken great pains in the Notes to the *Letter* to collect a vast number of expressions which occur in the Greek liturgy.[19] The petition "have mercy on us through the *Theotokos,*" or its equivalent, is very common. The Greeks often call Mary "our Lady," whereas this title is rare in Latin prayers. Even in the Holy Sacrifice of the Mass there are almost continual allusions to her; the same holds true for the other office books; but in the Latin Offices, addresses to her rarely get beyond the Antiphons.

Other Eastern schismatical bodies agree with the Greek Orthodox Church in their honors paid to the Blessed Virgin.[20] With good reason could Newman cite the words of Renaudot: "No one has accused the Orientals of deficiency in the legitimate honors which are the right of the *Deipara;* but many have charged them with having sometimes been extravagant in that devotion and running into superstition, which accusation is not without foundation."[21]

Newman points out two telling consequences of these considerations, namely, that the usage which is to be found in each of the separated parts of a religious communion after a split has taken place, tells in favor of its existence prior to the separation. In this case, the agreement of Orthodox, Nestorian, and Jacobite with the Latins in honoring the Blessed Virgin proves that these honors must have been substantially the same in the "undivided Church." Further, the passages cited by Newman from the formal ritual of the Greeks "are more compromising to those who propose entering into communion with them, than such parallel statements as occur in

---

[18] Ibid. 155.

[19] Ibid. 153–164.

[20] Diff. II, 163.

[21] Ibid. The Collyridians, a sect of Nestorians, worshipped Mary as a goddess.

unauthoritative devotions of the Latins."[22]

A letter of William Palmer to Newman may be adduced in further confirmation of what has been said on the attitude of the Greek Church towards devotion to the Blessed Virgin. The writer addressed these lines to Newman after the Letter to Pusey had appeared, and narrates a curious fact about relations between the Orientals and Non-jurors of England. He writes as follows: "For myself I have always admired the Christian simplicity and good sense of those Greek Patriarchs, who correspond with certain Non-jurors in the early part of the last century. The Non-jurors having admitted the intercession of the Blessed Virgin and the Saints, but having a scruple about invoking them for fear of treading on the honor due to God, the Greeks replied: 'We may here say of you in the words of the Psalmist, There were they afraid where no fear was, nevertheless though the ground of your objection, though mistaken, is a kind of piety, we will not insist much upon this point; but since you agree in the doctrine of the intercession of the Saints, say only sometimes at the end of your prayers, "By the prayers of Thy most holy Mother and all Thy Saints" and we are one.' Considering what was their own custom, how strongly they held to it, and how stiff they were in all matters of faith and necessary discipline in this correspondence, their largeness on this point is extremely remarkable, and shows that they thought that if only the principle or root were honestly admitted, the practical developments to come of it might safely be left to grow again of themselves; and that the precise volume or form to which they might attain in this or that local Church at this or that time was not a matter of essential importance, so long as there were no *arrière pensée* working in those who were less demonstrative against those who were more."[23]

Consequently, it is evident that the legitimacy of devotion to our Lady is sufficiently grounded both in the Fathers and in

---

[22] Ibid. 164.

[23] I am indebted for this letter to the Rev. Father Bacchus, of the Birmingham Oratory. William Palmer, spoken of here, **is** author of *The Patriarch and the Czar*. He became a Catholic.

the Eastern Churches, and hence we may ask with Newman: "What height of glory may we not attribute to her? and what are we to say of those who through ignorance, run counter to the voice of Scripture, to the testimony of the Fathers, to the traditions of East and West, and speak and act contemptuously towards her whom her Lord delighteth to honor?"[24]

V. Psychological Analysis of Devotion to Mary

The lessons taught Newman by his profound study of the development of Christian doctrine, served him in good stead when he had to show that the Catholic's belief concerning the Mother of God is substantially the same as that of early Christianity. In his *Letter* Newman condenses, as it were, his whole *Essay on Development* into a few pages pregnant with a deep psychological analysis of devotion to our Lady. This devotion may at times seem to open the way to excesses, abuses, or superstitions, yet for all that, it remains doctrinally well-founded. Whatever errors or misconceptions may creep in, are not so much the fault of the devotion itself, but of human nature, which, because of its fallen condition, ever tends to extremes.

Newman's basic principle for proving the legitimacy of Marian devotion, apart from Antiquity, is the same as that which serves as a nucleus for the *Essay on Development*, namely, the psychological evolution of an idea. As a germ, as something living that grows, the idea expands and leads to innumerable conclusions.[25] By this method Newman proves that no line can be satisfactorily drawn between primitive and modern teaching on the Blessed Virgin for the simple reason that it is so difficult, if not impossible, to draw the line clearly between right and wrong, truth and error. Wherever there is life, there is motion and continual change.

In the natural order, living things grow into their perfection, decline, and then die. Nothing can stop this process;

---

[24] Diff. II, 61.

[25] Cf. Dev. 33 sqq.

disorders may be combated, but the process itself cannot be eradicated. The same holds true, and more so, in the world of ideas. Attempts may be made to stifle them, to hinder the course of their development, or, on the other hand, they may be given free scope and in case of excesses be exposed and restrained after their occurrence. No other ways lie open. Of the two alternatives offered, it seems more advisable to give full liberty of thought and only afterwards to repress abuses if they occur.[26]

This is Newman's principle on ideas in general; if this is true of all energetic ideas, how much more so in matters of religion. The exposition of the effects of religious ideas is so vivid and at the same time verified by common experience that it is necessary to cite Newman at considerable length:

"Religion acts on the affections; who is to hinder these, when once roused, from gathering in their strength and running wild? They are not gifted with any connatural principle within them which renders them self-governing and self-adjusting. They hurry right on to their object, and often in their case it is, the more haste, the worse speed. Their object engrosses them and they see nothing else. And of all passions, love is the most unmanageable; nay more, I would not give much for that love which is never extravagant, which always observes the proprieties, and can move about in perfect good taste, under all emergencies. What mother, what husband or wife, what youth or maiden in love, but says a thousand foolish things, in the way of endearment, which the speaker would be sorry for strangers to hear; yet they are not on that account unwelcome to the parties to whom they are addressed. Sometimes by bad luck they are written down, sometimes they get into the newspapers; and what might be even graceful, when it was fresh from the heart and interpreted by the voice and the countenance, presents but a melancholy exhibition when served up cold for the public eye.

"So it is with devotional feelings. Burning thoughts and words are as open to criticism as they are beyond it. What is

---

[26] Diff. II, 78, 79.

abstractedly extravagant, may in particular persons be becoming and beautiful, and only fall under blame when it is found in others who imitate them. When it is formalized into meditations and exercises, it is as repulsive as love-letters in a police report."[27]

Holy minds readily adopt the language of another that suits their own religious sentiments: and hence any ridicule of the language they use seems a direct insult upon the object of their homage. What appeals to them will also have an appeal to the multitude the religion of which is "ever vulgar and abnormal," "tinctured with fanaticism and superstition."

"A people's religion," continues Newman in his classic analysis, "is ever a corrupt religion in spite of the provisions of Holy Church. If she is to be Catholic, you must admit within her net, fish of every kind, guests good and bad, vessels of gold, vessels of earth. You may beat religion out of men, if you will, and then their excesses will take a different direction; but if you make use of religion to improve them, they will make use of religion to corrupt it. And then you will have effected that compromise of which our countrymen report so unfavorably from abroad—a high grand faith and worship which compels their admiration, and puerile absurdities among the people which excite their contempt."[28]

Religion is based upon reason and so develops into theology. But since its preoccupation is with supernatural matters, reason can go only a certain distance when it runs into mysteries which it cannot explain. To pursue them is to run into error. The Arians used logic and lost the truth; the Fathers and Doctors of the Church went as far as reason would take them, and left the unexplainable portion of their expositions to faith. "Good sense and a large view of truth must serve as the correctives of logic."[29]

---

[27] Diff. II, 80.

[28] Diff. II, 81. Newman as an Anglican admired the intrinsic majesty and truth in the Roman Church; he admitted that it, above all, possessed the stimulants of popular devotion. Cf. V. M. II, 99.

[29] Diff. II, 81–82.

It may happen at times that individuals possess a false devotion to the Blessed Virgin, yet it is undeniable that Mary holds a position all her own in the Catholic system, a position that is distinct from Christ's the sole Mediator. She is the center of a range of thoughts distinct from that concerning the divinity and the office of her Son. Well could Newman say of the Arians that they had left Christ a creature and were found wanting, though they had said more about Him than did Catholic writers about the Blessed Virgin. He clinches his whole argument in a word: "The votaries of Mary do not exceed the true faith, unless the blasphemers of her Son come up to it. The Church of Rome is not idolatrous, unless Arianism is orthodoxy."[30] If Protestants object to the honors paid to Mary, it is because they have no very high notions of the divinity of Jesus, and consequently are easily led to mistake the honor paid to her, for that which is alone due to her Eternal Son.[31] Were we to place our Lord in the center which we assign to His Holy Mother, "we should only be dragging Him from His throne and making Him an Arian kind of God; that is, no God at all. He who charges us with making Mary a divinity, is thereby denying the divinity of Jesus. Such a man does not know what divinity is."[32]

This had been the accusation launched by Newman against Protestants who had forgotten or were forgetting the true natures of Christ; in fact, they were losing sight of the fundamental tenet that Christ was God.[33] Newman draws a delicate portrait of the beautiful role of the Blessed Virgin in regard to us; she does not hold the same relation as Jesus, who is our God and our Judge. She is our Mother and consequently full of tenderness and love. "Our Lord cannot pray for us as a creature prays, as Mary prays; He cannot inspire those feelings which a creature inspires. To her belongs, as being a creature, a natural claim on our sympathy and familiarity, in that she is

---

[30] Dev. 144.

[31] Ibid. 145.

[32] Diff. II, 85.

[33] Cf. P. S. III, 170; Mix. 345 sqq.

nothing else than our fellow. She is our pride,— in the poet's words, 'Our tainted nature's solitary boast.' We look to her without any fear, any remorse, any consciousness that she is able to read us, judge us, punish us. Our heart yearns towards that pure Virgin, that gentle Mother, and our congratulations follow her, as she rises from Nazareth and Ephesus, through the choirs of angels, to her throne on high, so weak, yet so strong; so delicate, yet so glorious; so modest and yet so mighty."[34]

No one can view the Blessed Virgin in her true light without feeling his affections stirred to their depths. Moreover, it is Christ Himself, who has made His Mother so great, so lovable and has Himself taught us how to love her. "Did not the All-wise know the human heart when He took to Himself a Mother, did He not anticipate our emotion at the sight of an exaltation in one so simple and so lowly? If He had not meant her to exert that wonderful influence in His Church, which she has in the event exerted, I will use a bold word, He it is who has perverted us. If she is not to attract our homage, why did He make her solitary in her greatness, amid His vast creation? If it be idolatry in us to let our affections respond to our faith, He would not have made her what she is, or He would not have told us that He had so made her; but far from this, He has sent His Prophet to announce to us, 'A Virgin shall conceive and bear a Son, and they shall call His name Emmanuel,' and we have the same warrant for hailing her as God's Mother, as we have for adoring Him as God."[35]

VI. MISCONCEPTION REMOVED: DEVOTION TO MARY DOES NOT INTERFERE WITH HONOR DUE TO GOD

Besides explaining the difference of position between our Lord and His Blessed Mother, Newman opposes actively the assertion that Catholics practice idolatry in regard to the Blessed Virgin or, at least, that the honor paid to her, interferes with that due to God alone. Pusey himself even affirmed that,

---

[34] Diff. II, 85.
[35] Diff. II, 86.

as a matter of fact, a certain number of Catholics do stop short in the Blessed Mary.[36] The process of Newman's conversion had been worked out in proportion as his difficulties in this regard were removed. He himself at one time thought that as a practical system Rome had supplanted the Blessed Trinity, heaven, and hell, by the Blessed Virgin, the Saints and purgatory, and that Mary had become the dispenser of mercy in place of her divine Son.[37] Education, environment, a constant tradition—all these combine to fix deeply in the minds of many non-Catholics, the strange notion that our Blessed Lady *must necessarily* relegate her Son to a secondary position, if she is honored in any fashion whatsoever. That is taken as an accepted fact, against which argument is considered a mere waste of breath. But is it really as they would have it?

Newman had already anticipated in his *Essay on Development* his answer to this assumption, reiterated by Pusey. The *Essay* and the *Letter* complete each other in this matter.

The supposed difficulty or objection had already been solved dogmatically in the fourth century when the death-blow was inflicted upon Arianism. At that time the principle was laid down that to exalt a creature was no recognition of its divinity. Arians had elevated Christ to the highest possible limits, leaving Him, however, a creature, and hence, since they adored Him, they really lay open to the charge of idolatry. There is no parallel possible between them and the defenders of Mary's prerogatives. In these modern times, those who mistake the honor paid to Mary for that to be rendered to Jesus may be assimilated to the heretics of old, who had false notions concerning the Divine Person of Christ. In most cases this is at the root of the objection.

The devotional thoughts centering in Jesus and in His Mother are entirely distinct and do not obscure one another. The question is one of pure fact: is the accusation made by Protestants really borne out in the event? Newman had long

---

[36] Cf. I Eir. 107.

[37] Cf. V. M. II, 369.

felt the necessity, during his Anglican days, of keeping clear and undimmed the correct belief in the Incarnation. The Catholic Church had furnished him with the key to success in this regard: Mary's title of Mother of God was the "Open Sesame."[38] It could protect the faith of Catholics from a specious Humanitarianism. Can it be proved in reality that there are Catholics who, through false devotion to Mary, forget Jesus? Certainly not for the bulk of Catholics. "There is this broad fact the other way—that, if we look through Europe, we shall find, on the whole, that just those nations and countries have lost their faith in the divinity of Christ, who have given up devotion to His Mother, and that those, on the other hand, who had been foremost in her honor, have retained their orthodoxy. Contrast, for instance, the Calvinists with the Greeks, or France with the North of Germany, or the Protestant and Catholic communions in Ireland. As to England, it is scarcely doubtful what would be the state of its Established Church, if the Liturgy and Articles were not an integral part of its Establishment."[39]

The fear that any honors paid to Mary were an encroachment upon the supreme worship due to God, has certainly not been justified. "They who were accused of worshipping a creature in His stead, still worship Him so purely, they, wherever obstacles to the development of their principles have been removed, have ceased to worship Him altogether."[40]

With a vivid touch Newman explains the event and its source: "The Church and Satan agreed in this, that Son and Mother went together; and the experience of three centuries has confirmed their testimony, for Catholics who have honored the Mother still worship the Son, while Protestants who now have ceased to confess the Son, began then by scoffing at the Mother."[41] Mary remains ever the minister of Jesus; her glory

---

[38] Cf. Mix. 346, 347.

[39] Diff. II, 92; cf. M. D. 69.

[40] Dev. 426.

[41] Mix. 348.

is for the sake of her Son. Thus, facts prove the truth of Father Faber's words: "Jesus is obscured because Mary is kept in the background."

The observation of Newman made more than sixty years ago has been repeatedly confirmed by experience since that time. These last years particularly have witnessed a bold dissection of the divine Person of Christ in most of the sects. To be convinced of this, it is not even necessary to look into Protestant dictionaries, books, or magazines; the daily press is used as the battling-ground for overthrowing faith in Christ's divinity. On the other hand, where there is a serious effort among Protestants to return to the teaching of the Fathers, there is also a corresponding endeavor to give the rightful place to devotion to Mary.[42]

Newman insists with objectors that the *tone* of devotion to the Blessed Virgin differs from that paid to Jesus or to the Trinity. "The supreme and true worship paid to the Almighty is severe, profound, awful as well as tender, confiding, and dutiful ... towards St. Mary, the language employed is affectionate and ardent, as towards a mere child of Adam, though subdued as coming from her sinful kindred."[43] To be convinced of this profound assertion one need but compare the *Dies Irae* with the *Stabat Mater,* the Office for Pentecost or Trinity Sunday with that of the Assumption. The fact is, though the human tends to supplant the divine, devotion to Mary leaves intact the worship of Jesus. Forbidding worship of the Saints will never teach men the worship of God. A very significant remark is made by Newman, that "great and constant as is the devotion which the Catholic pays to the Blessed Virgin, it has a special province and has far more

---

[42] Among the so-called Anglo-Catholics, devotion to our Lady is much in honor. A booklet written by the Anglican rector Baverstock teaches the devotion of the Rosary. (Cath. Lit. Ass'n, London.) A timid cult of Mary has raised its voice in the German *Hochkirche* (Cf. *Dublin Review,* Vol. 174, Jan. 1924). A contemporary German says that the Our Father is soon put aside when not accompanied by the Hail Mary. (Bartmann, *Christus ein Gegner der Marienkultus?* p. 10.)

[43] Dev. 427.

connection with the public services and the festive aspect of Christianity and with certain extraordinary offices which she holds, than with what is strictly personal and primary in religion."[44]

Further, this difference is exemplified by the books intended for the educated classes as well as for the ordinary people, such as the *Spiritual Exercises of St. Ignatius, Imitation of Christ, Spiritual Combat,* etc. These are almost entirely devoted to a consideration of Christ or of the great truths of faith. The Blessed Virgin is scarcely mentioned in them. Those intended for the use of the faithful and which refer directly to the Blessed Virgin, emphasize the place held by devotion to her and demonstrate conclusively that this devotion cannot interfere with the relations existing between the soul and its Creator.[45]

The personal religion of Catholics, even of the most ignorant, distinguishes clearly between adoration of God and worship of Mary. How different is their attitude concerning the Real Presence in the church and a statue of our Lady. Mary hardly enters into the Mass service, which is a direct sacrifice offered to God alone. Communion is a solemn, unequivocal act of faith in the Incarnate God.[46]

In order to judge correctly of Catholic devotion to our Lady, it does not suffice for a Protestant to examine expressions according to his own views and condemn them for what they seem to say to him. He must remember that Catholic authors are writing in general for Catholics and hence permit themselves observations or expressions which they know will not be misunderstood. These authors are writing for members of their own household, as it were. To form a just idea of Marian devotion, representative authors ought to be chosen, men remarkable for the sanctity of their lives and the solidity

---

[44] Dev. 428. Card. Wiseman signaled this passage for special commendation. Cf. Diff. II, 93.

[45] Dev. 428 sqq. The booklets mentioned here were among those presented to Newman by Dr. Russell on the occasion of their correspondence relative to Transubstantiation and devotion to our Lady.

[46] Diff. II, 95, 96.

of their doctrine. Even for Saints, Neman lays down the useful canon: "It never surprises me to read anything extraordinary in the devotions of a Saint. Such men are on a level different from our own, and we cannot understand them ... they are beyond us, and we must use them as patterns, not as copies."[47]

VII. SUPERSTITIONS DOCTRINALLY EXPLAINED

Newman has no intention to deny that superstitions have crept into the cultus towards the Blessed Virgin; these are rather to be expected, for, as he has already explained, religion and, consequently devotion, is something living and will run to decay. Because they do almost necessarily occur from the infirmity of man's nature, does not thereby justify or excuse them.

By explaining the development of devotion as analogous to the germination and growth of an idea, Newman indicates the reason for superstition. Besides the psychological reason, he adduces one that is *doctrinal*. Why are Protestants so scandalized at what they consider not merely the vulgarity, profaneness, and superstition of certain Catholics, but their flippancy, lack of reverence, and perfunctory, mechanical fashion of fulfilling their most sacred duties? Newman ascribes it to a difference of doctrinal viewpoint. Many Protestants hold, in fact, that faith cannot exist without love and obedience; whereas Catholics maintain that faith and love, faith and obedience, faith and works are separable. For the Catholic, faith is the sight of the unseen; for the Protestant it may be the equivalent of obedience or trust. The latter rather defines faith by its effects, and hence considers it no true faith unless good works follow.[48]

In the Catholic creed, faith is a spiritual sight and hence may be perfectly distinct from the desire, intention, or even power to act in conformity with it. Though grace may be lost in a baptized person, the faculty of faith remains unless

---

[47] Ibid. 97.
[48] Diff. I, 268–270.

resistance to grace eventually leads to infidelity. Thus, sinners may have a vivid perception of things unseen, yet have no desire or affection for them. Knowledge exists without love. The Church strives continually to bring her unfaithful children back to God and succeeds, to a certain extent, though there may be frequent subsequent relapses. The good and holy unite to counteract the evil influences that tend to drag down the masses. "Good and evil (are) mingled together in all conceivable measures of combinations and varieties of result; a perpetual vicissitude; the prospect brightening and then overcast again; luminous spots, tracts of splendor, patches of darkness, twilight regions, and the glimmer of day; but in spite of this moral confusion, in one and all a clear intellectual apprehension of the truth."[49] In a Catholic country, the ideas of heaven and hell, Christ, the Blessed Virgin, Angels and Saints, the Blessed Sacrament, the Mass, etc., are taken for granted as facts brought home to the individual by faith, but colored by the respective mind of each one.

The Protestant who becomes bad may drift into infidelity, because according to the principle of private judgment, practically everything is taken as a mere opinion; but a bad Catholic generally retains hope as well as faith, even though he has lost charity. He "seeks to evade the difficulty; he looks up to our Blessed Lady; he knows by supernatural faith her power and her goodness; he turns the truth to his own purpose, his bad purpose; and he makes her his patroness and protectress against the penalty of sins which he does not mean to abandon. ... Hence the strange stories of highwaymen and brigands devout to the Madonna. And their wishes leading to the belief, they begin to circulate stories of her much-coveted compassion towards impenitent offenders; and these stories fostered by the circumstances of the day, and confused with others similar though not impossible, for a time are in repute. Thus, the Blessed Virgin has been reported to deliver the reprobate from hell, and to transfer them to purgatory; and absolutely to secure from perdition all who are devout to her, repentance not being

---

[49] Diff. I, 275.

contemplated as the means."[50]

These and innumerable other apparent inconsistencies may be run across in the lives of some Catholics; the mixture of seriousness and levity, the familiarity with sacred things, etc., are the consequences of mixed multitudes having faith. The truths of religion stand as facts of which sin does not obliterate the impression.[51]

VIII. Attitude Toward Abuses

As to abuses which have existed and do exist, there is only one attitude possible—that of utter repudiation. Newman is categoric in this regard, as must be every right-minded Catholic. Certain Catholics at times misinterpret the dictum that "no honor is too great for the Blessed Virgin,"[52] and so permit themselves unwarranted exaggerations or excesses in her regard. Thus, it is intolerable to put Mary on the same level with the Divinity; Jesus is the sole necessary Mediator, and Mary cannot have a direct, immediate part in the august work of Redemption. Mary herself could not endure such manifestations of false devotion to her, for no creature possesses a love like hers for her Divine Son. She would consider any one a traitor who preferred her to Jesus.[53] "How do we show our love for her by wounding her in the apple of her eye?" justly demands the celebrated Oratorian. However, where occasion for offense is offered, it is necessary to carefully weigh the full import of an expression. Thus, if properly understood, we may say that Mary's prayer is omnipotent; that she is the center of all things, since creature and Creator met and became one in her womb. Again, certain expressions may be true for particular circumstances, times, and places, though

---

[50] Diff. I, 279.

[51] Ibid. 288, 289.

[52] Newman's confessor at Rome, a Jesuit, had given him a clear-cut rule for guidance in devotion to Mary when he said: "We cannot love our Lady too much if we love our Lord a great deal more." Cf. Diff. II, 21.

[53] M. D. 75.

abstractedly false; thus, it may be maintained in some instances that certain individuals cannot be saved without personal devotion to the Blessed Virgin.

A fundamental distinction is important in this matter, namely, the difference between intercession and invocation. No Catholic maintains that it is indispensable for salvation to pray to the Blessed Virgin, or to the Saints. What authors, such as St. Alphonsus, do hold is that God gives no grace except through Mary, that is, through her intercession. It may be quite true that Mary's intercession is a necessary part of the economy of Redemption. She intercedes for all, and that according to the will of God. God reveals His desires to her and she in turn prays for the fulfillment of his will.[54] We have no proof that the Saints in the primitive Church invoked Mary, and yet they are saved. Even though some may have gone so far as to speak of the necessity of devotion to Mary as a means of salvation, they do not impose a *sine qua non* condition. The necessity is not an absolute one, but a moral necessity. In Catholic countries, for example, where the atmosphere is, as it were, impregnated with devotion to our Lady, a Catholic might be running a great risk were he, through neglect or disrespect, to give up deliberately a universal practice and turn away his thoughts from the Blessed Virgin.[55]

There can be no hesitation about putting away expressions which, taken in their absolute, literal sense, as is done by Protestants, are exaggerated and false, though in all probability the writers did not use them thus. So we have phrases and sentences such as these, which Newman puts together: "that the mercy of Mary is infinite; that God has resigned into her hands His omnipotence; that it is safer to seek her than to seek her Son; that the Blessed Virgin is superior to God; that our Lord is subject to her command; that His present disposition towards sinners, as well as His Father's, is to reject them, while the Blessed Mary takes His place as an Advocate with Father and Son; that the Saints are more ready to intercede with Jesus

---

[54] Diff. II,

[55] Ibid. 106; Pusey IV, 120.

than Jesus with the Father; that Mary is the only refuge of those with whom God is angry ... that ... we are clothed with the merits of Mary, that she is Priestess, present in the Holy Eucharist; that elect souls are born of God and Mary, etc., etc."[56]

Newman's judgment on these expressions, which easily give rise to false views, is emphatic: "Sentiments such as these I freely surrender to your animadversion; I never knew of them till I read your book. ... They seem to me like a bad dream. I could not conceive them to have been said.... They defy all the *loci theologici.* There is nothing of them in the Missal, in the Roman Catechism, in the Roman *Raccolta,* in the *Imitation of Christ,* in Gother, Challoner, Milner, or Wiseman, as far as I am aware. They do but scare and confuse me. I should not be holier, more spiritual, more sure of perseverance, if I twisted my moral being into the reception of them; I should but be guilty of fulsome frigid flattery towards the most upright and noble of God's creatures, if I professed them—and of stupid flattery too; for it would be like the compliment of painting up a young and beautiful princess with the brow of a Plato and the muscle of an Achilles. And I should expect her to tell one of her people in waiting to turn me off her service without warning. Whether thus to feel be the *scandalum parvulorum* in my case, or the *scandalum Pharisœorum,* I leave others to decide; but I will say plainly that I had rather believe (which is impossible) that there is no God at all, than that Mary is greater than God."[57] Of course Newman admits that these sayings may not have so crude a meaning as they seem to have when taken on their face value independently of the context. Their authors probably never understood them in the literal sense. Nevertheless, they are "calculated to prejudice inquirers, to frighten the unlearned, to unsettle consciences, to provoke blasphemy, and to work the loss of souls."[58]

How thoughtless and blind, for example, to imagine that Mary, the all-holy, the sinless one, could be less shocked at

---

[56] Diff. II, 113, 114.

[57] Ibid. 114, 115.

[58] Ibid. 115.

wilful sin than her Son, and that she will be the intercessor of those who have no intention to amend their evil ways. Is it possible that she could hate sin less and love sinners more than our Lord does?⁵⁹

Her present mission in heaven, as it was upon earth, besides acting as Tower of David in defense of the Incarnation, besides interceding for men on earth, is to refer all her glory to her divine Son. She does not shine for herself, but as the Morning Star, she is the reflection of the Sun of Justice, her Redeemer as well as ours. When she appears, we know that He is close at hand.⁶⁰ In this wise may be applied what Newman advocated as a young Anglican preacher, that we should never separate Mary from her Divine Son, but for a different reason. How could she, as he had then supposed, prove a veritable snare for any who manifest their reverence for her person and dignity? How is it possible that she, who had been so highly honored, could eclipse in our minds the honor of Him who honored her?⁶¹ On the contrary, those who are most devout to Mary are perforce led to an intense devotion to our Lord. Dr. Russell had called Newman's attention to the fact that the greatest Saints in the Church were characterized by a great devotion to our Lady.⁶²

Where superstitions or abuses existed or crept in, the authorities of the Church were at hand to apply suitable remedies.⁶³ Sometimes it is advisable to forestall or eradicate abuses; at other times silence and forbearance are the best policy to pursue amid the mistakes, excesses, and superstitions of individuals or classes of Catholics. The Church has a very complex office to fulfill and consequently may make every effort to put a restraint or hindrance upon abuses, and actually

---

⁵⁹ M. D. 12. Cf. V. M. II, 214, 215.

⁶⁰ Ibid. 77.

⁶¹ Cf. P. S. II, 132.

⁶² Cf. above, p. 50. The great modern servants of the Blessed Virgin, such as Blessed Grignon de Montfort and Father Chaminade, both indicate devotion to her as the great means to attain to a resemblance with Christ.

⁶³ V. M. I, p. lxii.

does intervene. Thus, the wild notion of our Lady's presence in the Eucharist was condemned by Benedict XIV; the same punishment was meted out to the use of the title "Queen of the Sacred Heart of Jesus," and certain novel representations of the Madonna and Child, lest the faithful, deviating from the paths of true piety, be led to ascribe power to Mary as issuing from her divine maternity, beyond its due limits.[64]

Frequently, however, it is more expedient to leave excesses to the gradual operation of the opinion of educated Catholics rather than resort to direct and immediate condemnation.

IX. CHARACTER OF DEVOTION

In his *Letter to Pusey,* Newman seems to overlook an exposition of what he would consider a suitable devotion for the class of people for whom he was writing. His work was primarily apologetic; he was defending the devotion to Mary against false conceptions and at the same time proving its legitimacy. He had shown that devotion was founded on a solid doctrinal basis. Mary stands at the head of creation as the perfect masterpiece of the divine Artist.[65] Devotion must be the consequence of considerations on her dignity, her grandeurs, her sanctity. Dogma is something fixed, but devotion is free.[66] Faith remains ever one and the same, but a wide range is left for judgment and inclination in the matter of devotion. "No one interferes with his neighbor; agreeing as it were to differ, they (Catholics) pursue independently a common end, and by paths distinct but converging, present themselves before God."[67]

He who lays down the rule that devotion is something free should be the last one to indicate any special forms. Consequently, it sufficed for Newman to lay down principles, correct false impressions, and discountenance abuses in reference to devotion. The forms would take care of

---

[64] Diff. II, 107.

[65] Ibid. 85, 86.

[66] Pusey IV, 120.

[67] Diff. II, 29.

themselves, depending on the temperament of the individual.

Diversity of taste is largely determined by national and individual characteristics. Pusey recognized this fact when he wrote: "I do not presume to prescribe to Italians or Spaniards, what they shall hold, or how they shall express their pious opinions."[68]

Newman puts down some very wise rules concerning what he believed to be the sound devotion appropriate to English Catholics, who by their national good sense are protected from some of the extravagances to which other peoples more sentimentally inclined may be liable. The primary rule is to follow the safe guidance of the Holy See, which is ever conservative in the matter of devotion. The ordinary people as a rule do not go after a foreign style of devotion, though the educated class may be influenced by it for a time.[69] Newman characterizes a suitable type of devotion: "There is a healthy devotion to the Blessed Mary, and there is an artificial; it is possible to love her as a Mother, to honor her as a Virgin, to seek her as a Patron, and to exalt her as a Queen, without injury to solid piety and Christian good sense—I cannot help calling this the English style." Newman ever gave his preferences to English habits of devotion as showing less singularity than by trying to introduce what was novel or exotic.[70]

Prayer-books which give the true character of English devotion are to be found in great abundance; it is to these that objecting Protestants ought to appeal in order to give a fair judgment. Such works as the *Garden of the Soul,* the *Key of Heaven,* etc., besides the semi-authoritative *Raccolta* may be cited as instances. The latter collection seems almost extreme in its carefulness to avoid whatever might savor of

---

[68] Ibid. 99; cf. also Pusey IV, 122.

[69] Newman admits that he himself had been subjected for a time to the influence of Continental devotions. He had been warned at his conversion against the effects of Italian compositions upon English Catholics. Cf. Diff. II, 21, 22.

[70] Ibid. 20.

exaggeration in its invocations of the Blessed Virgin. To sum up his point, Newman tells his friend Pusey: "On the whole I am sanguine that you will come to the conclusion that Anglicans may safely trust themselves to us English Catholics, as regards any devotions to the Blessed Virgin, which might be required of them over and above the rule of the Council of Trent."[71]

Nevertheless, Newman assured his friend that the honor of our Lady was dearer to him and his fellow-Catholics than the conversion of the country. He had good reason to expostulate with the sincere Pusey for his hostile stand to Catholic devotion. Breaking through his habitual reserve, he gave vent to his own deep feelings on the subject when he said: "Have you not been touching us on a very tender point in a very rude way? Is it not the effect of what you have said to expose her to scorn and obloquy who is dearer to us than any other creature? Have you ever hinted that our love for her is anything else than an abuse?"[72]

The duties to our Lady are summed up in the cult of veneration, the cult of love, of imitation and invocation. The last form is peculiar to Catholics and to those who follow the cult to its logical consequences.

Because of her eminent dignity the Blessed Virgin receives a cult special to herself. She cannot be put on the same level with the Divinity, for she is but a mere creature. Hence, she cannot receive the worship of *latria,* or adoration, which is reserved to God alone. Since she is above all the Angels and Saints, she receives a superior sort of worship than they, not specifically diverse, but differing only in degree. This cultus is designated as *hyperdulia.* Elevated to the highest possible dignity on earth, she is next to her divine Son in glory. He has made her Queen of heaven, Queen of Angels and Saints, Mother of all living, Refuge of sinners.[73] If Jesus venerates, honors her so much, that He has put her next to Him in glory, that He wishes her to intercede for us, what limits can be set to

---

[71] Ibid. 103.

[72] Ibid. 116.

[73] Mix. 363; cf. Diff. II, 108, 112.

our veneration of her?[74]

No one can contemplate her beauty without feeling a strong emotion at the sight of her exaltation. She has a claim on our sympathy and familiarity; she is the pride, the glory of our fallen nature. She must necessarily attract our homage in order that our affections might correspond to our faith.[75]

This homage, however, is to be more than a mere silent contemplation.[76] Hers is not an earthly beauty, dangerous to look upon; she is rather "the Morning Star, the harbinger of day, breathing purity, telling of heaven and infusing peace."[77] Her sphere is to guide us on to Jesus. We owe her a veneration, a respect, as to the most highly favored of creatures. By exalting her, we cannot be unfaithful to Jesus; on the contrary, we honor Him by honoring her, for her Divine Son cannot but be zealous for her glory.[78]

Furthermore, Catholics owe the Blessed Virgin a cult of love. Can any one love God above all things, without at the same time possessing at least a small degree of love for His own Blessed Mother? Of all creatures, she is the closest to God, the first object of our love. United to us as Mother of men, she merits our love; she ought to have the first place in our love after Jesus, since "she is the first of creatures, the most acceptable child of God, the nearest and dearest to Him."[79]

Love is the most natural sentiment of children for their mother; let uninitiated ears take offense at the supposed extravagances of love's language.[80] This noblest of human sentiments will make all of Mary's children rise in defense of her honor and dignity.[81]

---

[74] P. S. VII, 79; P. S. II, Sermon 12: "The Reverence due to the Virgin Mary."

[75] Diff. II, 85, 86.

[76] Such was largely the nature of Newman's Anglican devotion; he feared then that Mary might prove a snare to us. Cf. P. S. III, 387; II, 133 sqq.

[77] Mix. 358, 359.

[78] M. D. I, 75.

[79] M. D. I, 4.

[80] 80 Diff. II, 80.

[81] Ibid. 115.

Love particularly incites to imitation. The true child of Mary cannot be such unless he attempts in his measure to reproduce in himself her virtues; her devotion to Jesus, her meekness, her simplicity, her modesty, the faith of her "who received God's message by the Angel without a doubt; her patience, who endured St. Joseph's surprise without a word; her obedience, who went up to Bethlehem in the winter and bore our Lord in a stable; her meditative spirit, who pondered in her heart what she saw and heard about Him; her fortitude, whose heart the sword went through; her self-surrender, who gave Him up during His ministry and consented to His death; above all, ... her purity, who rather than relinquish her virginity was willing to lose Him for a Son."[82]

Finally, our Lady demands a cult of invocation. When once Newman comprehended its legitimacy, he could not help but insist upon it. Though distinct from intercession, it is intimately connected with the latter. The Blessed Virgin intercedes for us, for she is our great Advocate; we in our turn must call upon her with trust and confidence, knowing that "God gives no grace except through Mary."[83] Her Son will deny her nothing that she asks for.[84] Since she is so powerful and yet so amiable, we can have recourse to her in all our necessities. Our invocations of her will not be of the sterile variety, consisting in idle, vain, or pompous addresses, but rather heartfelt salutations and earnest prayers for her gracious assistance in our needs. She will ever be at our side to guide us in the dark night and across the bleak wilderness of this world to our everlasting home, to our Lord Jesus. What joy, what love, what happiness, what emotion will fill our breasts in that day when we can gaze upon the awful beauty of her, of whom Newman wrote:

---

[82] Mix. 374, 375.

[83] Diff. II, 105.

[84] M. D. I, 71.

"And you never could name that conceivable best,
To exhaust the resources the Maker possess'd.
    But I know of one work of His Infinite Hand,
Which special and singular ever must stand,
    So perfect, so pure and of gifts such a store,
That even Omnipotence ne'er shall do more."[85]

---

[85] V. V. 288.

CONCLUSION

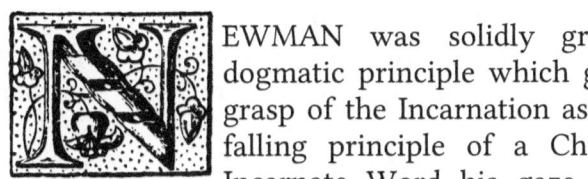EWMAN was solidly grounded in the dogmatic principle which gave him a firm grasp of the Incarnation as the standing or falling principle of a Church. From the Incarnate Word his gaze was necessarily directed towards her from whom Christ derived the substance of His manhood. Where Anglican doctrine was precise, Newman was clear-cut and categoric in his expression. Though holding firmly the Communion of Saints, he did not as an Anglican clearly see the doctrine of their intercession involved in it, and hence his language is vague and indefinite, but becomes clearer as time advances. In the second phase of his development he comes to regard the question of the intercession of our Lady and the Saints as left open by the Anglican formularies. The same holds true for his views on invocation, though he himself never admitted them, as not being sanctioned by the Anglican Church. As for the Roman practical system, particularly in what concerns devotional manifestation to our Lady, he was unreserved in his condemnation during the first period of his career. These categoric assertions gave way to hesitation and eventually to complete silence on Rome's so-called "abuses." The kindly intervention of Dr. Russell of Maynooth with his own studies on the development of doctrine smoothed his practical difficulties and brought him to the true Church of the Apostles.

His experiences as an Anglican, together with his deep patristic formation, made him the apologist *par excellence* of

Catholic devotion to the Blessed Virgin. His clear conception of its doctrinal basis together with a thorough knowledge of Antiquity, marked him out as the recognized teacher for Catholics and non-Catholics alike. The latter can find in his remarkable Letter to Pusey the means of removing what for many is their great *crux* as regards Catholicism.

That Mary is the Mother of God, that she is the Second Eve—these are the two great centers of his doctrine, as exposed in the Second Part. In these two great facts of the divine maternity and the spiritual maternity of Mary, he directs himself to an explanation of Mary's grandeurs and her prerogatives.

Would Newman look for the reason of Mary's dignity, her virginity, her sanctity, her Immaculate Conception, her Assumption, her intercessory power, he turns towards Mary's close relationship with the Incarnate Word, who had to be born of a Virgin as alone befitting His infinite holiness. This Virgin had to be holy because holiness and divine favor go together; further, she was in intimate intercourse with the Fount of holiness for more than thirty years. She had to be holy in her conception, for Jesus would have naught to do with sin. As the most devoted of sons, He could not permit His Mother to witness the corruption of the tomb. In heaven, Mary's intercession is all-powerful with Him, because Jesus cannot refuse anything to His Mother, who was His only near relative on earth.

Newman's Mariology is particularly characterized by his deduction of the dignity and privileges of Mary, from her role as Second Eve. The doctrine of the Second Eve as he shows (and there lies the great strength of his argumentation), is as old as Christianity itself; in fact, Newman goes farther and sees it foreshadowed in the oracle of Genesis, announcing the woman who would one day crush the head of the serpent. This parallel between Mary and Eve has held a prominent place in the minds of the faithful throughout the ages. The early Fathers, as well as the Doctors of the Church, have all emphasized this great position of Mary. In the nineteenth century itself, a good servant of the Blessed Virgin, Father

Chaminade, based the consecration of Christians in general to the Mother of God on this position. To the members of the Society of Mary which he founded, he presented Jesus as the model of their devotion, for Jesus associated His Blessed Mother in all the mysteries of His life and of the Redemption.[1]

Newman considers Mary's position from a particular aspect, for he finds this doctrine the special one, the primitive view, the *prima facie* view of the Blessed Virgin in Antiquity. In this doctrine he finds the reason for Mary's exaltation, as clearly demonstrated by the apocalyptic vision of the Woman. Mary must be as fully endowed as Eve. Eve the Virgin, brought forth death, Mary the Virgin, brings forth life; Eve was filled with grace to be the mother of the living, though in fact she became the mother of death; Mary, the true Mother of the living, had to have greater grace, greater holiness. Like Eve, she had to be conceived immaculate. Had Eve not sinned, she would have been spared the corruption of the grave; the second and greater Eve was spared this humiliation. Mary appeared to the Fathers as Eve's Advocate, and in this role she exercises her maternal solicitude on behalf of the children of men. Since all this is true of our Lady, faith must have devotion as its consequence, to which no limit can be set, provided her condition as creature is recognized.

Newman's doctrine, which is seen to be consistent and to form a harmonious whole, has served as a model to subsequent Marian writers who insist on the solid doctrinal basis for this devotion, one of the most beautiful in Catholic life. His own defense of devotion to our Lady was a serious protest against the puerile absurdities and unwarranted exaggerations to which some writers have given expression under pretext of honoring the Mother of God. He has demonstrated beyond doubt that a virile solid true devotion can exist without running to stupid extravagances. He accomplished for the nineteenth century in England, what a Bossuet, a Francis de Sales and

---

[1] Cf. Chaminade, *Petit Traité de la Connaissance de Marie*. This complete abandonment to the service of the Blessed Virgin, in imitation of Christ's filial devotedness to His Mother, has been elevated to the dignity of a vow of religion and recognized as such by the Church.

several others did for the seventeenth century in France, where indiscreet devotees of our Lady advocated a multiplication of petty practices as being the essential of true piety.

A follower of Petavius, Canisius, Bellarmine, Newman has led the way for Catholics in their defense of the truth against the attacks of Protestants, who are blinded by prejudice and ignorance in most cases. Following the standards of critical research, Newman has proved that Catholics can trace the beginnings of their devotion to Mary, down to the primitive Church—not that it existed in precisely the same forms as at the present time, but that these forms are the logical consequences of what was held concerning her in the earliest ages of Christianity. He prepared the way for the numerous works that have appeared in recent years on the teachings of the early Fathers relative to our Lady. On his conversion he had deplored the absence of a historico-dogmatic school among Catholics, but now his desires are being realized to the full. The history of Mariology in the first five centuries of which he practically gives an epitome is being studied in detail and developed to its just proportions.

www.ingramcontent.com/pod-product-compliance
Lightning Source LLC
Chambersburg PA
CBHW022000160426
43197CB00007B/206